GETTING Good AT GETTING Older

by Richard Siegel & Rabbi Laura Geller

BEHRMAN HOUSE

Behrman House, Inc.
Millburn, New Jersey
www.behrmanhouse.com

Edited by Aviva Gutnick, Emily Wichland, Diana Drew
Design by Elynn Cohen, Terry Taylor
Cover design by Zatar Creative

Special thanks to the Morning Minyanaires of Congregation Beth El in
South Orange, New Jersey, for their contributions to this project. —AG

Cover images: Man playing guitar, hands on challah: Photos by Bill Aron; Richard Siegel in kayak: Photo by Bill Siegel;
tourists: photo by Roger Geller; volunteer: ESB Professional; Shutterstock; birthday: Monkey Business Images, Shutterstock.
Photo credits: p19: Pixelrobot, Dreamstine.com; p24, 42, 67: Bill Aron; p31: David Behrman and Vicki Weber; p95:
Shalea Oretzky; p119 and p235: wavebreakmedia, Shutterstock; p130, 213, 221: Wikimedia Commons; p132: Terry Pullan; p153:
Meal Train; p156: Fair Trade Judaica; p192: Philippe Vahe; p198: Jane Menster; p211: Roz Chast,
book cover of Can't we talk about something more PLEASANT? (New York: Bloomsbury USA, 2016).
Reprinted by permission of Bloomsbury Publishing Plc.; p258: bbernard, Shutterstock; p261: mickyso, Shutterstock.

ISBN 978-0-87441-985-6
Printed in the United States of America.

Library of Congress Cataloging-in-Publication Data

Names: Siegel, Richard, 1948- author. | Geller, Laura, 1950- author.
Title: Getting good at getting older / Richard Siegel and Rabbi Laura Geller.
Description: Millburn, New Jersey : Behrman House, 2019. | Includes index.
Summary: "A tour for all of us "of a certain age" through the
resources and skills to navigate the years between maturity and old age,
told with warmth, humor, and more than 4,000 years of Jewish experience
to the question of how to shape this new stage of life"— Provided by publisher.
Identifiers: LCCN 2019039579 | ISBN 9780874419856 (paperback) | ISBN 9781681150543 (ebook)
Subjects: LCSH: Older people–Life skills guides. | Older people--Conduct of life.
Classification: LCC HQ1061 .S48496 2019 | DDC 305.26—dc23
LC record available at https://lccn.loc.gov/2019039579

Visit www.behrmanhouse.com/ggago for more resources
Visit rabbilaurageller.com for information about book events and
to read more about Getting Good at Getting Older.

5 7 9 8 6 4

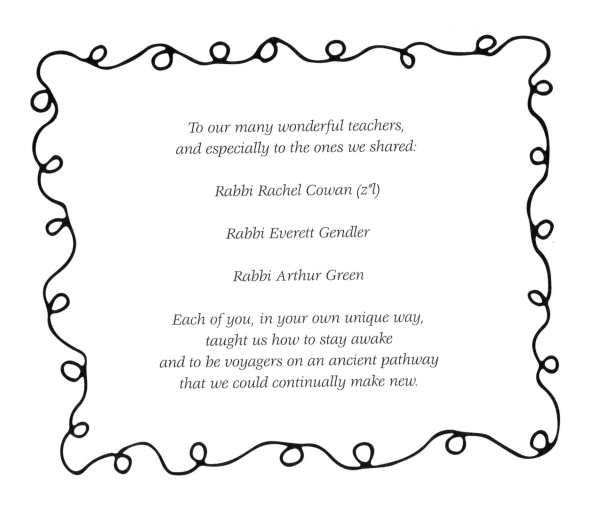

To our many wonderful teachers,
and especially to the ones we shared:

Rabbi Rachel Cowan (z"l)

Rabbi Everett Gendler

Rabbi Arthur Green

Each of you, in your own unique way,
taught us how to stay awake
and to be voyagers on an ancient pathway
that we could continually make new.

Contents

Author's Note

This is the introduction I never wanted to write.

When Richard and I began working on this book, we were both in our sixties. We imagined that we would bring the wisdom of a rabbi and an educator to the questions of how all of us get older—how we can do it wisely, and with a sense of humor. And we imagined that it might even help the two of us get better at getting older together. But then, Richard was diagnosed with cancer.

In the face of that bad news, working on the book actually helped Richard, me, and us as a couple navigate all the issues surrounding his illness. Our years of discussion, research, and writing about the art of aging—which is the essence of this book—gave us a shared vocabulary and an intimacy that enabled us to face his cancer with honesty, with humility, and, believe it or not, even with humor. Getting good at getting older isn't just a bumper sticker. It's a mind-set that sees this stage of life as an invitation to a road trip, perhaps even a magical mystery tour.

What that meant for Richard was staying awake to what he was experiencing, being prepared, knowing the people he loved would be able to flourish after he died, that they would know how much he loved them, and that he could come to understand the legacy he was leaving behind.

Richard died one month short of his seventy-first birthday.

As unprepared as any of us is for a loved one to die, I was prepared. I had a list of all his passwords, I knew all his account numbers, our children knew what decisions he would make at the end of his life. And because we had imagined this road trip to getting older together, we had a clear sense of the projects we wanted to work on, including continuing to be curious about reimagining aging. That brings me comfort even as I continue the work without him.

When that moment comes for someone you love, I know that having thought about the issues this book raises will be as helpful for you as it was for me.

But let me be clear: This is a book about life, meant to empower, delight, challenge, and whet our appetite for whatever comes next.

Richard galvanized a generation of Jews to take ownership of their Jewishness through his writing and teaching. Through this book, he hoped to similarly infuse *our* generation with ownership of how we get good at getting older as we move into our sixties and beyond. Though his death came too early, he leaves an important legacy. What you take from this book will be a part of that.

I am grateful to have been his partner.

Laura

Introduction

Do you remember the '60s—the bumper stickers that read "Question Authority," the marches, the music, the energy? We believed that we could change the world, that we were invincible and immortal, that anything was possible. The book that captured the ethos of that generation was the *Whole Earth Catalog*, a do-it-yourself manual of the American counterculture. Among its opening lines is this: "We are as gods and might as well get good at it."

Now that we are in our 60s (more or less) we know that we are neither invincible nor immortal. In fact, we are all too human. Perhaps our mantra should now be: "We're getting older and we might as well get good at it."

We changed the world once and now we can do it again. We are in this new stage of life, between midlife and frail old age, that doesn't even have a name. Let's approach it as we approached our younger years, with energy, with ambition, with intentionality, and with chutzpah.

We are now living approximately 30 years longer than people were a century ago, thanks to advances in medicine, education, and science. These are *decades* now tacked on to midlife, a whole life stage our parents and grandparents never experienced. What will we do with those extra years? In the Okinawan language, there is a word connected to all the stages of adult life: *Ikigai* (eek-y-guy). It means "the purpose for which you wake up in the morning."

What is our purpose now—when we're more distant from the work or child-rearing that used to fill our days? How can we get good at finding meaning and purpose in the time we have left? Now that more years have been added to our lives, how can we add more life to our years?

We boomers are used to being culture makers and culture changers. We can continue on this path as we challenge the conventional view of aging—as a time of decline—and instead view it as a time of possibility and opportunity. We can develop new practices, new behaviors, and new wisdom about these years, transforming prevailing ideas about aging and shaping a different vision for ourselves and for society at large. Ageism, sadly, is real, a prejudice still sanctioned in polite society. Older people often aren't considered for jobs for which they are qualified. Growing older is the butt of jokes and birthday cards. Marketers covet what's young and fresh and new. Older people can feel invisible or ignored, even though huge numbers of us boomers and beyond have lifetimes of experience, talent, and energy and want to put all that to good use.

It's up to us to confront and challenge assumptions about aging, both in the world and within ourselves. We may not even realize when we buy into ageism. We say 60 is the new 40. Seventy is the new 50. But that's just a way of pretending that we aren't really growing older. Internalized ageism manifests even in the difficulty we have at finding words to describe this stage of our life. What word do you prefer: Retired? Maybe you're not. Senior? Those senior discounts at movies or restaurants are nice, but many of us don't like the actual word. Elder? Sounds too old. Sage? Too pretentious. We accept ageist stereotypes: that wrinkles are ugly; that it is sad to be old; that old people are incompetent. And, most of all, we view older people as "other," not us—not even "future" us.

Guess what? Seventy is not the new 50. Seventy is simply a new 70.

Here's an alternative for what to call us: perennials. As Dr. Laura Carstensen from the Stanford Center of Longevity says, "The symbolism is perfect. We're still here, blossoming again and again. It also suggests a new model of life in which people engage and take breaks, making new starts repeatedly. Perennials aren't guaranteed to blossom year after year, but given proper conditions, good soil and nutrients, they can go on for decades. It's aspirational."

This change in mindset is good news. It means that we get to make the rules for how we want to live these years, and we don't have to conform to notions of what being a certain age should look like. We also don't have to accept the story of competition for resources between generations and instead can tell the story of the benefits of bringing older people together with younger people with different skills and energy. It turns out that a lifestyle that celebrates independence and autonomy rather than building community is bad for everybody's health. If we ask new questions about social policy concerning housing, recreation, transportation, higher education, health care, or information technology, the changes we make in our world will change our future and the futures of those who follow us.

Back in 1973, Richard and his friends created *The Jewish Catalog: A Do-It-Yourself Kit*. It empowered a generation to take back Judaism from the staid hands of our elders and reshape it for our times. In *Getting Good at Getting Older*, the two of us—Richard as a Jewish communal leader and Laura as a rabbi—have created this guidebook to frame a new way of approaching aging, with tools and resources we can use to inhabit this phase of our lives and, in doing so, change the world around us. Now that we are the elders, we hope that instead of staid hands, we bring a sense of humor and curiosity as we ask what guidance Jewish wisdom can offer us now. It turns out what was true in the '60s is still true today: We have to create the traditions we are looking for. This book offers do-it-yourself tools shaped by more than 4,000 years of tradition for gaining wisdom, getting along, getting better, getting ready, giving back, and giving away.

We do not presume to prescribe an antidote to aging. Nor do we offer a solemn sermon about living life to the fullest. We know that growing older is hard. But growing older can also be so much more than simply growing old.

Let's get good at it—together.

1

Getting Good at Gaining Wisdom

Occasionally we meet an older person we admire and think, "I want to be like that when I grow up—wise, joyful, grateful, compassionate, patient, funny, curious, optimistic." As Estelle Reiner said in the classic deli scene from *When Harry Met Sally*, "I'll have what she's having." Some of these qualities might be beyond our capacity—can we really cultivate "funny"?—but others might be within reach. The question for us boomers is this: What can we do now to become the 85-year-old we someday hope to be? Psalm 90 says: "Teach us to number our days so we may attain a heart of wisdom." What do we do now to acquire a heart of wisdom?

You can't just order these traits in a restaurant. There is no shortcut.

We once saw the following sign on a storefront:

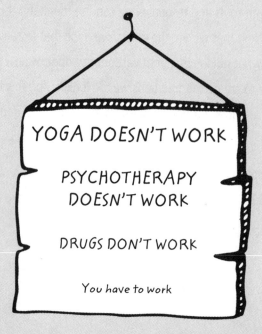

YOGA DOESN'T WORK

PSYCHOTHERAPY
DOESN'T WORK

DRUGS DON'T WORK

You have to work

> Life is about not knowing, having to change, taking the moment and making the best of it, without knowing what's going to happen next. Delicious ambiguity.
>
> —Gilda Radner, *It's Always Something*

We all have to work on ourselves to attain a heart of wisdom.

The book of Job notes that "with age comes wisdom and with length of days understanding" (12:12). However, the influential social psychologist Erik Erikson observed that "lots of old people don't get wise, but you don't get wise unless you age."

As we will see in the chapters that follow, there are many ways to cultivate wisdom in the second half of life. A practice of personal and spiritual review can lead from self-discovery to personal transformation. Looking at the bigger picture, we change the world for the better by starting with ourselves. Spiritual practices—mindfulness, journaling, spiritual direction, slowing down—can help us, among many things, better prioritize, handle stress, improve our self-esteem, and strengthen family connections. One thing we learn as we grow older is that wisdom isn't a static destination but an ongoing accumulation of knowledge, insight, and experience. Lucky for us, opportunities for lifelong learning abound, whether by ourselves, with a friend, in a small group or a large class, or online; whether by studying texts, traveling, or acquiring new skills. As we learn more about ourselves and those around us, we may be inspired to create new ways to acknowledge and celebrate those special moments and accomplishments as poignant markers of and motivation for our continued growth. As Rabbi Zalman Schachter-Shalomi shows us, our own hearts and souls are laboratories to cultivate the skills we need for what he calls "eldering." As he advises, "As you become more skillful in harvesting the fruits of a lifetime, you will embark on an adventure in consciousness that will lead to a more noble, useful, and fulfilling age."

I WANT TO BE Like THEY ARE.

CHAPTER 1   Changing Your Life for (the) Good

Words of Wisdom

Most of us have clearer strategies for how to achieve career success than we do for how to develop a profound character.... Change your behavior and eventually you rewire your brain.

—David Brooks, The Road to Character

There are many ways to change your behavior, rewire your brain, and cultivate a heart of wisdom. We and our contributors offer five practices to help you do that.

Personal Transformation

by Rabbi Laura Geller

Mussar is a Hebrew term that means "instruction," "correction," or "ethics." Although the roots of mussar are in the tenth century, it has resurfaced in contemporary Judaism largely as a result of the work of Alan Morinis, founder of the Mussar Institute. In his book *Everyday Holiness: The Jewish Spiritual Path of Mussar*, Morinis describes mussar as "a path of spiritual self-development. It means working on yourself, but not for the sake of your self. . . . Its purpose is not that you will gratify all your desires but that you will become the master of your desires, so you can fulfill the potential of your higher nature."

The mussar tradition is based on the notion that everyone has "soul traits" (*middot*), such as humility, patience, honor, enthusiasm, and generosity, but each of us possesses those traits in different measures. Through concerted attention, we can refine those traits, keep them in balance, and not let them go to extremes. Consider humility: too much and you become a doormat, too little and you become arrogant.

How can we practice balancing these traits? Begin by identifying specific traits to focus on, what Morinis calls your "spiritual curriculum." He recommends focusing on a different trait each week. Where to start is up to you. If you look around the living room and have a hard time seeing the floor, "order" is likely to be a trait on your list. If someone cuts you off on the freeway and you scream through the windshield, then "equanimity" might belong there as well.

Morinis suggests some daily practices to help us work on our traits.

Adopt a daily reminder phrase.

Find a text or saying that captures the trait for you. For instance, if you want to cultivate humility, your phrase could be "No more than my place, no less than my space." Read over the phrase and concentrate on it when you wake up in the morning.

Develop an exercise for the times you're tempted to forget about working on the trait.

Keeping with the humility example, when you're inclined to speak up in a one-on-one conversation or a group setting and have already done so many times already, ask yourself: WAIT (Why Am I Talking?). If you don't have a good reason, don't talk. This is a way to cultivate humility.

Practice journaling.

At some point in the day, perhaps bedtime, reflect on the past 24 hours and notice how your trait of the week was manifest. Writing about this will help you become more aware of the choices you've made, big and small.

Many of us struggle with similar character challenges, so even better than working through them on our own is to share the practice with a partner and come together periodically with a larger group to reflect on the process. A group also creates a kind of accountability for the work you're doing.

Paying attention to our soul traits is good practice throughout our lives. One that is particularly important for us to focus on as we grow older is gratitude. As Dr. George Vaillant, director of the Harvard Study of Adult Development and the author of *Aging Well*, observes, "[Those] who have aged most successfully are those who worry less about cholesterol and waistlines and more about gratitude and forgiveness."

Why 13 Traits?

The traditional mussar practice is based on studying 13 traits, one at a time, then repeating the cycle with the same list of traits. Why?

"Each trait is practiced for one week before you move on to another trait. Some weeks you may be tempted to extend the trait work for another week—perhaps you were making enormous progress, or just the opposite. . . . [But] we want to work each trait with our greatest energy. When we extend beyond a week, our interest and resolve begin to wane, the freshness of the trait dwindles, and we likely find ourselves falling back on old habits."
—Edith Brotman, *Mussar Yoga: Blending an Ancient Jewish Spiritual Practice with Yoga to Transform Body and Soul*

Some common traits that people choose to actively cultivate include:

- Gratitude
- Forgiveness
- Humility
- Generosity
- Enthusiasm
- Compassion
- Order

- Patience
- Simplicity
- Honesty
- Responsibility
- Strength
- Equanimity

MUSSAR UP CLOSE: GRATITUDE

Daily phrase: Awaken to the good and give thanks.

Exercise: The Jewish practice of saying 100 blessings each day is an interesting challenge. Although some blessings are related to commandments, most are simply expressions of gratitude. For instance, upon waking up in the morning, instead of hitting "snooze" on the alarm clock and muttering "Oh God!" try saying a blessing, such as the traditional morning prayer: "I am grateful to You, Living and Eternal Spirit, that You have returned/restored my soul to me in mercy. Great is Your faithfulness." Or make up your own.

Adopting this practice would mean that 100 times a day we stop, look around, and notice some little miracle, something we might otherwise take for granted. These expressions of gratitude need not be traditional prayers. For instance, one of our editors has a friend who recently went through chemo for breast cancer. She is a real foodie and struggled to eat throughout treatment. Some days the food she loves tasted good; other days she couldn't choke it down. And she got really depressed about that. As a way to cope, she started saying a prayer of thanks each time something tasted the way it should, so it was something she could enjoy: "Thank You, God, that this yogurt tastes like yogurt today." "Thank You, God, for introducing me to liver, which I never would have tried before, but at this moment it inexplicably tastes great and is providing nutrients I really need." She's on the other side of treatment now and her taste buds have returned, but she has an entirely different and much deeper appreciation for food—and she's keeping up her gratitude practice.

Given how much and how often many of us eat, just focusing on gratitude blessings for food will go a long way toward that 100 a day. As part of your mussar practice, try to pay special attention to what you are eating, not just what it looks like but also how it grows, where it came from, who brought it to you, and all the people whose labor made it possible for you to enjoy it—growers, farmworkers, packers, grocery store workers. How does that consciousness change your behavior toward all those people and the conditions under which they work?

You can find mussar groups in your community online or perhaps through your local synagogue or JCC.

Journaling: Take it one step further and write down your reactions to the practice in a journal, and see how that makes you feel.

A traditional prayer book often has lists of gratitude blessings, such as when you see the ocean, a rainbow, or a friend you haven't seen for a while or when you hear good news. Once you get started, you will undoubtedly find many more than a hundred moments to express your gratitude each day. In all these moments, saying a blessing—a traditional one or one you compose on your own—helps you notice what you are experiencing and enables you to find the good in it for which you can be grateful.

Getting to know ourselves as we age is one step to growing wiser. Particularly as we get older and reflect on the many chapters of our lives, mussar, or character development, is one of the most powerful practices to help us change our behavior. Another is mindfulness.

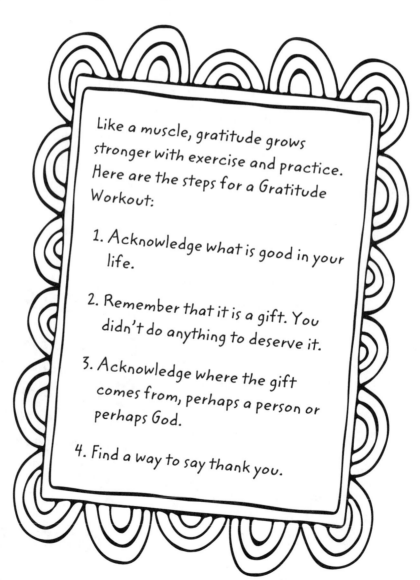

Like a muscle, gratitude grows stronger with exercise and practice. Here are the steps for a Gratitude Workout:

1. Acknowledge what is good in your life.

2. Remember that it is a gift. You didn't do anything to deserve it.

3. Acknowledge where the gift comes from, perhaps a person or perhaps God.

4. Find a way to say thank you.

Mindfulness

by Sylvia Boorstein

It is hard not to notice that mindfulness, a practice for establishing clarity and balance in the mind, has taken off out of its original Buddhist context and made it into mainstream American culture: mindful parenting, mindful eating, mindful childbirth, mindful gardening. Down the street from where I live, a studio advertises "Mindful Chiropractic." Every time I pass the sign I think, "I certainly *hope* so. The alternative would seem to be Haphazard Chiropractic."

Sylvia Boorstein is a cofounding teacher of Spirit Rock Meditation Center in Marin County, California, where we both have studied with her, as well as in workshops and retreats sponsored by the Institute for Jewish Spirituality.

It seems to me that this upsurge in interest in mindfulness is at least partly the result of demographic changes. When I began to practice meditation 40 years ago, I was surrounded by young people taking time, often just after college, for personal spiritual questing. It was part of the zeitgeist of the era. At 40, I was often the oldest participant at mindfulness retreats, but now classes are full of gray-haired people past retirement age. People at this stage, like younger people, yearn for experiences of abounding love and joy that are typically a part of contemplative experience. They also want to feel that their lives are still meaningful and that the losses they are beginning to experience are manageable.

I think it is fine that *mindfulness* has such super-special, almost mystical meaning. Acting mindfully enhances the possibility of making wise choices (in any activity) and therefore reduces unnecessary strife and enhances possibilities for happiness. A wise mind that is completely relaxed is definitely a divine experience. However, it's not mystical as much as sensible. Here's a simple overall instruction for developing mindfulness: Pay attention, carefully and deliberately, to whatever you are doing, with the goal of living in a way that is gratifying to you and everyone else.

I was giving a talk at a local school about mindfulness and the importance of paying attention when a sixth-grade boy asked, "How can I tell that I'm not paying attention? When I'm not, I don't know that I'm not." That was a valuable and true observation. We do sort of know that we are daydreaming, fantasizing, or ruminating about something from the past or worrying about what is coming up, but usually we just continue to be preoccupied until we have the sudden awakening: "Oh my goodness, I'm not at all present. I've missed the whole first act of the opera"; "I missed that whole explanation from this salesperson and need to ask him again"; "I lost interest in what my wife was saying and I missed the rest of her story, and now I need to respond"; "I know I came in the front door and put my keys deliberately where I knew I'd be able to find them, and now I don't remember where they are." Does this ever happen to you? We lose memory capacity as we age, but training our attention to stay present for current experience on behalf of wise discernment and wise action in every situation is beneficial at any age.

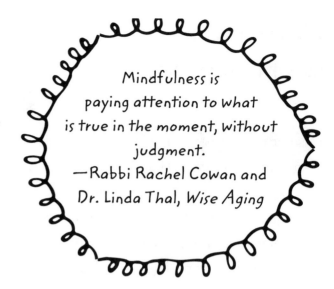

Mindfulness is paying attention to what is true in the moment, without judgment.
—Rabbi Rachel Cowan and Dr. Linda Thal, Wise Aging

THE ELEMENTS OF MINDFULNESS

Mindfulness has two components. One is steadiness of mind: the ability to keep from easily becoming distracted. We develop this steadiness, often called "concentration," by bringing attention to an aspect of our current situation, such as the feelings of breathing in and out that become more prominent when we sit down and close our eyes to meditate. We can also develop concentration with open eyes, walking at a steady pace (perhaps around a track or around the block) and attending primarily to the feeling of feet alternately connecting with the ground. Plain, steady, repetitive, neutral sensations are perfect for calming the mind into a steady, balanced state.

The second component of mindfulness is clarity: being able to recognize different impressions, feelings, opinions, and other responses that follow one after another as we move through an experience. We don't always recognize these prompts to action. Consider these scenarios:

- You are walking down a street and a pleasant smell of pizza wafts into your nostrils, followed by the awareness that you are hungry, followed by the discovery that you've veered off course and into the pizzeria and have bought a slice and are walking out without remembering that you were already late for your next meeting that includes lunch.

- You are standing at the copy machine and hear that the candidate you did not support just got elected. The sudden rise of fear and anger in you leads you to say, "I can't believe who voted this way—idiots!" before you realize that your colleague is standing next to you wearing a button endorsing the winning candidate.

- You are at a large family wedding, and a cousin approaches you and makes what you consider a snarky remark about your not having kept in touch. Your indignation arises. You are just about to rebut the remark but notice that the cousin probably has had a bit too much to drink, and remembering what good friends you were in childhood, you instead hug the cousin and feel pleased that you have avoided ruining an otherwise good relationship.

Clarity of mind is what makes the difference between the first two examples of distracted, impulsive action and the last example of conscious, attentive reflection. We think, "This feeling is arising in me, and now this impulse, but . . . I can wait, let the impulse pass, and feel relieved not to upset either of us." In other words, mindfulness is acting with clarity, with the support of steadiness of mind, on behalf of peace in our own mind and peace for others.

Just as there are exercises for cultivating concentration, there are exercises for cultivating clarity. I often think to myself, "Right now I am very happy." Or "Right now I'm starting to feel irritable, so I am thinking of what will soothe this. Maybe I'm hungry. Maybe I'm tired. Maybe I'm confused."

Of course, it would be great if every time our mind felt "off" we could sit quietly for a few moments to steady it again. Most of us live at a pace that does not allow for that. An alternative is being mindfully aware. For example, recognize that "I'm really grumpy. I'll just need to be careful now not to be impulsive in what I say or do." I call it TIO, "Thinking It Over."

Think it over.

Spiritual Direction

by Rabbi Ruth H. Sohn

Ruth Sohn is a longtime friend and colleague of ours. She directs the Spirituality Initiative and the Leona Aronoff Rabbinic Mentoring Program at HUC-JIR in Los Angeles and co-directs the Yedidya Center's Morei Derekh Jewish Spiritual Directors Training Program.

Spiritual direction is another powerful practice for those of us entering—or already well into—this stage of life.

When Cheryl first came to me for spiritual direction, she was anticipating big changes in her life. In just a few months she would turn 65 and welcome her first grandchild into the world. Within the next two years, she planned to retire from a high-powered business career and sell her business. Cheryl anticipated a changing relationship with her husband and eagerly looked forward to having more time to travel and pursue other interests.

To prepare for these changes, Cheryl sought help to consider who she had become as a person. What was she pleased with and what did she want to change? How could she prepare herself to meet the anticipated and still unknown changes she knew were just around the corner? She had recently come to feel that the demands of her business career had taken a toll on her natural capacity for compassion, and she wanted to correct that. This proved a rich area for exploration and growth, including the discovery that compassion for herself could be even more challenging than compassion for others—and just as transformative.

Cultural anthropologist Mary Catherine Bateson calls Cheryl's new stage of life "later adulthood," a time that invites exploration and discovery as well as the chance to reclaim parts of ourselves we may have neglected or forgotten over the years. We ask ourselves:

- What has been the meaning of my life thus far?
- What questions, yearning, and mystery draw me forward now?
- What relationships are most important to me today?
- Is there work in the world I am still called to engage in?

WHAT IS SPIRITUAL DIRECTION?

Spiritual direction, first developed by Christian desert mothers and fathers in the third century, is practiced today by people of virtually every religion and spiritual orientation. Also known as "spiritual companioning," spiritual direction invites us to explore and deepen

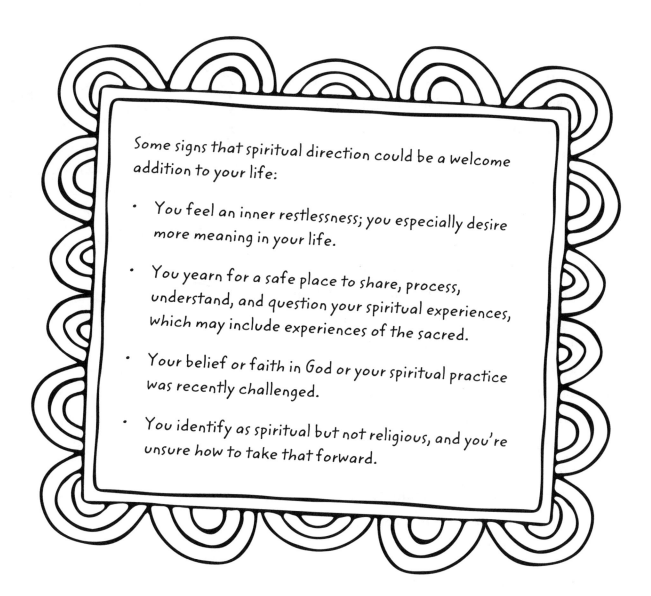

Some signs that spiritual direction could be a welcome addition to your life:

- You feel an inner restlessness; you especially desire more meaning in your life.

- You yearn for a safe place to share, process, understand, and question your spiritual experiences, which may include experiences of the sacred.

- Your belief or faith in God or your spiritual practice was recently challenged.

- You identify as spiritual but not religious, and you're unsure how to take that forward.

our connection with the sacred—however we experience it: God, the Divine, the Holy, the Mystery, our higher purpose, our inner soul—and to consider how this connection might make a difference in how we want to live.

The term *spiritual direction* refers to an internal invitation: What can we do to bring our inner and outer lives into deeper alignment with each other, to move closer to the "hidden wholeness" that educator Parker Palmer, in his book *A Hidden Wholeness*, suggests is "the deepest yearning of our soul"? Spiritual direction can open us to our heart's desires for greater connection, love, service, and gratitude. It can help us identify that which is torn or broken in our lives and the world and often opens for us new stirrings and clarity about potential paths we can take toward healing.

WHAT IS JEWISH SPIRITUAL DIRECTION?

Jews of past generations knew the practice of meeting with a trusted spiritual guide to engage in deep listening, spiritual counseling, and guidance—for example, the rebbes and spiritual advisors of the Hasidic and Orthodox movements—but many Jews today are unfamiliar with the formal practice of spiritual direction. How did we lose our connection to this contemplative, prayerful form of one-to-one guidance and support?

We baby boomers grew up in a Jewish world shattered by the Holocaust, in which the word *God* often raised more questions than answers. In Jewish Community Centers, Federations, and even synagogues, the emphasis was on fighting anti-Semitism, ensuring Jewish survival and continuity, and supporting the State of Israel. Questions about God, if voiced at all, were more likely to be "Where was God in the death camps?" or "How could God have allowed this to happen?" rather than "When and how do I sense the Divine in my life?" or "How am I being invited to respond more fully to this moment?" Spiritual experience and concerns were so absent in Jewish organizational and even religious life that many Jews turned East, to Buddhism and Hinduism, in search of spiritual awakening. In fact, many of the best-known teachers of Eastern meditation and mindfulness practices in the United States—Sylvia Boorstein, Jack Kornfield, Sharon Salzberg, Jon Kabat-Zinn—are Jewish.

> Talking about or belief in God is not necessary to benefit from spiritual direction. It can be a powerful practice for those of us who are "spiritual but not religious."

Today there is renewed interest in Jewish spiritual practices both traditional and contemporary, including Jewish spiritual direction. Jewish spiritual direction is distinct in that it helps us connect experiences of the holy to Jewish vocabulary and tradition, explore Jewish pathways that sustain the inner life, and inspire participation in spiritual community.

BRING IT ON.

SPIRITUAL COURAGE

HOW IS SPIRITUAL DIRECTION DIFFERENT FROM THERAPY OR PASTORAL COUNSELING?

Therapy and pastoral counseling are oriented toward problem-solving. Therapy seeks to deepen our understanding and help us adjust to the emotional challenges of life. Pastoral counseling offers insight into how religious wisdom and tradition can help us understand and respond to life and its challenges. In spiritual direction we attend to the stirrings of the soul, the "still small voice" within us. We take time to notice where the Divine is showing up in our life and nurture our unfolding relationship with the mystery or oneness that many call God. A spiritual director supports us as we strengthen and deepen our inner life.

Spiritual direction helped David face the unanticipated early death of his wife. He deeply appreciated how spiritual direction helped him access his connection with "something bigger than myself" months before his wife's leukemia diagnosis. When she died just three months later, he found he was more in tune with and accepting of the range of emotions that welled up again and again, often in sudden surges of feeling. As he moved through the difficult places of intense grief and painful loss, he always emerged stronger. Over time his readiness to accept and be with these difficult feelings allowed him to open more deeply to gratitude, a calm presence, and an inner strength that surprised him.

Meeting regularly with a spiritual companion can help us get better at getting older by offering a way for us to explore what is moving under the surface of our daily interactions and activities. It makes it possible to hear the desire for more loving connections and identify opportunities to make a difference in our lives, the lives of others, and our surrounding world. Spiritual direction can call forth gifts still waiting to be discovered and shared as you come to see the story of your life as a sacred journey. And that can change your life.

Journaling
by Merle Feld

Journaling is a fourth practice
that deepens our sense of life as a sacred journey.

The spiritual practice of journaling, sublime in its simplicity, is an opportunity for opening, a means to record the journey of your days, ordinary and extraordinary. It's a way to better see and explore your inner world. Use it to give yourself the gift of quiet time, solitary time, to find the silent places within and to listen carefully.

Richard met Merle and studied with her in the early years of Havurat Shalom Community Seminary in Somerville, Massachusetts. She is the founding director of the Albin Rabbinic Writing Institute, helping rabbinical students and rabbis from all denominations explore their spiritual lives so they can serve others more effectively as spiritual leaders.

The process is simple but transformative. It's a way to encounter your deepest self, as some are able to do through prayer, meditation, or spending time in nature. You begin by identifying a feeling—longing, confusion, exultation, fear—and then you find words to express those emotions. As you write, with no one to impress, giving your judgmental self a "time-out," you reach for understanding, listening for the stories that beg for explication, for meaning making. It's an opening for you to be kind, loving, and completely truthful with yourself, and then to see the surprises, insights, and comfort that can emerge.

HOW TO BEGIN A JOURNALING PRACTICE

Buy yourself one of those hardcover, black-and-white-marbled composition notebooks at your local office supply store—the kind of notebook you might remember from third grade, that you carried as you walked to school in the fall, crunching the leaves underfoot, your heart stirring at the hope of new beginnings. The hardcover means you can sit with it on your lap anywhere; no need for a desk, just sit and write—the original "laptop." I also love these notebooks because they're cheap and therefore not threatening. Perhaps you, like me, are intimidated by those exquisitely beautiful journals people buy to give as gifts. I can't guarantee that what I write will be as wonderful as the notebook itself; I'm afraid of spoiling it—an invitation to writer's block. With a notebook I paid a couple of bucks for (or less), I feel at ease.

Why write by hand? In my experience, it connects us much more deeply to the heart, to the authentic, to the unexpected. Computers are great because they let us go faster, faster. Journaling, though, is all about slower, slower. (If you try to write by hand and it doesn't work for you, go with whatever works; make friends with your laptop and give it a name as your new treasured companion.)

With the means to write, find a quiet place where you won't be disturbed. At first it will help to write in the same place to reinforce the habits that will support a practice, but as you develop your capacity to focus and go deep in the writing, you'll be able to block out distractions and write anywhere, anytime.

WHEN TO WRITE? HOW OFTEN TO WRITE?

Establish a routine. Look at your weekly schedule and identify regular pockets of time—early in the day before others even rise; as part of your lunch break; in the evening hours as you wind down for sleep. Designate small blocks of time on your calendar, two or three days a

A Group Encounter

Writing with a friend or a group of friends can provide an extraordinary opportunity for spiritual encounter. You can do this weekly, with partners using the same prompts or texts as take-off points or writing as "parallel play," each focusing on your own subject. After writing, you can share what you've written or just talk about what you've written; both are profound ways of coming to know one other. Similarly, you could convene a spiritual writing group once a month, once a season, perhaps designating one participant each time to provide prompts. Several years ago, on a major anniversary of my mother's death, I gathered a small group of women friends to write and share together. We each came with photos and stories. We remembered, cried, and laughed together. We ended the evening closer than we'd ever been. The possibilities for such groups are limitless.

week—write your name on your calendar to indicate commitment. Try different times of day and see what works for you and how often during the week feels best.

HOW MUCH TIME SHOULD YOU SET ASIDE?

A half hour is enough time to let your mind relax, your thoughts drift, to write and be spacious. If that's not possible, even the busiest person has 10- to 15-minute pockets in the day to claim for themselves. You'll be amazed how deep even such a short experience of writing can be.

Listen to yourself as you would listen to the people you most dearly love: with rapt attention and tenderness, curiosity, compassion. Then let the stories, your thoughts and feelings, tumble onto the page. Relax and let the details of special moments return to you as you write. You can try the rich experience of journaling on your own or enjoy special time of intimate sharing with a writing partner or a small group of friends.

Going Forward

Above all, a journaling practice is about connecting with yourself. As the process unfolds, you'll discover that journaling can offer the rich reward of sparking new growth, deepening self-understanding, heightening awareness, and softening or even healing old sorrows.

Tech Shabbat
by Tiffany Shlain

The fifth practice, one that has been a particular challenge for us, is taking a break from tech, unplugging for one day a week.

In 1997 I first met my partner in everything, Ken Goldberg, who practiced Shabbat. I found it profound but also sexy when he, as a busy robotics professor, said, "I never work on Saturdays. It's Shabbat. We need one day off." It's sexy to have deep wisdom guide you. As a cultural Jew, I was intrigued.

We first encountered Bay Area artist and educator Tiffany Shlain through her mind-bending, award-winning short documentary film *The Tribe*, which tells the history of the Jewish people through the herstory of the Barbie doll.

Fast-forward to 2007: We're married, we're parents, and the iPhone is released. We now have this addictive, compelling device in our pockets, ready for a hit of distraction, entertainment, or escape. I remember us placing our two cellophane-wrapped white boxes on the kitchen table and I struggled to convey why I felt as if opening them would be a detriment to our relationship. But, of course, we opened the boxes and were soon mainlining data, text, emails, and calls like everyone else.

I love technology. I have always been one of the first people to try things out and experiment with different creative uses of it. I know the benefits that technology can bring to our lives, businesses, relationships. But I see over and over again that connecting broadly is meaningless unless you also connect deeply.

In 2009 my father died and our daughter Blooma was born within days of each other. I thought a lot about life, death, the meaning of it all. It was all happening too fast, and technology seemed to speed up time and interrupt the present moment like an assault. Reboot, an organization I am a part of, planned a National Day of Unplugging and asked me to join them. I was ready.

So there I was, unmoored by losing one of my strongest connections, my father. I looked at the other people I loved deeply in my life and knew I had to do things differently if I wanted to live in a way I felt good about—where I wasn't moving so fast all the time. I wanted to slow. it. all. down. Albert Einstein said that time is relative to your state of motion. With all this texting, tweeting, posting, and emailing, we're making our minds move faster, which accelerates our perception of time. It seemed there wasn't a day that went by when I didn't think, "How did it get to be 5 p.m.?"

I recruited my family to join me. We were ready to bring some presence back. The day we participated in the National Day of Unplugging was so good, clean, and present that we decided to make it a weekly practice, a modern interpretation of a very old tradition. It is the best thing we have ever done.

People ask, "Is it hard?" At the beginning I did have the phantom limb sensation of reaching for my phone to look something up or call or text someone. But I keep a piece of paper out with a big black pen, and for the first couple hours I jot down whatever combination of to-dos or reminders tumble from my head. Then I feel set free. And Sunday morning it's like a dam breaks; rested and recharged, I'm at my most productive and creative.

Some people say, "We have too many events on Saturday. How would I coordinate with people? This will never work with my family." My answer to that is to print out a schedule on Friday afternoon.

"What if people need to get in touch with you in case of an emergency?" We have a landline for just that purpose.

What about the email, the voice mail, the texts that pile up? They'll still be there tomorrow, and I've never missed something important because I took 24 hours to recharge.

You can come up with a lot of reasons not to unplug. But I've found a lot more compelling reasons why you should. According to a recent Nielsen survey, the average American adult spends 74 hours a week staring at a screen—and the majority of that time is stressful. Our tech Shabbats have become a secret force field of protection to give us the strength, perspective, and energy for the other six days.

I also now experience what I had heard so many times from my parents when I was a child: Life continues to speed up the older you get. My tool to slow things down is to turn things off.

So taking a tech Shabbat is a kind of magic that slows down time and makes every connection better. What more could we want?

When I reflect back on my favorite moments—when I really felt present and connected with the people in my life—I usually find they're on our tech-free days. I want these times to feel as long as possible, and unplugging is what makes that happen.

CHAPTER 2

Cooking Up New Rituals

by Rabbi Laura Geller and Richard Siegel

Laura received a call from a 55-year-old woman as the woman was on her way to clean out her parents' apartment just after she and her brother had moved their mother into an assisted living facility. The woman asked, "Rabbi, what is the prayer you say when you begin to close up the home you grew up in?" I thought, "What a good question. There should be a prayer at a moment like this." The answer was not in any standard clergy handbook . . . yet. Creating the right prayer and saying it before she and her brother began to dismantle the home transformed their experience from a chore into a sacred act.

Rituals like this matter. Traditionally, rituals and ceremonies mark important transitions that a community wants to reflect on and use as teachable moments. As individuals, we too can infuse moments like these with meaning. And, over time, if enough people see particular transitions as significant, then what matters to our communities begins to change.

Case in point: The Jewish religious school curriculum in the 1950s and '60s often included a class about life-cycle rituals: circumcision (*brit milah*), redemption of the firstborn son (*pidyon haben*), bar mitzvah, marriage, and death. The curriculum made it clear that what mattered was the experience of boys and men, not that of girls and women. What else didn't seem to matter? Anything that happened between marriage and death.

In the late 1960s and '70s, inspired by the women's movement, Jewish women insisted that their

Words of Wisdom

There are moments you remember all your life.

—"This Is One of Those Moments," from the Yentl soundtrack

experiences be recognized as part of the overall Jewish experience. So began a transformative moment in Jewish life, as women created new rituals to celebrate key moments in their lives: welcoming girls into the covenant, weaning, previously hidden experiences such as abortion and miscarriage, and the onset of menopause. Such rituals can now readily be found on the internet, and many have made their way into rabbis' manuals and seminary and religious school curricula.

Now it's our turn. As we move into and through this next stage of our lives, we will encounter many events, occasions, transitions, beginnings, and endings, and we might want to pause and reflect on their deeper significance and emotional resonance. Just as we have anticipated and prepared for previous meaningful moments in our lives—coming of age, getting married, having a child—we can anticipate and prepare for these later-in-life experiences as well. Rituals, both religious and secular, can help remind us about what really matters and connect us to our traditions and our authentic selves.

How can we create new rituals? Let's think of it as akin to preparing a meal. First, we recognize that we are hungry for something to nourish us at a particular milestone. Then, we choose the setting and with whom we want to mark the moment—our guests. Finally, we mix together the ingredients to create something special.

Moments to Celebrate

What follows are certain moments in this stage of life that we'll remember for the rest of our days—some gladly and some with a sense of loss—and a number of ideas about how to mark them.

UNTIL 120: A MAJOR BIRTHDAY

Any milestone birthday is an opportunity to reflect on our life's journey and the time that has passed since the last one. It could be 50, 60, or even 100. Is this a time of celebration or reflection? Other years may also have particular significance to us. Maybe it's a birthday by which we have outlived one of our close relatives. One woman we know considered turning 44 a huge milestone because that was the age at which her mother had died.

While anthropologists often distinguish between ritual and ceremony, we are using these terms interchangeably. Much of what we describe here can be considered rites of passage, marked by three phases: Consider retirement, for example.
1. separation (from work).
2. limbo (not sure what to do next).
3. reintegration ("rewire" into new stage).

For some Jews, 83 is a major birthday. Psalm 90:10 says, "The span of our lives is 70 years," and a tradition has developed to celebrate a second bar or bat mitzvah 13 years later, at the age of 83. How would you celebrate this differently from your first one? Or if you didn't have a first one, what would it mean to you to have one now?

CHILDREN GROWN AND FLOWN

For many of us, a young adult leaving home for college or work is a moment that matters. Imagine marking it with a separation

Laura blessing Richard on his 70th birthday.

ceremony, such as the Prayer for a Journey (page 34), or a discussion sparked by the biblical text of Noah's ambivalence about leaving the safety of the ark. Another moment of transition might involve transforming the room that once belonged to a child into an office, a guest room, or a meditation space. Before you do, what memories from that room do you want to hold onto? What memories might you want to let go? What do you want to keep from the room and from among your children's things? What do you want to give away?

STOPPING FULL-TIME WORK

Retirement isn't what it used to be. *Rewirement* might be a better word for this transition. Some of us stop working full-time but still work part-time; others seek an "encore career," either as a volunteer or for a salary. For many of us, this is a major transitional moment, often suffused with ambivalence and mixed emotions. How might you want to mark it? And with whom?

BEGINNING A NEW ADVENTURE

The biblical Abraham and Sarah, both well past midlife, are called to "go forth from your land . . . to the land that I will show you" (Genesis 12:1). Whether moving across the country to live near your kids, going back to school to learn a new skill, or volunteering with an organization working with at-risk teens, our path forward is

Embracing Havdalah

Havdalah is a Jewish ceremony that separates "special" time from "ordinary" time—the Sabbath from the rest of the week, for example. It focuses on endings and beginnings and the importance of paying attention to both. It is short and literally sweet, with blessings over sweet wine and fragrant spices, as well as the flame of a braided candle. The ceremony also includes an invitation to the prophet Elijah to bring the promise of renewal to individuals and to the world. (Some also welcome Miriam, the sister of Moses, who represents clarity and celebration.) The symbols and themes of havdalah can be embraced, either on Saturday night or at a different time, to mark a transition from one stage to another, such as sending a young adult child off to college or beginning retirement.

rarely laid out for us. Filled with anticipation and anxiety, what commitments would you like to make or what hopes would you like to express as you start down this road? What do you need to let go of to lighten your load?

DOWNSIZING

When our kids have finally left home, do we want to move or downsize? How do we say good-bye to those homes? How do we help our parents (or, when the time comes, ourselves) leave home to move into a retirement community or assisted living? What can we, our families, and our communities do to mark these leavings and then welcome new beginnings?

BECOMING A GRANDPARENT (OR A GREAT-GRANDPARENT)

Jewish tradition celebrates the transmission of values and family stories (and recipes!) from one generation to another. Becoming a grandparent or a great-grandparent can be a moment of great joy, acknowledging that our master story continues. What words of wisdom, photographs, stories, or signature dishes would you like to pass on to your grandchild or

Farewell, Family Home!

Saying good-bye to the house where you raised your children isn't easy, but it's easier if you actually say good-bye.

Our daughter, her boyfriend, my husband, and I walked through the rooms of our home, stopping in each one to share good memories and to honor the room for its service.

After our journey through time, space, and love, we shed a few tears, toasted the house, and sent it on its way to shelter and protect a new family.

Before this ritual, we were stuck, painfully holding on to the house we had built 27 years before when our daughter was born. But after the ritual, we felt joy and contentment as we realized how rich those years had been and how ready we were to let go and move on.

An unforeseen benefit is that our daughter's boyfriend now feels more connected to the life and history of our family and says he can't wait to be part of the new memories we make together in our condo. We can't wait, either.

—Penny White, Los Angeles

great-grandchild? In what setting? At what moment? What prayer might you write for that moment when you first meet your new family member?

SURVIVING A LIFE-THREATENING ILLNESS

Jewish tradition has a brief ritual to give thanks for having survived a dangerous situation. After being called to the Torah during a synagogue service, the survivor says, "Holy One of Blessing, whose Presence fills creation, You bestow favor upon the undeserving and have bestowed favor upon me." To which the congregation responds, "Amen. May the One who has been gracious to you continue to favor you with all that is good." Another version of this is: *Thank God I made it through.* Is this how you would want to recognize this moment? If that doesn't feel meaningful to you or you are not part of a congregation, how, when, where, and with whom could you acknowledge the experience?

RENEWING MARRIAGE VOWS

We change, and our relationships change, as we get older. How could we express our love for our spouse now? What new commitments would we like to make? What would we like our children to know about our expectations for and of each other?

In renewing our vows, we might spell out the lessons we've drawn from our marriage so far and how we envision our later years together—akin to a road map for ourselves and our loved ones.

REMOVING A WEDDING RING AFTER DIVORCE OR THE DEATH OF A SPOUSE

Putting on a wedding ring is a central part of a marriage ceremony and is a public declaration of marital status. When or with whom do we remove the wedding ring after the death of a spouse? Does divorce at this stage call for a different kind of ritual than what is traditional earlier in our lives?

Rabbi Rachel Adler has created a new form of marriage contract, a brit ahuvim (covenant of loving partners), that eliminates the problematic aspect of traditional marriage where a woman is literally acquired by a man. Check out her award-winning book Engendering Judaism.

Recipe for a Ritual: The Ingredients

In creating a ritual of your own, think through the various elements that will make this ritual meaningful both to you and to your guests. Keep in mind your spiritual intention in crafting this ritual.

TIME

Consider the dimensions of time.

Time of day. Morning is a time of energy, optimism, and light. Doing a ritual in the morning can energize us as we proceed through the rest of the day. Evening offers calm, pensiveness, darkness. Performing a ritual in the evening can help people wind down from the day. It's a more relaxed time, making the festivities mellow and peaceful.

Weekend or weekday. Weekday rituals are generally shorter than those performed on weekends and tend to draw family and close friends only. Weekend rituals can be longer and are more likely to draw from a larger circle of friends and colleagues. If you're so inclined, weekends present a special opportunity to use the Sabbath as a focal point, such as an event built around a Friday night dinner, a morning Torah reading, or an early evening *havdalah* service. If you celebrate the Sabbath on Friday (Muslims) or Sunday (Christians), your ritual held on the Sabbath could include a Sabbath theme as well.

Season. You may draw on elements from a particular season, or even a seasonal holiday, to enrich personal rituals. For instance, the Jewish holiday of Sukkot, a fall harvest festival that symbolizes the ingathering of fruits and friends, could be a good time to celebrate a retirement or the completion of a major project. Shavuot, the late spring celebration of the giving of the Torah, might be a good time to celebrate a major intellectual achievement, such as writing a book or finishing a course of study. Hanukkah, observed in winter at the time of the solstice, the darkest time of year, celebrates moving from darkness to light, decline to renewal, which could be a good time for a ritual relating to divorce or healing from addiction or trauma.

> Rituals should not be too long or too short. Just as in cooking, even with the best recipe and ingredients, overcooked or undercooked food isn't very good.

PLACE

Location can enhance the significance, poignancy, and resonance of just about any ritual. Inside or outside? In a home or at a synagogue? At a site that has symbolic or personal meaning, such as the park where you first met your partner? At a special destination—in Israel, for example? You don't have to conduct the ritual in a space deemed sacred by the community, like a synagogue. On the contrary, conscious and attentive choice of space will make the space sacred wherever it is.

PARTICIPANTS

Who attends will have a profound impact on the experience. Do you want the ritual to be small and intimate, where you share personal thoughts and emotions with your closest friends and family members, or open to a broader community, where you can publicly express your feelings?

Most important, decide what roles you want the participants to assume. There are four primary roles:

> *Subject*—The person or group marking the transition. You may be celebrating a milestone birthday or the completion of a major project, or your family may be closing

up the family home. If it's a group, each member of the group should have a role, whether scripted or of their own choosing, that enables them to offer their own contribution to the ritual.

Community—People who feel connected to the moment you are commemorating and whose relationships you would like to recognize. These may include relatives, friends, or others who have had a part in what is being celebrated.

Officiant—The person who directs the action and helps plan the event. This could be a clergyperson or a dear friend.

Witnesses—The larger community—friends, family, colleagues—with whom we may want to celebrate our special moments. They are not passive observers; rather, they are there to attest to the moment being marked and lend it a deeper degree of gravitas and warmth. You may want them to sign a program or other memento from the event as an official record of their presence.

A New Seder

The frame and elements of the Passover seder can be used as the basis for celebrating a variety of other special moments, particularly transitions from a condition of confinement or constriction to one of liberation or expansion. At least since the late '60s, with (Rabbi) Arthur Waskow's Freedom Seder, seders have been created to celebrate different types of liberation, including feminism, LGBTQ experience, and freedom from addiction. Maybe it's time to develop an "overcoming ageism seder." Use the structure of the seder's Four Questions to spark an intergenerational conversation about how people of all ages feel about growing older, or reframe the Four Children as the Four Elders.

TONE

Establishing the right tone is perhaps the most difficult aspect of a ritual to calibrate. Virtually any moment can be an opportunity for quiet reflection or exuberant joy. In reality, most occasions involve a little of both.

Reflect on and discuss with family, close friends, and also perhaps a clergyperson how you want to mark an occasion. In some ways, this reflective process is the essence of the experience, and the ceremony is just the culmination. Is renewing marriage vows a moment of joy for the miracle of the endurance of love? Do you want to dance to '60s music and strobe lights? Or is this a bittersweet moment, acknowledging the long journey to this point and the inevitabilities on the road ahead? Would soft candles and Bach sonatas be more appropriate?

Witnesses to a Wedding

Quakers ask everyone attending a wedding to sign the wedding certificate. They are all witnesses.

One Jewish couple, Vicki and David, had all the guests at their wedding sign their *ketubah* (the Jewish marriage document). The *ketubah* had the required signatures, and it was especially meaningful because all those who were with them at the wedding had signed it.

OBJECTS

Part of what gives ritual emotional impact is the intentional use of objects that evoke meaning or memory. Think of candles and candleholders (to cast light and warmth) or the blanket a family friend knit for you when you were a baby. Among the objects often used in Jewish ceremonies are wine cups (to offer blessings), spice boxes (to inhale sweetness), and prayer shawls (to be enveloped by the moment).

Since life-cycle rituals look both forward and back, incorporating an object from an earlier stage of life or a previous generation infuses the ritual with a powerful poignancy. For example, using the cup with which you were married in a recommitment ceremony or the bar mitzvah cup of your adult child in a ritual celebrating becoming a grandparent could add depth and meaning to the ceremony. In addition, you might introduce a new object with the intention of handing it down to future generations.

Ritual objects don't have to come from the world of sacred symbols. Your great-grandmother's brisket pot could serve as a vessel to collect written memories from family members at a ceremony marking the closing up of a home. Throwing away keys to an office could symbolize the beginning of retirement and a new sense of freedom from the world of work.

Mix It All Together

Central to any ritual, whether traditional or new, is the action symbolizing that a change is happening: A new name is given, a promise is made, a blessing is invoked. You might create a ceremonial action from scratch, as did a former competitive swimmer who celebrated turning 70 by swimming 70 laps at a pool party. You could borrow from Jewish tradition, such as breaking a glass at the end of a wedding to symbolize that love endures even in the face of a still-broken world, or from other traditions, say, by including gentle yoga to express gratitude for an able body. The deeper the connection with known rituals, the deeper the emotional, intellectual, and spiritual impact the action will have. Here are some ideas to consider in forging your new ritual.

GET RID OF SOMETHING

Letting go of the emotional baggage that weighs us down can be cathartic.

Jewish tradition recognizes this and makes this symbolic shedding part of some holiday rituals. For example, before Passover, traditional Jews search for crumbs of leavened food—bread, cookies, pasta, etc.—that were overlooked in cleaning their homes and then burn those items, symbolizing the elimination of anything that puffs us up or weighs us down. Similarly, on the afternoon of the first day of Rosh Hashanah (the Jewish New Year), many Jews go to a body of living water—a river, a lake, a pond, or an ocean—and throw chunks of bread into the water as a symbol of casting off their sins.

Adapt these rituals to identify and let go of unfinished business in your own life. Such casting off—whether it's making a list of what you want to get rid of and then burning the list or tossing a symbolic object into water—can be quite liberating. Imagine adding this into rituals for divorce, sobriety, or any transition from a narrow place.

GIVE SOMETHING

Share your abundance of resources or time. Organize your friends to contribute squares for a quilt for a colleague who is entering an assisted living facility. Invite your friends and family to volunteer with you at a food pantry or a homeless shelter. Connect with a project to register people to vote or to lobby elected officials.

Or borrow from Jewish tradition and incorporate tzedakah into your ritual. *Tzedakah* comes from the Hebrew root meaning "justice." It's not an act of generosity but rather an obligation to share some of the gifts we have been given. Donate to an organization or cause that is important to you. Ask others to do the same. Include a line on your invitations that says: "In lieu of gifts, please consider a contribution to XYZ organization, whose good work doing [fill in the blank] I admire and support."

OCCASIONS FOR SPECIAL BLESSINGS

UPON SEEING AN OLD FRIEND

UPON SEEING THE OCEAN

UPON SEEING A RAINBOW

UPON HEARING GOOD OR BAD NEWS

UPON SEEING SOMEONE VERY BEAUTIFUL

UPON SEEING SOMEONE WHO MAKES YOU FEEL UNCOMFORTABLE

EAT SOMETHING

Embody the moment. Food and drink conjure up many associations, such as the Jewish tradition of using wine to symbolize joy and seal many blessings, or apples and honey to usher in any new beginning.

MAKE A COMMITMENT

Make or renew promises in writing. In Jewish tradition, a written marriage contract outlines the promises a couple make to each other. Renew your vows on a significant anniversary, adding new promises related to growing older. Put new commitments in writing at transitional moments, such as the birth of a grandchild or the start of an encore career.

MAKE NOISE

Create mood and strengthen community with music or song. Words reach our consciousness, but music touches our hearts. Any instrument—or even a recording—can be used to play music or accompany singing. Mix a drumming circle into your ritual. Bring in echoes of other cultural traditions with a harmonium or a sitar. The shofar and tambourine have special Jewish resonances.

There is nothing like singing—or even playing a recording—to set a mood and create a communal feeling. Whether it's songs without words that are meant to be repeated (*niggunim*)

or songs by contemporary musicians that form the soundtrack of our lives, share the music that has shaped the experience of who you are.

SAY A PRAYER, MAKE A BLESSING

Sanctify the moment. Whether you recite or adapt traditional blessings or offer prayers you make up yourself, there's no limit to the number and type of blessings that can be composed and recited to sanctify a new ritual.

Prayer to Mark a New Beginning

The traditional Jewish blessing for a special occasion is called the *Shehecheyanu*. "Holy One of blessing, whose Presence fills creation, who has kept us in life, sustained us, and brought us to this time."

Prayer for a Journey

A prayer called *T'filat Haderech* may be most appropriate. "As we set out on our journey, may it be Your will that we be guided on the paths of well-being and protected from all harm and evil on the way. Bless the works of our hands and grant us grace, loving-kindness, and compassion in your eyes and in the eyes of all who see us. Holy One of Blessing, whose Presence fills creation, who listens to prayer."

Don't underestimate moments of silence.

IMMERSE SOMETHING

Purify, renew, heal, celebrate. Immersion in water—whether it's the washing of hands, feet, or the whole body—is integral to many traditional cultures and is also the final step in converting to Judaism. Today the ritual bath (mikvah) can be seen as a spiritual tool for everyone to mark transitions. Some may be around healing, such as from abuse, divorce, or completing a month or year of mourning. Others may be moments to celebrate milestones such as reaching menopause, a birthday, coming out, or beginning a new adventure.

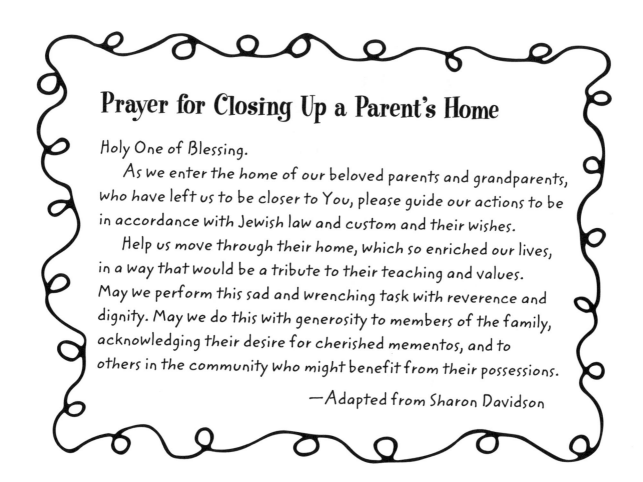

Prayer for Closing Up a Parent's Home

Holy One of Blessing.

As we enter the home of our beloved parents and grandparents, who have left us to be closer to You, please guide our actions to be in accordance with Jewish law and custom and their wishes.

Help us move through their home, which so enriched our lives, in a way that would be a tribute to their teaching and values. May we perform this sad and wrenching task with reverence and dignity. May we do this with generosity to members of the family, acknowledging their desire for cherished mementos, and to others in the community who might benefit from their possessions.

—Adapted from Sharon Davidson

CHANGE A NAME

Acknowledge who you are now. Change your name; change your luck. A Jewish tradition teaches that everyone has three names: the one your parents give you, the one others call you (such as a nickname), and the name you acquire for yourself that reflects the essence of who you are.

When called to begin their journey, Avram's and Sarai's names are changed to Avraham and Sarah with the added Hebrew letter *hay*, which is one of the names of God. Jewish tradition offers the possibility that changing your name can change your life. People who immigrate to Israel, whether for religious or secular reasons, often take on a new name that reflects their connection to the land and the people. When someone is ill, it is not uncommon to add a new name to theirs, such as Chaim, meaning "life," or Raphaella, meaning "healing."

A Dual Name Change

In a ceremony called "Becoming a Crone: Ceremony at 60," created for Marcia (Marty) Spiegel in 1988, taking on a new name took two forms. "I decided for ceremonial purposes to take on the name of Miriam. I had never had a Hebrew name, just the Yiddish Mushagolden. So when I am called up to Torah in the future, I will be called up as Miriam bat Hinda v'Abraham," she said.

In an additional part of the ceremony, Rabbi Sue Elwell bestowed upon Marty the title *Chachama*, "Wise Woman," because our elders deserve a title of honor, "those who have lived and survived years of joy and pain. From them we can learn of love and loss and life."

WEAR SOMETHING

Signal the connection between life stages.

Something Old

The subject of a ritual often is adorned in special or symbolic clothing. Examples of special clothing that might be worn while performing a new ritual include the tallit that you used at your bar or bat mitzvah, if you had one; a *kittel* (white smock) you might have worn at your wedding or on Yom Kippur; your wedding dress (or the veil?) that might still fit; the shawl your grandmother made for you; your grandfather's watch.

Something New

Invite participants to help create a garment to be used in the ceremony. Distribute material in advance to be decorated by friends and sewn together prior to the ritual.

Serving the Meal

Rituals generally consist of an opening, a closing, and a transformational middle, the phase when the subject of the ritual moves from one state to another. Pay attention to all three phases. Help your participants make the transition from the everyday to the holy, and then help them move back into their everyday lives—for instance, with movement, music, or guided meditation.

Just as in cooking, when you're creating a ritual, you choose your ingredients carefully. Sometimes you want the food you are cooking to elicit childhood memories; other times you want to conjure up a sense of something adventurous; and sometimes you're seeking a new variation, inspired by older traditions. Your mother probably never cooked with kale, quinoa, or some of the spices and herbs that we use today. And, of course, preparations can change with the introduction of new resources, such as the food processor or the internet as a giant recipe book. Remember also that the best and most interesting cookbooks include the story behind the dish, so think of the moment you are marking as the story that evokes the flavors, smells, and tastes of the experience.

B'tayavon—Enjoy the meal.

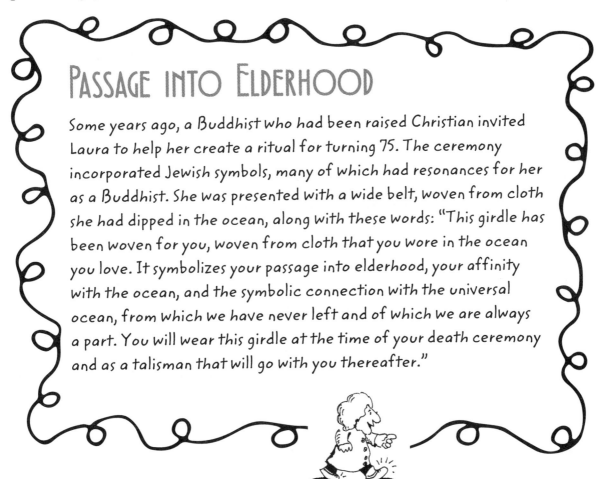

PASSAGE INTO ELDERHOOD

Some years ago, a Buddhist who had been raised Christian invited Laura to help her create a ritual for turning 75. The ceremony incorporated Jewish symbols, many of which had resonances for her as a Buddhist. She was presented with a wide belt, woven from cloth she had dipped in the ocean, along with these words: "This girdle has been woven for you, woven from cloth that you wore in the ocean you love. It symbolizes your passage into elderhood, your affinity with the ocean, and the symbolic connection with the universal ocean, from which we have never left and of which we are always a part. You will wear this girdle at the time of your death ceremony and as a talisman that will go with you thereafter."

Putting the Life in Lifelong Learning
by Richard Siegel

Continuing to learn new things is a critical element in successful aging: as a deterrent to Alzheimer's and other forms of dementia, an antidote to depression, a buffer against loneliness. Learning something new is energizing and empowering. Even when it is difficult—or particularly when it is difficult—learning a new skill or gaining a deeper understanding about some area of interest stimulates new pathways in our brains, lights up our endorphins, helps us gain a sense of achievement, and helps us grow. When we are learning, we are living. It makes us feel alive.

Lifelong learning is the ongoing pursuit of knowledge, which gives us a sense of connection to our community, strengthens our ties to our fellow citizens, and enhances our personal growth. In Jewish tradition, learning for its own sake is a core value, and it has nothing to do with schooling or with enhancing professional development. It is an essential activity, an expectation, an eagerly anticipated source of enjoyment. It is understood as a way to connect with Divinity and to see the world anew.

Getting Started

Other than learning serendipitously from new experiences in the course of your life (like figuring out how to be a grandparent), how do you go about intentionally learning something new? To get started, here are some questions to consider:

- What interests you? What are you curious about?
- With whom do you want to be learning—by yourself, with a partner, in groups small or large?
- What type of learning are you interested in— experiential, practical, learning for its own sake?

Words of Wisdom

When you stop learning, you start dying.

—Congressman Thomas Brooks Fletcher (D—Ohio), 1936 (often mistakenly attributed to Albert Einstein)

- How much time do you want to spend learning—short term, long term, lifelong?
- Are you willing to pay for the experience and, if so, how much?

Self-Directed Learning

Self-designed learning is flexible. You do it alone, on your own schedule, at your own pace. Take something you're curious about or enjoy doing and design a project around it. Train for the San Francisco–LA annual AIDS Ride. Learn Spanish with language-learning software. Watch every movie in the top-10 lists of the *New York Times* film critics' end-of-year review. Read the complete works of Shakespeare.

Here's a suggestion: Before going to see a play or hear a concert, study up in advance. For a play, pick up a copy of the script and read it. If it's an older play, the library will probably have a copy. If it's a new play, you might be able to buy the script online or at least read the reviews. For classical music, get a copy of *The Norton Scores: A Study Anthology* at the library or online. Listen to a recording of the pieces you will hear (several online music services have good collections of classical music) and follow along with the score. (*The Norton Scores* include guides for how to listen to the pieces.) Also read up on the group who will be performing and any featured soloists. The experience of both live theater and classical music is immensely enhanced by advance preparation.

JEWISH TEXT-BASED SELF-STUDY OPPORTUNITIES

The weekly Torah portion. One of the oldest Jewish study practices is to read the weekly Torah portion. To get started, set aside some time every day to read that week's portion. (You can find it by googling "weekly Torah portion.") There are several excellent translations and commentaries available that can make Torah

> Our friend Henry Saltzman likes to present himself with self-imposed learning challenges. For example, he set out to read one novel by every writer who has received the Nobel Prize in Literature. After he finished this, he wrote: "My 'project' continues apace. I googled 'international literary prizes' and discovered a quite varied and numerous group from which to select."

reading both aesthetically pleasurable and intellectually stimulating. If you do this regularly, not only will your understanding and appreciation of the text deepen, but you will also gain insight into the rhythm of the Jewish year.

Daf yomi. For the more ambitious, *daf yomi*, literally the "daily page," is a regimen practiced around the world to study the Talmud (the Oral Law). With 2,711 pages in the Talmud, reading one page a day takes about seven years, five months. The completion of the *daf yomi* cycle is celebrated at events worldwide. In 2012, for example, the celebration marking the end of that *daf yomi* cycle was attended by more than 90,000 people at MetLife Stadium in New Jersey!

> Check out who's sponsoring the Jewish learning sites you visit. They can range from very progressive to ultra-religious. Sample a couple of different sites to get a variety of perspectives.

Until fairly recently, participating in *daf yomi* was difficult for most people because the text is in Aramaic, and there were no decent English translations. But the publication of two good English translations—the Schottenstein Edition of the Babylonian Talmud, published by ArtScroll, and the Koren Talmud Bavli—makes the text accessible to people of all backgrounds. Additional resources are available to assist those who seek to complete the cycle, including audiotapes, online websites, and mobile apps with lectures covering every page of the Talmud.

Learning with a Partner

While self-directed learning can be an energizing and empowering experience, it lacks the social dimension that can make learning an opportunity for social engagement. Learning with a partner, a group of friends, or a large class has the advantage of building social networks and boosting the intellectual effort required by challenging your assumptions about or understandings of the material.

The experience of studying one-on-one with someone, particularly someone you already know, can be an immensely meaningful and intimate learning experience. It can deepen your understanding of what you are studying, as well as your relationship with your study partner. Studying text with another person one-on-one, known as *hevruta,* is a Jewish tradition dating back to the Talmudic period (200–500 CE). Whether you are studying Rilke's *Duino Elegies* or the book of Psalms, you and your study partner are not looking for the "right answers" but rather the dialogue that leads to discovery, the human exchange of fears, hopes, and experience that gives life to the words.

TIPS FOR PAIRED STUDY

Here are some helpful tips for *hevruta* learning:

Find a partner. It could be a spouse, a close friend, or a colleague with whom you feel some affinity. Studying with someone you love often brings more intimacy into the relationship. Face-to-face learning is ideal, but you can also learn together via Skype, telephone, or email. This could give new meaning to "texting."

Agree on a text. The best texts are evocative and open to multiple meanings. Many biblical, rabbinic, philosophical, and Hasidic texts work well because they can be broken up into short sections, generally involve stories, and have lots of openings to invite creative interpretation. Poetry of any kind is also ideal for this type of interaction.

Agree on the expectations. Both parties should take the commitment seriously. While schmoozing will be a natural part of each session, you should agree to focus on the text for a certain period of time and try to stay with it.

Set up a regular time to study together. It can be once a week or once a month. Make sure to confirm the next session before you leave the previous one.

Alternate reading the passage aloud. Words resonate differently, for the reader and the listener, when they are spoken.

Ask questions—of the text, of each other, of yourself. Try to figure out the text's explicit meaning. Then interrogate the text. Is something missing—for example, is one character's perspective left out of the story? Why? Is something implied but unstated? What

Do not say: "When I have the time I will study." You might never have the time. —Pirkei Avot 2:5

might those background assumptions be? Are there other ways of looking at the text? Finally, share with each other what you've learned from the text. How might it apply to your life? How does it reflect your own experience—or not?

Learning in Small Groups

Learning as part of a small group—from three people to no more than 20, as a practical maximum—has a number of advantages. It's small enough to be intimate and personal, and large enough to encompass a diversity of perspectives. Small-group participation can conjure up feelings of responsibility and accountability, which might motivate you to prepare, attend, and participate. To accommodate everyone's schedule, it's often difficult for these groups to meet more often than once a month, so it's best to study something that doesn't require continuity from one session to another—for example, cultural experiences, books, plays, exhibitions, or films.

FINDING LOCAL SMALL GROUPS

Local small-group learning opportunities are often posted in libraries (either on site or on their websites), bookstores, synagogue bulletins, or community center newsletters.

One popular online source is Meetup.com. Once you sign up (it's free), you can search for local groups that share your interests, whether in books, film, theater, health and wellness, sports, the outdoors, or a myriad of other subjects. Some are open to people of all ages, some geared to specific demographics, like the book group in our neighborhood called "Baby Boomers and Friends Book Club II—L.A. West."

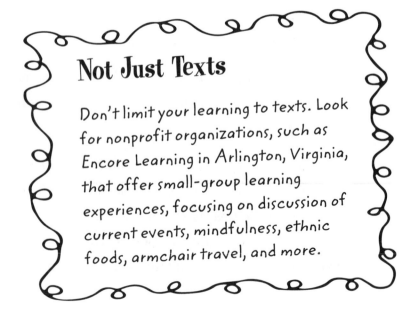

Not Just Texts

Don't limit your learning to texts. Look for nonprofit organizations, such as Encore Learning in Arlington, Virginia, that offer small-group learning experiences, focusing on discussion of current events, mindfulness, ethnic foods, armchair travel, and more.

Learning in Large Groups

Schools and colleges are the traditional and familiar settings for large-group learning, but the format also includes online courses, travel seminars, workshops, and retreats. Large-group learning typically has the benefits of a knowledgeable instructor, a curriculum, and a reading list specially curated for the course. You have the advantage of learning from and interacting with a diverse group of people or you can be anonymous. To combine the best of both worlds, consider taking courses with a friend or colleague.

CHOOSING A LARGE-GROUP LEARNING EXPERIENCE

Local colleges, universities, and community colleges. Many allow nonmatriculated students to audit regular classes, generally with a registration fee, and some have specially designed classes for community residents. On a national level, Osher Lifelong Learning Institute (OLLI) targets people over 50 who are interested in the "sheer joy of learning" without examinations or grades. Check out the National Resource Center for OLLI at Northwestern University for locations of the 120 campuses and other resources for lifelong learning.

Travel. Travel combines the pleasure many of us derive from visiting new parts of the world with the desire to learn more about the sites than is available in most tourist guides. Many universities and travel organizations offer excursions that feature lectures and conversations with faculty experts who travel with the group.

Online. With major universities branching out into online education, in the form of adjunct courses for matriculated students, online learning has expanded to offer professional certifications and professional education credits, as well as courses for lifelong learners looking for something on a sophisticated intellectual level. Massive open online courses (MOOCs) can sometimes have a global audience of thousands of people. There are no admissions requirements, even for courses offered by the most elite universities, and they are generally free, although there is often a small charge for a certification or "statement of achievement" (SOA), if desired. The most common MOOCs have start and end dates, although you can do the work on your own time. With so many students taking the courses, you can't expect individualized attention from the instructor; however, there are often active discussion boards for conversation with other students taking the course.

With all the options for learning available to us—from book groups to self-guided study, from online courses to worldwide travel—we are living in an ever-expanding classroom. As Albert Einstein says of our challenge in getting good at gaining wisdom, "Wisdom is not the product of schooling but of the lifelong attempt to acquire it."

CHAPTER 4

Discovering Your Inner Pilgrim
by Rabbi Vanessa Ochs

Richard first encountered Vanessa Ochs when she was an undergraduate at Tufts University and came to Havurat Shalom on Shabbat morning. Laura met Vanessa years later in the context of their work together on Jewish feminist projects. Now a professor at the University of Virginia, Vanessa writes and teaches on a wide range of topics, including new Jewish ritual, Jewish feminism, and the relationship between Jewish people and their things

Words of Wisdom

We depart seeking our most valuable treasure and return to find it in the very homes we left: our precious, renewed, and expanded souls.

—Rabbi Adina Lewittes

Although many of the techniques for gaining wisdom explored in part 1 involve "going in," whether through meditation, journaling, or exercises in eldering, there is much to be learned by "going out" and gathering experience from our closely observed encounters with the broader world. From Abraham and Sarah heeding God's call to "go forth . . . to the land that I will show you," pilgrimage has been, for millennia, a spiritual exercise in self-discovery. With travel on so many people's bucket lists, how can we transform the experience of tourism into an opportunity to grow our wisdom? —Laura and Richard

Travel can be a spiritual discipline and journeys can be sources of deep meaning and transformation, whether religious or secular. There are the historical Jewish pilgrimages (Sukkot, Passover, and Shavuot) that required the ancient Israelites to bring their sacrifices to the Temple in Jerusalem; the modern-day Birthright trips; the Hajj, the annual Islamic pilgrimage to Mecca; the journey to Lourdes in search of healing waters; and the Camino de Santiago, the path through Europe that culminates in Spain at the tomb of Saint James at Santiago de Compostela.

Well-known secular pilgrimages include the annual "Run to the Wall," in which Vietnam veterans motorcycle their way across the nation until they gather at the Vietnam Veterans' Memorial Wall in Washington, DC, to pay their respects, and civil rights pilgrimages to commemorate, among other events, the 1965 march from Selma to Montgomery.

Then there is a whole other category of pilgrim-like journeys that people make to places of special meaning: paying homage at

44 Getting Good at Gaining Wisdom

the home of a hero (Elvis's Graceland and Thoreau's Walden Pond are favorites), going back to Grandma's house, visiting the Lower East Side where your family might have lived generations ago, or traveling abroad to discover the place in the "old country" from which ancestors hailed.

I love to make pilgrimages to the Second Avenue Deli in Midtown Manhattan, where every few years I abandon my near-vegetarian diet and perform the beloved ritual of my New York childhood: having a pastrami sandwich on squishy rye bread, along with half-sour pickles and a shot of chocolate soda. (Take note: I have witnessed extremely pious fellow pilgrims who start the ritual with a bowl of matzah ball soup or a hot dog with everything on it.)

Pilgrimage transforms something potentially mundane—traveling away from home to a destination—into an act that bonds people to matters that are ultimately important to them. It takes something as potentially random as a particular place on the earth—even a specific rock—and transforms it into what some have called a "thin place," a place where heaven and earth meet.

Victor Turner, a noted cultural anthropologist, describes pilgrimage as a process, a complex multistep experience, often in the company of fellow travelers. Pilgrims prepare for their departure, sharpening their spiritual focus and gathering what they need for the journey. Perhaps they bring a journal to chronicle their days and give testimony to their soulful wrestlings. Among their fellow pilgrims, people possibly much unlike themselves, they risk a journey, collectively weathering the need for food, shelter, and hospitality; if there are spiritual or physical dangers, they surmount their vulnerabilities and overcome their challenges together.

The journey puts us in a liminal state—we are betwixt and between, neither here nor there. We are on a metaphorical threshold between who we were and who we are becoming. As China Galland, author of *Longing for Darkness*, wrote upon leaving her children and setting forth on her private pilgrimage in search of Tara, a female Buddha in the Tibetan tradition, as well as the Black Madonnas of Europe, "I felt uprooted, cried, and longed to turn back. Who is leaving? Who is returning? The same person never comes back."

Connecting Within and Without

As the historian of religions Mircea Eliade described it in *The Sacred and the Profane*, upon our arrival at the destination, as we move from the periphery to the center, we feel a profound connection not just to all who had been traveling with us but to all people. Turner called this experience of intense collectivity *communitas*. Perhaps we pilgrims feel connected to all others who had come to this sacred spot together in the past and will come in the future as well. Perhaps we feel a blurring of the distinctions that separate people. We inhabit a time outside of time; even though there are rules to follow, there is liberation. At the very least, they aren't following the everyday routines of home.

On our return journey back home from a pilgrimage, we recognize that we have changed. Most pilgrims feel obliged to bring back souvenirs for ourselves and for the loved ones left behind so they can have a "secondhand" taste of the experience. These objects convey some of the power of the experience. For example, pilgrims to the Hajj spend considerable time looking for objects to bring home—prayer mats, prayer beads, copies of the Qur'an, bangles, or images of Mecca—because these items are the touchstones for memory and gifts of love.

Pilgrimage: It's a Perspective

Can the sacred experience of classical pilgrimages infuse our more mundane travel with the possibility of meaningfulness? If we, in our journeys, assume the attitudes of a pilgrim, might our own lives be changed? Phil Cousineau, a world traveler and a student of classical pilgrimages, thinks so. In his book *The Art of Pilgrimage: The Seeker's Guide to Making Travel Sacred*, Cousineau acknowledges that while few actually set forth on pilgrimages, we all have the capacity to turn our trips into journeys that are more "soulful" if we adapt the heightened attentiveness and purposes of pilgrims. Challenge yourself when traveling to seek inspiration by grafting the steps of pilgrimage onto more mundane trips, breaking the trip into broad steps:

1. Contemplate what you are longing for in your life at this moment.
2. Anticipate your journey by reading poems and stories about the place you will visit.
3. See your preparations for departure, such as packing, as rituals that mark your separation and setting off.

4. Find ways to make the traveling itself holy for you—sing, write, step in a conscious way.

5. When you encounter challenges, face them honestly and reaffirm your purposes.

6. When you arrive, celebrate the marvel of the moment by imagining how your experience will allow you to give back. One way to do that would be to recite the Shehecheyanu blessing (page 34).

7. Find a way to bring back aspects of your journey once you return.

I am inspired by many of Cousineau's suggestions. For example, he suggests choosing a theme, such as the "deceptively simple things from everyday life, such as windows, doors, clouds, faces, children, café signs, bicycles, tilework, and bookstore facades." Take in the objects of your focus, notice them, draw them (even if you are not an artist) or take photographs. Then focus on the details. If you stick with it each day, you will come to recognize why these objects are calling your imagination, why they are attracting your love. It's about seeing with the heart, soulful seeing.

When I think about how to transform trips into deeper journeys of self-discovery, I inevitably turn to the poem "Tourists" by the Israeli poet Yehuda Amichai. The poet speaks critically of visitors whose pilgrimages to Israel are superficial. They end up feeling everything they anticipated feeling and do so on command, according to the itinerary established by their guide who treats them as consumers of "the Israel experience." His excellent advice is useful to both pilgrims and tourists seeking a greater level of meaning: Escape the bubble of your tour group. Experience the complexity of the place you are visiting. Observe and connect to real people. That, Amichai says, would be redemptive.

Seeking Restoration, Inspiration, Transformation

Of course, there are times when we have no inclination whatsoever to enhance our travel experiences, to be pilgrims-in-spirit. Sometimes, when we take trips, we have no desire to find ourselves or to gain wisdom. Our old selves are just fine, thank you, and our lives are already too supercharged with meaning. We just want to get away, have a break, find renewal in pausing and not filling up more. We don't always have to restore our spirits. We choose instead to relax on the sunny beach with a lime stuck into a Corona or seek distraction by going culture-hopping. And that's okay—it may not be soulful but it's restorative. The same person comes back more rested and maybe with a better tan.

Pilgrimage is indeed different from that kind of travel. The pilgrim is willing to be changed by the questions that motivated the journey. Why is this place calling me? What deep memories does it evoke—mine or my ancestors'? What feelings are sparked by what I experience?

The pilgrim welcomes seeing the world in a new way, captured in the last line of a poem by Mary Oliver: "I don't want to end up simply having visited the world."

Tourists By Yehuda Amichai

Visits of condolence is all we get from them.
They squat at the Holocaust Memorial,
They put on grave faces at the Wailing Wall
And they laugh behind heavy curtains
In their hotels.
They have their pictures taken
Together with our famous dead
At Rachel's Tomb and Herzl's Tomb
And on Ammunition Hill.
They weep over our sweet boys
And lust after our tough girls
And hang up their underwear
To dry quickly
In cool, blue bathrooms.

Once I sat on the steps by a gate at David's Tower,
I placed my two heavy baskets at my side. A group of tourists
was standing around their guide and I became their target marker. "You see
that man with the baskets? Just right of his head there's an arch
from the Roman period. Just right of his head." "But he's moving, he's moving!"
I said to myself: redemption will come only if their guide tells them,
"You see that arch from the Roman period? It's not important: but next to it,
left and down a bit, there sits a man who's bought fruit and vegetables for his family."

Exercising for Sages in Training
by Rabbi Zalman Schachter-Shalomi

These exercises will help you get started in the practice of spiritual eldering in the laboratory of your own life. They serve as a soul and mind gym in which to flex and develop your eldering muscles. As you grow stronger in your determination to become an elder and as you become more skillful in harvesting the fruits of a lifetime, you will embark on an adventure in consciousness that will lead to a more noble, useful, and fulfilling old age.

Approach these exercises with openness and a lightness of spirit. Be gentle with yourself and lighten up your expectations as to what kind of elder you "should" be. Do you know why angels fly? Because they take themselves lightly. If you apply this attitude to your own eldering process, you will have a more enjoyable journey through elderhood.

Exercise 1: Approaching Elderhood

Oftentimes, we unthinkingly accept the images of aging propagated by our culture, seeding our bodies and minds with the expectation of sliding into a weak and socially useless old age. In the first exercise, we will unearth the sources of our aging images (both negative and positive) and then reprogram our consciousness with the expectation of a vital and meaningful old age.

1. Prepare to write in a journal by sitting in a comfortable chair, closing your eyes, and relaxing your body. Take several deep breaths, emptying your lungs completely after each inhalation. Remain in a meditative state as you become quiet and centered.

Reb Zalman, who died in 2014 at the age of 89, was one of Richard's most important teachers. He was an early leader of the Havurah movement, which shaped Richard's spiritual life. His vision inspired *The Jewish Catalog* and the Jewish Renewal movement. All those multi-colored tallitot you now see in synagogues around the world, and group *aliyot*, where people bring their own life experience to the synagogue Torah reading, were among his many innovations.

The following 10 exercises in "spiritual eldering" or "life harvesting" were originally published in his groundbreaking book *From Age-ing to Sage-ing: A Profound New Vision of Growing Older*, coauthored with Ronald S. Miller (New York: Warner Books, 1995).

Here are a number of tips for getting the most out of these exercises:

Set aside specific periods of time for these spiritual exercises, the same way as you schedule physical exercise into your weekly activities.

Take your time in doing these exercises. Exploring them in an unhurried manner enables you to access information from the unconscious mind.

Deal with potential distractions before each session so that you can work undisturbed.

Don't approach these sessions as a chore. Consider them a gift that you give yourself.

Plan to do something pleasant to reward yourself after each session.

2. Spend some time exploring the question, "How do I feel about aging?" What do you look forward to and what do you fear? In this regard, you may want to consider these questions in terms of your profession, family life, finances, health, intellectual life, and spirituality. Write naturally without censoring yourself, telling the truth in your own language. Remember that there are no "right" or "wrong" answers in this exercise.

3. Now list negative models of aging that you have internalized from our culture, from sources such as literature, films, television, advertising, religious instruction, your family life, and older people you have known. Be specific in describing traits and attitudes that may be influencing your own aging process.

Words of Wisdom

You have to learn to do everything, even to die.

—Gertrude Stein

4. List positive models of aging that have influenced you. Have you acquired any traits and attitudes that are helping you become an elder?

5. In your mind's eye, make a composite of the good models and imagine what it feels like to walk in the shoes of such an elder. Do you have a useful role in society? Are you earning respect and recognition for your wisdom? Is growing older a blessing or a burden?

6. Visualize going through a routine day as your ideal elder, feeling confident, respected, and socially useful. Be as concrete and detailed as possible in imagining encounters with colleagues at work, loved ones, friends and associates, and mentees [protégés]. Know that by envisioning a positive future, you are seeding consciousness with the expectation of your own potential growth.

7. To end this exercise, read the Elder Creed:

An elder is a person who is still growing, still a learner, still with potential, and whose life continues to have within it promise for, and connection to, the future. An elder is still in pursuit of happiness, joy, and pleasure, and her or his birthright to these remains intact. Moreover, an elder is a person who deserves respect and honor and whose work it is to synthesize wisdom from long life experience and formulate this into a legacy for future generations.

Write in your journal any insights or questions that occur to you after reading the Elder Creed. Are you in the process of becoming this kind of elder? What personal and social forces could prevent you from claiming your full stature as an elder?

Exercise 2: The Cycles of Your Life

All of us experience dramatic changes as we move through childhood, adolescence, first maturity, middle age, and elderhood. However, grasping the larger pattern that unites these diverse stages of life often eludes us. The following exercise helps us to perceive the "pattern that connects" by partitioning the continuum of our lives into seven-year cycles in an attempt to discover how the parts are related to the whole. In general, memory becomes sharper and clearer when it's associated with partitioned time. Telling someone to remember the past in general terms usually does not yield good results; targeting a specific period of time works far better. When we ask someone to remember what happened during the April of his life, from ages 22 to 28, a person may respond, "When I was 28, I bought my first home and celebrated the birth of my second child." Focusing on specific periods of time acts like a magnet in the psyche, bringing to awareness all the "filings" (the experiences) that we need to recover our past and harvest our lives.

Once we have assembled the raw data of our experience, we can grasp the overarching pattern that was struggling to express itself through the ups and downs, the successes and failures that make up the rich texture of our lives. Seeing which experiences remain incomplete, we can take measures to express the unlived life that beckons from within. Perceiving the larger pattern of our lives, we can gain insight into how to harvest our lives and bring them to completion. Besides showing us directions for future growth, this exercise can help us cultivate an appreciation for all that we have had and enjoyed, even if our means were only modest by the world's standards. We can say, "I experienced friendship, a home and family, a useful career, and I grew in maturity over my life span." If we encountered sorrow and suffering, we can affirm, "By bearing these burdens, I grew in inner strength. I did something heroic."

1. Down the left side of a large piece of paper, list the seven-year cycles of your life: January, 0–7; February, 8–14; March, 15–21; April, 22–28; May, 29–35; June, 36–42; July, 43–49; August, 50–56; September, 57–63; October, 64–70; November, 71–77; December, 78–84 (and beyond).

2. Across the top, divide the remainder of the paper into three sections in which you write answers to the following questions for each of the 12 periods:

    a) What were the significant moments and events of each phase of life?

    b) Who were the people who guided and influenced you during each period?

    c) What did each phase contribute to the continuum of your life?

3. To deepen your memory of people and events, you may want to devote a separate page or more to various time periods. You can enhance your memory by attaching

photos to the paper, making sketches, writing little poems that evoke the era, or making a collage of newspaper and magazine clippings. Be creative in calling forth and harvesting the experiences of a lifetime.

4. Use this exercise to help recover memories of experiences that remain incomplete and that you can bring to completion as part of your eldering work. You also can use the exercise for working on forgiveness, recontextualizing difficult outcomes, mining the past for its untold riches, and discovering a future direction for growth.

Exercise 3: Turning Points

Like the preceding exercise, "Turning Points" helps you survey your life with panoramic vision. By revisiting some of the highlights of our personal history, we can contemplate the unfolding pattern of our life. Once we move from the past to the present with an awareness of the larger panorama, we can reach toward the future with a greater sense of optimism and confidence. Because we can perceive a direction toward which our life has been moving, we can address the question, "Where would I like to be in five years?" without giving way to paralyzing anxiety. By contemplating the past, we consciously can begin shaping our future without conforming to external goals and standards. We can follow the promptings that come from within, constructing a life based on self-knowledge and the hard-earned autonomy we have developed over a lifetime.

1. Sit in a comfortable chair, relax your body, and prepare to write in a journal. Take several long, deep breaths to put yourself in a meditative state of mind.

2. Write down your earliest memories of your:

- first Holy Day
- first day in school
- first love; first kiss
- first and most recent experience of illness
- high school
- college

- first job
- first significant achievement
- first failure
- career changes
- marriage and children (including births and weddings)
- first and most recent experience with death (including your ideal departure)

3. On a piece of paper, make a [horizontal] time line on which you place the significant turning points of your life. Begin with your birth on the far left and fill in the experiences until you arrive at the present time.

4. Place a point beyond the present time to indicate the near future. Now ask yourself the question, "Where do I want to be in five years?" Using your imagination, project yourself into the future and see yourself living your ideal life as a fulfilled elder. Where do you live? What is the quality of your relationships? What activities give your life meaning?

5. Spend some time in your journal exploring the life that you envision for yourself as an elder. Because you are dealing in the realm of possibility, you may want to return to this exploration on a number of occasions until a clear sense of purpose and direction emerges.

Exercise 4: Journey to Our Future Self

Many perplexing questions confront us as we make our way through the unexplored terrain of spiritual eldering: How should I plan my retirement? What lifestyle should I choose? How should I grow intellectually and spiritually? What is the meaning of my life? For insight into these questions, we should seek out the most reliable and knowledgeable sources, including books, magazines, continuing education classes, and retirement counselors. But as elders in training, we also need to contact an inner source of wisdom to receive guidance from our spiritual Self. In meditation we can make an appointment to visit our realized Self, the Inner Elder who is already enlightened and who can inspire us with compassionate wisdom to carry on our struggles for self-knowledge. This enlightened Self dwells beyond space and time, yet has an intimate relationship with our personality. Establishing a permanent relationship with our Inner Elder can provide us with guidance for all aspects of daily life.

1. Sit quietly, close your eyes, and for a few moments follow the inflowing and outflowing of your breath as you become calm and centered.

2. Count slowly from your actual age to 120, the biblical age of accomplished wisdom. At the same time, visualize in your mind's eye walking up a set of stairs leading to the door of your Inner Elder. When you knock on the door, your realized Self, the embodiment of boundless compassion and wisdom, greets you with a warm embrace. As you gaze into the Inner Elder's eyes, you feel unconditionally loved and reassured about your progress so far.

3. As a pilgrim confronting the highest, most all-embracing source of wisdom, ask the Inner Elder for guidance about an issue that you have been puzzling over. The guidance that you seek may range from practical concerns ("Should I continue working at my present position or take early retirement?") to the most metaphysical inquiries ("What is the meaning of my life?" "Is there continuity of life after physical death?"). After posing your question, remain in a state of receptivity, allowing an answer to imprint itself in your consciousness as a sign, symbol, or an inner sense of knowing.

4. When you receive your answer, rest in the silence for a while. Then, as you look again into the eyes of your enlightened Self, you receive these parting words of encouragement: "Journey on with confidence and with blessings as you proceed on your path. Visit me again whenever you need further guidance."

5. With deep gratitude, take leave of your Inner Elder and with joy and confidence walk down the stairs to your point of departure. Sit quietly for a few moments, slowly open your eyes, and return to normal consciousness.

6. Record your impressions and intuitions in your journal. As you establish a long-term relationship with your realized Self, over time you will begin to trust the guidance that comes from within and begin incorporating it in your everyday life.

Exercise 5: Healing a Painful Memory

Life review sometimes involves reaching back into the past to repair events and relationships that caused us pain or disappointment. We can mend our personal history because time is stretchable and therefore subject to reshaping through the use of contemplative techniques. To heal the part of ourselves that is still imprisoned in the past, we can return to the scene of a questionable decision or a bruised relationship and apply the balm of our more mature consciousness. In this way, we can forgive ourselves for actions undertaken without the benefit of the more enlightened awareness we now have. By recontextualizing the past, we can release the defenses that obstruct the expression of our natural love and spontaneity and recover a sensitivity and sense of innocence that we may have lost in becoming our mature selves.

1. Sit in a comfortable chair, close your eyes, and begin breathing in a slow, rhythmic manner. With each breath, feel yourself reaching further and further into the past until you return to a time of emotional turmoil and pain. Do not resist the memory; with

all your strength and awareness, make contact with your younger self who felt alone, misunderstood, unconsoled, or hurt.

2. Now let your elder self reach back with reassurance from the present and hold your anxious younger self in its arms. Visualize this embrace in your mind's eye as your mature self blesses the younger self that is smarting with pain and self-doubt about its present course of action.

3. Reaching through the fog of anxiety, the elder self says, "I come with assurance from the future. You are going to make it. You lived through this difficulty, healed from it, and learned important lessons that matured into wisdom. You acted courageously, you grew in strength and character, and in the end everything worked out well. Be at peace: Even though it seems impossible now, unforeseen blessings will result from your present course of action."

4. Still feeling the embrace of your elder self, let go of the cramp around the pain. Reach into the pain, hugging, consoling, and finally sanctifying it by offering it as a sacrifice for the good of all humanity. In this way, you elevate and ennoble that which you took to be worthless and ignoble.

5. As you let go of the burden of the past, focus your attention on your breathing and become aware of the increased energy, the buoyancy of feeling, and the sense of courage that are now available to you. Breathe in a sense of well-being and give thanks for having rescued and harvested a holy spark of your life.

6. Sit quietly for a few moments and then record your observations in your journal. Instead of writing a narrative, you may prefer to paint a picture, write a poem, play some music, or go for a meditative walk in nature.

Exercise 6: Giving Yourself the Gift of Forgiveness

Because all of us have unhealed scar tissue from past relationships, practicing forgiveness plays a major role in spiritual eldering work. When we heal our major woundings, along with the minor bruises that accompany intimate relationships, we release feelings of anger and resentment that armor our heart with defensiveness, drain our energy, and reduce the level of our vitality. Forgiveness work has two dimensions. First, we need to take responsibility for initiating acts of forgiveness. This means overcoming our passive attitude that makes forgiveness dependent on the other person's apology. Second, we need to forgive ourselves for our contribution to the misunderstanding.

Because this kind of enlightened behavior does not come easily to us, we need to train ourselves in this noble and beneficial practice. By gaining proficiency in the art of forgiveness, we can learn how to transmute our sorrows into the capacity to love, enabling us to reach out to others with a spontaneity and openness that will add emotional richness and enjoyment to our lives. As you practice the following exercise, you will discover through firsthand experience why forgiveness is one of the greatest gifts that we can give ourselves.

1. Sit quietly and take a few deep breaths to center yourself.

2. In your mind's eye, visualize being in the presence of someone toward whom you have unresolved anger or resentment, someone who has wronged you and toward whom you harbor a grudge. As you contemplate this person's actions, consider how your lack of forgiveness keeps you chained to this relationship, drains your energy, and disturbs your emotional equilibrium.

3. Place yourself in your adversary's shoes for a moment and investigate whether your own unacknowledged needs and expectations or a misunderstanding in communication contributed to the upset or rupture in your relationship.

4. Allow your awareness to move back and forth between yourself and the other person, giving you an enlarged perspective and objectivity with which to view the relationship.

5. Imagine that the two of you are bathed in a ray of golden sunlight that melts your resentment and allows forgiveness to take root within your heart. Rest in the warmth of this sunlight for a while.

6. With a sincere desire to mend the relationship, say, "I forgive you with all my heart and wish you nothing but unalloyed goodness. And I forgive myself for my complicity in creating this misunderstanding. May neither of us have to suffer any further painful consequences from our past encounter."

7. Now visualize being in the presence of your former antagonist and mending your relationship with kind words and gestures. As you contemplate this auspicious encounter, feel how a great weight is being lifted from you and how a sense of inner peace is replacing it.

8. Slowly open your eyes and relax for a few moments. When you return to everyday awareness, record your observations in your journal.

Exercise 7: A Testimonial Dinner for the Severe Teachers

This exercise uses the broad perspective of time to reframe hurtful relationships and situations. With this perspective, you welcome people back into your life, thanking and blessing them for the unexpected good fortune that resulted from the apparent injustice that was inflicted upon you. Besides coming to terms with these "severe teachers," we can use this exercise to investigate how our own behavior unconsciously may have contributed to our victimization. As we witness our behavior from an objective [perspective] that was unavailable earlier in life, we can take responsibility for actions on our part that unwittingly led to personal suffering. In this way, we can end the blame game and reclaim a sense of personal empowerment.

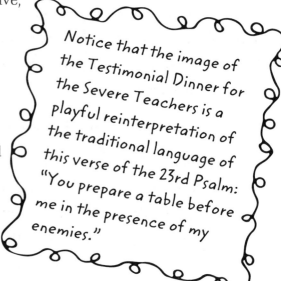

Notice that the image of the Testimonial Dinner for the Severe Teachers is a playful reinterpretation of the traditional language of this verse of the 23rd Psalm: "You prepare a table before me in the presence of my enemies."

1. Sit in a comfortable chair, relax your body, and take some long, rhythmic breaths to center your mind.

2. Divide a piece of paper into three columns. In the first column, list the guests you are inviting to this testimonial dinner, those who have wronged you in some significant way. In the second column, describe the apparent injustice that was inflicted on you. In the third column, describe the unforeseen benefits, the unexpected good that resulted from their actions.

3. Using the broad perspective of time, say to each of the offending parties, "I understand now that you did me a great deal of good by your actions when you did _____, for which I want to thank you. I understand now that it was difficult for you, and it was difficult for me. But now that I forgive you, I am grateful for your contribution to my life."

4. As you consider how each of the offending parties treated you, ask yourself, "What part did I play in being victimized? Did I have an unconscious agenda that made me an unwitting collaborator in this scenario?" If you uncover ways in which you sabotaged yourself, extend the same courtesy to yourself that you just extended to your severe teachers. Forgive yourself. As you free yourself from the blame game and take responsibility for yourself, you can release the energy that has been tied up in resentment and redirect it into your conscious growth as an elder.

Exercise 8: Doing Your Philosophic Homework

In addressing the philosophic homework, elders work on synthesizing wisdom from long life experience. Contemplating the past as well as the future, they seriously investigate the "big questions" that have occupied humanity's greatest thinkers since time immemorial: Where do we come from? Why are we here? Where do we go after we die? What is our purpose? What is our place in the universe? To whom are we answerable? Is there inherent in life a way of being harmonious with it? In doing your philosophic homework, you confront these questions not as an interesting intellectual exercise, but as an impassioned examination of your ultimate values and commitments. In the following exercise, you will use socialized meditation [meditation with a friend] to investigate one of the issues that humanity has wrestled with for millennia. Sitting in spiritual intimacy with a trusted friend, you will induce yourself into a state of deepened awareness and attempt to gain clarity on this major philosophical question.

1. Sit quietly with a friend who has agreed to work with you on the philosophic homework. Both of you should close your eyes for a few moments and take long, deep breaths to quiet and center yourselves.

2. When you open your eyes, your partner will pose a question to you, such as, "What do you believe about the soul and the afterlife?" or "What is the purpose of your life?"

3. As your partner listens in silence, providing a safe, supportive field of attention for the exploration to take place, speak from your heart about this subject without censoring yourself. Explore your thoughts and feelings without trying to impress either your friend or yourself. Forget about what Socrates, Jesus, Confucius, and Muhammad have to say about this issue; speak from the immediacy and the authority of your own experience. Continue for 10 minutes or so and then close your eyes and return to silence.

4. When you open your eyes, pose the same question to your partner and listen attentively as he or she wrestles with the issue. When your friend has finished, close your eyes and be silent for a few moments.

5. Now write in your journal whatever insights emerge from this session. You also

might want to paint a picture, sculpt, or express your discoveries through any of the expressive arts. You also can use your insights as a launching point for further solo meditation.

Exercise 9: Letters of Appreciation

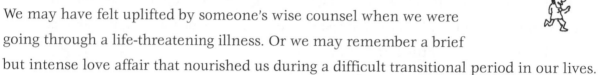

As elders, we often feel the desire to express our heartfelt appreciation to those people who have helped us on our life journey. We may have had a brief encounter with someone who changed our perspective at a crucial turning point in our youth.

We may have felt uplifted by someone's wise counsel when we were going through a life-threatening illness. Or we may remember a brief but intense love affair that nourished us during a difficult transitional period in our lives.

We can write letters to such people expressing our gratitude and appreciation. By writing "How wonderful it was to have a friend like you" or "You mean a lot to me, even though we haven't communicated to each other for some time," we acknowledge our interconnectedness with the many people who have contributed to the inner richness that we now feel as elders. As elderhood takes root in our psyches, we increasingly need to communicate what people really mean to us, how they have nourished our lives, and how we have benefited from knowing them. By sending letters of appreciation to our children, spouse, close friends, relatives, neighbors, and the spiritual teachers who have influenced our development, we gain closure in our relationships while widening the circle of our compassion.

Make a list of people whom you would like to invite to a Thanksgiving Reunion of the Benevolent Teachers. These are the people to whom you will write letters of appreciation. In writing each letter, try to communicate the essential qualities that make the person unique and the ways in which you have grown because of your association with him or her. Don't hold yourself back: Express the "mushy" sentiments that you may have avoided articulating over the years. Now is the time to open your heart and to speak with unadorned simplicity and straightforwardness. When the letters are written, you may choose to mail them or to have them mailed posthumously. (Because of unique circumstances in relationships, some people may prefer to wait until after their deaths before having their letters sent.) In either case, your actions not only will bring closure to your relationships but also strengthen the social web that is in danger of being fragmented and atomized by the exigencies of modern life.

Exercise 10: Acting as an Elder of the Tribe

Like tribal elders of the past, today's spiritual elders are wisdom-keepers, entrusted with the responsibility of maintaining the well-being of our families and communities. When they serve in the public sphere, elders bear witness to enduring values that transcend shortsighted political partisanship. Motivated by broad cultural and planetary concerns, elders call into question our overreliance on consumerism and our continued assault on the planet's ecological health. Guided by an ecological sensibility, they urge us to make political and consumer decisions with the long-term consequences of our actions in mind. Serving as stewards of the community and the environment, they champion the causes of sane consumption, social justice, and cross-cultural understanding and cooperation.

The following exercise will help you get in touch with the sage within yourself who longs to make a contribution in the public sphere. By exercising your responsibility as an elder, you can serve as a leader in rebuilding our fractured communities and in safeguarding the health of our ailing planet Earth.

1. Sit in a comfortable chair and relax your body and mind by taking a few deep breaths.

2. Think back to all the animated conversations you have had with your children, relatives, friends, and colleagues at work in which you voiced solutions to world problems or to problems closer to home. Recall those occasions in which you spoke with such passion and clear-sighted vision that had you been a political leader, you would have inspired people to pursue an enlightened course of action on issues of local, national, or international importance.

3. Now imagine that you are addressing a Parliament of World Leaders. Standing at the podium, you speak fearlessly and eloquently, expressing your concerns about ecology, world hunger, the deprivation of civil liberties around the globe, religious and political intolerance, or any other issues that deeply move you. Invoking your authority as an elder, rebuke these leaders for failing to serve the interests of the planet and the next seven generations, who may inherit a severely compromised environment and a world divided by political, economic, and religious differences.

4. Still in touch with your moral and political convictions, open your journal and consider ways in which you can express your wisdom as an elder in the public sphere:

    a) How can you best serve the planet?

    b) How can you serve the nation?

    c) How can you serve the community?

    d) How can you be of service to your family?

    e) How can you best serve those who are in the process of becoming elders?

Tools and Resources

Chapter 1: Changing Your Life for (the) Good

MUSSAR

Morinis, Alan. *Everyday Holiness*. Boston: Trumpeter Books, 2007. An introduction to the history, theory, and practice of mussar, by one of the pre-eminent contemporary teachers of the tradition.

The Mussar Institute (www.mussarinstitute.org). Founded by Alan Morinis. Advances the study and practice of mussar, through practitioner and facilitator training courses and online resources.

The Center for Contemporary Mussar (www.contemporarymussar.org). Nonprofit led by founder Rabbi Ira Stone (author of *A Responsible Life*) and Dr. Beulah Trey that offers distance learning, local small-group study, and training opportunities.

The Making of a Mensch (available through www.letitripple.org/ or www.rebootshop.org). Filmmaker Tiffany Shlain's ten-minute film explores the Jewish teachings of mussar, interpreted through a 21st-century lens.

MINDFULNESS

Boorstein, Sylvia. *That's Funny, You Don't Look Buddhist*. San Francisco: HarperCollins, 1997. This book explores how you can be both a "faithful Jew and a passionate Buddhist."

Kabat-Zinn, Jon. *Mindfulness for Beginners: Reclaiming the Present Moment and Your Life*. Boulder: Sounds True, 2012. An introduction to the practice of mindfulness by the founding executive director of the Center for Mindfulness at UMass Medical School.

Kaplan, Aryeh. *Jewish Meditation: A Practical Guide*. New York: Schocken, 1982. A classic and early introduction to the techniques of Jewish meditation.

Slater, Jonathan. *Mindful Jewish Practice*. New York: Aviv Press, 2004. Through rabbinic, liturgical, and Hasidic texts, the author offers a way to understand Jewish practices of study, prayer, and loving-kindness as openings to mindfulness.

SPIRITUAL DIRECTION

The Yedidya Center for Jewish Spiritual Direction (www.yedidyacenter.com). Dedicated to promoting the emerging practice of spiritual direction in the North American Jewish community.

Spiritual Directors International (www.sdiworld.org). Offers a directory of spiritual direction practitioners from all over the world.

JOURNALING

Feld, Merle. *A Spiritual Life: Exploring the Heart and Jewish Tradition.* Albany: SUNY Press, 2007. Journaling as a spiritual practice (see also www.merlefeld.com).

Progoff, Ira. *At a Journal Workshop.* New York: Putnam, 1992. Progoff's Intensive Journal Method draws on his interest in depth psychology and the humanistic application of Jungian ideas.

SHABBAT

National Day of Unplugging (www.nationaldayofunplugging.com/). A project of Reboot, an innovative organization that "affirms the value of Jewish traditions and creates new ways for people to make them their own."

Muller, Wayne. Sabbath: *Restoring the Sacred Rhythm of Rest.* New York: Bantam Books 1999. A moving and thoughtful book that draws on the wisdom of several traditions to offer Sabbath as a powerful practice.

Chapter 2: Cooking Up New Rituals

Ritualwell (www.ritualwell.org). Provides models of Jewish rituals to commemorate special life moments, including milestone birthdays, grandparenting, becoming an elder, menopause, and retirement.

Jewish Sacred Aging (www.jewishsacredaging.com/). Wide-ranging website with resources that explore the implications of the revolution in longevity for all generations, drawing on the wisdom of Judaism.

Mayyim Hayyim (www.mayyimhayyim.org). This Boston-based organization provides a refreshingly contemporary perspective on the mikveh experience and offers a resource guide with examples of many new rituals.

Ochs, Vanessa. *Inventing Jewish Ritual.* Philadelphia: Jewish Publication Society, 2007. Ochs explores the phenomenon of new American Jewish rituals and ritual objects being created today.

Chapter 3: Putting the Life in Lifelong Learning

TEXTS

Alter, Robert. *The Hebrew Bible: A Translation with Commentary.* New York: Norton, 2018. Combines contemporary scholarship with beautiful literary language and style.

Eskenazi, Tamara Cohn, and Andrea L. Weiss. *The Torah: A Women's Commentary.* New York: URJ Press, 2007. This extraordinary milestone is the first commentary written entirely by women scholars and rabbis. Finally, women's voices are in the Jewish conversation.

Fox, Everett. *The Five Books of Moses.* New York: Schocken Books, 1997. Also known as the Schocken Bible, this work draws on the acclaimed German translation by Martin Buber and Franz Rosenzweig and preserves the allusions and wordplay of the Hebrew original.

The JPS Tanakh. Philadelphia: Jewish Publication Society, 1985. If there is something approaching a standard Jewish translation of the Bible, it would be this. Edited by a committee of scholars, it was first published in 1917 and updated in 1985.

Sefaria: A Living Library of Jewish Texts (www.sefaria.org/) is a free online library of Jewish texts in English and Hebrew.

LEARNING ONLINE

The Daf Yomi Advancement Forum (www.dafyomi.co.il). This online resource center supplies free, multilevel English language resources for those studying Talmud according to the 7½-year *daf yomi* cycle.

MOOCs (Massive Open Online Courses). There are MOOCs on many online platforms, but the following offer the largest number of courses, from the largest number of institutions, in the broadest range of subjects:

Coursera (www.coursera.org). Founded by two Stanford professors, Coursera classes are taught by instructors in institutions all over the world, including museums.

edX (www.edx.org). Launched by MIT and Harvard University, edX offers free university-level courses from institutions around the world.

Udemy (www.udemy.com). Offers more than 45,000 courses. Anyone can create one, so use Udemy's rating system to see what others' experiences have been. Many courses are free, but not all.

My Jewish Learning (myjewishlearning.com) is a great platform for nondenominational self-paced Jewish study online.

Project Zug (www.projectzug.org). Takes classic Jewish *hevruta* (one-on-one) learning online and matches people from North American to Israel in weekly sessions, facilitated by teachers. Also can be used by institutions or organized groups who want to offer *hevruta* learning within their membership.

Derekh: Pathways to the Heart and Jewish Tradition (www.derekh.org). Online learning and resources created by Rabbi Eddie and Merle Feld for spiritual deepening for clergy and lay leaders.

A SOON-TO-BE CLASSIC

Kurshan, Ilana. *If All the Seas Were Ink: A Memoir.* New York: St. Martin's Press, 2017. Kurshan takes us on her 7½-year journey reading one page of the Talmud a day, and tying it into life's rhythms and disruptions.

TRAVEL LEARNING

Odysseys Unlimited (www.odysseys-unlimited-catalog.com/). Small-group guided tours for older adults with a balanced mix of traveling, sightseeing, cultural encounters, and free time.

Overseas Adventure Travel (www.oattravel.com). Small-group adventures for lifelong learners, typically over 50, who are interested in going off the beaten path and getting immersed in the local culture.

We love study tours offered by universities and museums, and by Road Scholar (www.roadscholar.org), the preeminent leader in educational travel.

RETREAT CENTERS

Chautauqua (www.jewishcenterchautauqua.org), in southwestern New York State, is open in the summer to explore social and political issues and to promote excellence and creativity of the arts. The Everett Jewish Life Center, one of Chautauqua's denominational houses, examines cutting-edge issues from a Jewish perspective with important Jewish teachers and thought leaders.

Esalen (www.esalen.org), in Big Sur, the epicenter for leaders and methodologies of the emerging New Age movement in the '60s, now offers more than 500 workshops a year in personal growth. Its East Coast counterpart is Omega Institute for Holistic Studies (www.eomega.org), in Rhinebeck, New York.

Institute for Jewish Spirituality (www.jewishspirituality.org). A unique cross-denominational resource center for developing and deepening your contemplative practice of Judaism, IJS offers retreats and training programs.

Kripalu Center for Yoga and Health (www.kripalu.org), in Stockbridge, Massachusetts, and the Feathered Pipe Ranch (www.featheredpipe.com), in Helena, Montana, offer classes and retreats built on yoga and the Hindu tradition.

Spirit Rock: An Insight Meditation Center (www.spiritrock.org), near San Rafael, California, and the Insight Meditation Society (www.dharma.org), in Barre, Massachusetts, offer contemporary American Buddhist retreats.

Chapter 4: Discovering Your Inner Pilgrim

Cousineau, Phil. *The Art of Pilgrimage: The Seeker's Guide to Making Travel Sacred.* San Francisco: Conari Press, 2012. Guidebook to the stages of a sacred journey, offering exercises, stories, and spiritual tools for the traveler.

Hoffman, Lawrence. *Israel: A Spiritual Travel Guide.* Woodstock, VT: Jewish Lights, 2005. Combines prayers, poetry, and spiritual teachings to help transform any trip to Israel into a spiritual experience.

General

The AARP website (www.aarp.org) is an all-around great information resource.

PART
2

Getting Good at Getting Along

Shortly after creating the first human being, God declared, "It is not good to be alone," and the world of relationships sprang into being. We are social animals, meant to live with others in families, clans, tribes, neighborhoods, communities, polities, and nations.

At the same time, as the philosopher Jean-Paul Sartre reminds us, "Hell is other people." Relationships require sharing, which does not come naturally. It means that we have to give up something: space, possessions, personal freedom. Even more, being in relationship makes us vulnerable. The closer we are to others, the more they can hurt us.

Getting good at getting older means holding both these truths at the same time. As we get older, it is more important than ever to maintain a robust social life. Bolstering our "social capital," to use the sociologist Robert Putnam's phrase, is key to maintaining our physical health, mental acuity, and emotional well-being. However, when people retire and no longer have the myriad interactions that work provides, as kids and friends move away, or when driving becomes problematic, loneliness and isolation may take root.

> Seeing your face is like seeing the face of God.

> — Jacob, upon reconciling with his
> brother Esau (Genesis 33:10)

It requires effort to care for an elderly parent, to nurture a still-unlaunched millennial, to keep in touch with old friends, to make new friends, to renew a life partnership, to pursue new interests. It may be confusing to figure out the tricky role reversals that come at our age and stage—becoming caregivers to our parents, being cared for by our children—and choreographing the sometimes-delicate dance we must perform to be present in the lives of our grandchildren. Those of us without children, or without an intimate partner, face different challenges. For all of us, it can be daunting to ask ourselves, "With whom do I want to grow old?" But relationships are what keep us alive and ultimately make life worth living.

Part 2, "Getting Good at Getting Along," explores a variety of social relationships and how they change as we get older. Here we also offer some tools for how to enhance the quality and quantity of our social capital.

CHAPTER 6

Honoring Your Father and Mother

by Rabbi Laura Geller

I have a distinct and surprising memory from childhood of asking my father why the Ten Commandments says that the reward for honoring your parents is a longer life. It is surprising because my father was not a particularly religious man and I didn't often ask him questions like that. What made it distinct was his answer. He told me: "Honoring your parents is harder than it sounds. Even though I love my mom and dad, your Nana Stella and Papa Sam, it isn't always easy to honor them, to take care of them and to do some of the things they want me to do when I am also taking care of you and Mom. But I bet that because you and your brothers see Mom and me taking care of our parents now that they are old, you will take care of us when we get old . . . and so we will live longer."

He was right. Before my father died in the early '80s, my brothers and I did take care of him as he aged. We are still taking care of my 96-year-old mother. And he was right that taking care of parents and figuring out what it means to honor them is actually harder than it seems.

Our tradition, as well as my father, understood how complicated honoring parents could be. The commandment appears twice in Torah, in Exodus 20:12 and Leviticus 19:3. The first time it says, "Honor your father and your mother"; the second time it says, "Revere your mother and father . . . I am Adonai your God." The Talmud asks, "Why add 'I am Adonai your God'?" The answer: "There are three partners in creating a human being: the Holy One, the father, and the mother. The Holy One says, 'When a person honors his father and his mother, it is as though they are honoring Me'" (BT *Niddah* 31a).

No wonder it sometimes feels as though we need to be angels to really honor our parents: The standard seems to be superhuman.

According to these rabbinic ancestors, there is a significant difference between "honor" and "revere." Revere relates to maintaining a parent's dignity, while honor means caring for a parent's physical needs—food, clothing, and safety. But then the rabbis ask, "At whose expense do you care for parents' physical needs and at whose expense do you maintain parents' dignity?" Their answer: We care for parents' physical needs out of our parents' savings, at least until they run out of money, and we maintain our parents' dignity at our own expense, through the gift of our time and presence.

Of course, most of us want to make sure that our parents' physical needs are taken care of and that they maintain their dignity. But how do we translate these values into real-life experience, especially given all the other demands on our time and attention? How is it different if we live far away? What if it gets in the way of caring for our own children or grandchildren? What happens if our siblings or our own partners disagree on how it should be done? What are the particular challenges if our relationship with our parents is difficult, strained, or estranged?

What Is Enough?

Honoring and revering our aging parents can be overwhelming, and we may be inclined to ask ourselves, how much is enough? Our rabbinic ancestors recognized the problem but couldn't agree on the answer. One rabbi said there are no lengths too great, and another acknowledged that some demands from our parents are simply irrational or impossible to fulfill. So it is up to us to set our limits based on our resources—financial, geographical, emotional—and those of our parents and siblings. For the needs that extend beyond what we can handle, we must find other ways to provide that care.

This is not just a modern problem. Maimonides (the 12th-century Jewish sage) specifically ruled that a child can pay others to look after a parent if it is too distressing for the child to do so on his or her own (Hilchot Mamrim 6:10). Perhaps knowing that this has been a problem for adult children and their parents for so many generations can ease our own feelings of guilt and distress that we may not be able to provide the hands-on care our parents might

want and need from us. But even so, not all of us
have the financial resources to hire caregivers and
care managers.

Because there are few government resources
available to families with aging parents, most
families simply cobble together a caregiving plan as
best they can. If adult children (and their spouses) are willing to share the responsibility of
caregiving, the financial and emotional burden on the adult children might be eased a bit. If
not, one adult child generally ends up shouldering the entire financial and emotional burden,
including interviewing and choosing prospective caregivers, introducing them to aging
parents, and working them into the family routine. Many adult children also find that they
must do all the shopping for their aging parents, maintain their parents' house (if the parents
insist on remaining in their own home), take care of bill-paying, and handle or oversee every
other detail of their parents' lives. Most caregivers end up spending thousands of dollars of
their own money in this effort, either through direct outlays, lost wages, or having to give up
jobs or businesses entirely.

So besides saving for children's college tuition and your own retirement, it might also make
sense to set aside money to help cover the cost of care for aging parents. Caregiving—
especially round-the-clock, in-home care—is very pricey, and few elderly people have saved
enough to cover that cost themselves. If you don't need to dip into that account, so much the
better.

Whatever our financial resources, there is also the real challenge of our emotional
resources—how much time, energy, and even physical strength we have in order to both
honor and revere our parents. How do we deal with our own guilt or the sadness in our
parent's voice when she says, "I wish you didn't have go home so soon."

After my father died, my mother's first instinct was to stay in the home they had shared.
Honoring her desire to be independent and at the same time worrying about her safety living
alone was a delicate dance for me and my brothers. But when she went out for an errand and
left the kettle on, she understood that she couldn't live alone anymore. In a way, we were
lucky that happened; she came to the conclusion on her own. Our friends have had a harder
time convincing their aging parents that it was time to move.

My mother, now 96, lives in a retirement community, and my brothers and I are continually
trying to figure out the best ways to work as a team. One of us has taken over her finances

and coordinates her health care. We have a skilled patient advocate to manage her doctor appointments and supervise her caregivers, who enable her to stay in the independent living section, because she refuses to move to assisted care. My brothers and I consult regularly via phone with each other and with the patient advocate, the social worker in her community, and, most recently, the hospice nurse and my mother's primary caregiver. My other brother and I, who live far away, call my mother every day and visit as often as we can. Still, it feels as though I am never doing enough. And still, sometimes, my brothers and I disagree on what's best for her.

As we deal with the challenges of our parents' aging, we need to take a breath and allow ourselves to be present in the moment, paying attention to what is happening not only with our parents but also with ourselves and our siblings. We need to recognize our own sadness as we see our parents, who might have once been so vibrant in our minds and lives, becoming frail and dependent. It's also necessary, scary as it may be, to accept and face our fears about our own aging and mortality that our parents' situations raise for us. With self-awareness, these experiences can help us grow in wisdom and understanding.

Some Steps for Making Decisions about Our Parents

At least 25 percent of adult children are involved with the care of a parent, and the care we provide often changes as our parents—and we—age. When we were younger we were called the "sandwich generation," sandwiched between our young children, our work, and our parents. Now, as we are pressed harder—between frail parents needing our attention, adult children often looking for our help, and dealing with our own health issues and those of our partners and friends—the sandwich has become a panini.

In *Facing the Finish: A Road Map for Aging Parents and Adult Children*, life transitions expert Sheri Samotin outlines some steps that can help us as we care for our aging parents.

PANINI GENERATION

STEP 1: ASSESSMENT

Ask yourself some of these questions:

- Is my focus on both parents or just one? If both are still alive and still together, do I expect one to care for the other? If a move to a higher level of care is necessary for one, what are the implications for the other?
- What are my parents' physical, cognitive, and emotional conditions?
- What financial and human resources are available to provide help?
- Should I consider asking my parents to move closer to me or consider moving closer to them?
- Do I understand that my parents, as long as they are cognitively capable, are entitled to make their own decisions, even if they make "bad" ones, and that I don't get to take over?

STEP 2: CLARITY

Get clear about what you are willing and able to do for your parents, given the other demands on you. Obviously, if you are partnered, have siblings, or are parents of adult children, decisions such as these need to be shared with your partner and siblings and perhaps your own children, since these will affect them too. It's even more challenging with blended families.

STEP 3: CONVERSATION

Talk with your siblings and other loved ones who are closely involved with such decisions. These conversations are complicated, and it's easy to fall back into old patterns that might have been beneficial when you were children but are less useful now. Whatever you can do to get on the same page is worth doing, including talking with friends  who have navigated similar situations, with a professional counselor, or with trusted clergy to help you avoid stepping on what might be old land mines, such as how you felt you were treated as a child or whom Mom or Dad really does love best.

Then you can move on to the more practical questions, such as what skills and availability you each have that could be useful to your parents. If the time comes when your parents need direct help, which of you ought to be doing what? Who ought to be paying bills, managing their financial affairs, interacting with doctors and others involved with your

Tips for Having the "Talk" about No Longer Driving

According to AARP, warning signs for older drivers include having crashes or close calls, slower response times, and less confidence behind the wheel. Health more than age determines when people need to stop driving.

The National Institute on Aging (nia.nih.org) offers the following advice about having the "Talk" about driving:

Be prepared. Learn about local services to help someone who can no longer drive. Identify the person's transportation needs.

Avoid confrontation. Use "I" messages, rather than "You" messages. For example, say, "I am concerned about your safety when you are driving," rather than "You're no longer a safe driver."

Stick to the issue. Discuss the driver's skills, not his or her age.

Focus on safety and maintaining independence. Be clear that the goal is for the older driver to continue the activities he currently enjoys while staying safe. Offer to help him stay independent. For example, you might say, "I'll help you figure out how to get where you want to go if driving isn't possible."

Be positive and supportive. Recognize the importance of a driver's license to the older person. Understand that he may become defensive, angry, hurt, or withdrawn. You might say, "I understand that this may be upsetting" or "We'll work together to find a solution."

parents' lives? Do you imagine that your partners or children will also have some responsibility for your parents? What are your parents' financial resources, and what are your and your siblings' expectations of how they ought to be used? Should you consult with a professional who can lay out for you and your siblings the options that might be available to your parents?

STEP 4: MORE CONVERSATION

As you (and your siblings and other loved ones) become clearer about the next steps for your aging parents and ideally before a crisis occurs, begin discussing care plans with your parents. Samotin sets out some best practices for these ongoing conversations, including choosing the right time (for example, not in the midst of a family celebration) and deciding in advance who will facilitate (for example, you, your sibling, or an objective facilitator). Most important at this stage is to try to imagine what this transition is like for your parents, who might deny that they need any special help or need to make changes in their lifestyle. This is not a one-time conversation but an ongoing discussion.

A few years after my mother had been living in her new home but still driving, we had another conversation. It was obvious to everyone, except my mother, that she shouldn't be driving anymore. My brothers and I decided to encourage her to give her car to her granddaughter as a graduation gift. At first our mother protested: How would she get around? How could she still be independent?

We shared with her research we had done about ride-sharing options in the community where she lived, and we showed her how to access gogograndparents.com, which makes it easy for a person who doesn't have a smartphone to use any phone to call an Uber or Lyft. Over time, and especially after her granddaughter made an impassioned request, she relented, eventually feeling very generous as opposed to incompetent and—this was key—able to explain to her friends why she was giving up her car in a way that made her feel good. It was certainly a more elegant solution than just taking away her keys.

Remembering and Appreciating

Now, some nine years after gifting her car to my daughter, my mother, safe in her graduated care retirement community, has Alzheimer's disease.

My mother is becoming more childlike as she ages, and she seems to enjoy singing songs she remembers from when she was younger. On a recent visit I reminded her of a song my dad used to sing to her:

Believe me if all those endearing young charms

which I gaze on so fondly today

were to change by tomorrow and flee from my arms

like fairy gifts fading away.

Thou would still be adored

as this moment thou art

let thy loveliness fade as it will

and around the dear ruins each wish of my heart

would entwine itself verdantly still.

(Lyrics by Thomas Moore)

In the middle of singing it with her, I burst into tears, gazing as I was on her fading self, these "dear ruins," remembering my late father, and, yes, imagining a time in the future when one of my children will be singing those words to me. Then my mother asked me what "verdantly" meant. I told her it meant she was still growing, and that made her smile.

Her adult children are still growing, too.

"Honor your father and your mother, in order that your days be long on the land that Adonai, your God, is giving you" (Exodus 20:12). The Torah doesn't tell us that it is easy or that all the solutions will be elegant. But it does suggest that there is a reward. For me the reward is not that I will necessarily have a longer life, but that I will have a more peaceful heart.

CHAPTER 7

Caring for (and Feeding) Adult Children
by Ruth Nemzoff

Ruth Nemzoff is a resident scholar at the Brandeis Women's Studies Research Center and a board member of InterfaithFamily.com. We were first introduced when we came across her very helpful book *Don't Bite Your Tongue: How to Foster Rewarding Relationships with Your Adult Children* and discovered that we have many friends and colleagues in common.

Words of Wisdom

The legend engraved on the face of the Jewish nickel—on the body of every Jewish child!—not IN GOD WE TRUST, but SOMEDAY YOU'LL BE A PARENT AND YOU'LL KNOW WHAT IT'S LIKE.

—Philip Roth,
Portnoy's Complaint

When our children were young and they depended on us for everything, our role was clear: to protect them. But now that they are adults, what is our role? Most of us will be parents of adult children for longer than we were parents of dependent children. The very notion of "adult child" is an oxymoron. They are adults, independent in so many ways, yet they are still our children—we love them and still want to protect them. The challenge and opportunity of this stage in our lives is to transform that relationship from one of dependency to one of mutuality and interdependence.

Ambiguity, lack of definition, past habits, and social customs put parents and adult children in a quandary: How do we relate to each other as we change over the course of our lives? We need each other for the beginning of life, the end of life, and all the transitions in between. Healthy relationships with those with whom we have shared years of experience are critical to enhancing our sense of well-being and can add texture and joy to our lives.

The relationship between parents and adult children is a mix of choice and obligation. Whether we choose to place more emphasis on one or the other depends on culture, history, religion, and competing loyalties. The fifth commandment reminds us to honor our father and mother, though the exact formula for how to fulfill that obligation remains unclear. We cannot assume that we should expect the same from our children that our parents expected of us. For example, while you may have felt obliged to care for your in-laws financially and physically, your children may see this as choice. (Too bad for us!) When we do not discuss our expectations with our adult children, problems can arise and fray our relationship. When expectations are clear, we have greater opportunity for pleasure, open communication, and positive shared experiences.

Don't allow striving for perfection to be the enemy of progress. You and your children have been disagreeing since your two-year-old wanted the apple both whole *and* cut into slices. A good relationship is not synonymous with a smooth one. Controversy and conflict are part of its texture. Intimacy and irritation go hand in hand. The challenge in fostering a successful relationship is to find the right combination of nurturing and autonomy for you and each of your children at various stages of development.

When Does Adulthood Begin?

The markers of adulthood are changing, for better or worse, leaving no clear end to childhood. Our laws even blur the distinction: at age 16 you can drive in many states; at age 18 you are responsible for your own contracts, but you can stay on your parents' health insurance until age 26. Many of our children have full adult responsibilities but still may be on the family dole.

Adulthood used to mean being able to support yourself. Now many of our children are unable to do so even if they are not slackers, perhaps because the economy does not reward social service work or because of the duration of professional training. Others are traveling the "scenic" route to adulthood—taking time literally to travel perhaps, or accepting unpaid internships to gain experience.

Finding the Right Balance Is a Blessing

Many of our children vacillate from being independent to wanting assistance, and many parents fluctuate between wanting to protect their children from what they see as bad choices to trusting in their capability to do things themselves. By trial and error, and lots of honesty, we can find the right balance between being there and letting go, being intrusive and being helpful, being controlling and being empowering, being infantilizing and being respectful.

The rewards of finding the right balance are huge: a satisfying relationship with one's adult child is a blessing. In times of crisis, parents and children can help each other, such as when poor health strikes either generation, finances dry up, or support systems unravel. Many studies show that communication and care across the lifetime increase the quality of life for both parents and adult children. Aging parents who have maintained connections with their children are less likely to become depressed and more likely to receive adequate elder care. Adult children who have longstanding healthy relationships with their parents are more willing to be actively involved in their aging parents' care. It seems to be well worth it to work hard to get this right.

Tips for Getting It Right

Finding—and then maintaining—the right balance between concern and overbearance is an ongoing process that requires building up your internal resources. Here are some pointers for figuring this out for your family:

- *Know yourself.* Be honest with yourself. Sort out what you are doing for your kids and what you are doing for yourself. In your interactions with them, try to be aware of your motivations. Are you responding out of judgment, criticism, or kindness? There is a parent and a child within each of us; we move back and forth from our most adult selves to our most childish behaviors. Apologize when you act like a child, and try to call upon your most mature self.

- *Forgive your parents.* Our parenting is influenced by the ways our parents parented us, for better and worse. What kind of relationship would you have wanted with your parents once you became an adult? See if you can expand your repertoire of behaviors. If you fall into old negative patterns, you get the same old negative responses. Find new sources of insight. Ask friends how they might handle specific situations.

- *Know the environment.* Remember how hard it was for our parents to accept what we were perfectly comfortable with when we were the age of our adult children? The world is still changing, so some of what our kids do might be as hard for us to accept as what we did was for our parents to accept. What might have been taboo for us is now more acceptable, such as gender fluidity. Try not to worry about a previous generation's biases or other people's judgment. That's hard to do, but if you are thoughtful about keeping an open mind and heart, you might even learn something new about the world from your children.

- *Find the right degree of separation.* For the first six months of our children's lives, we carried them everywhere. Over time, we watched them walk across the room, go to a friend's house, and eventually, to school. We never let them go completely but instead gave them a longer rope, experimenting to find the degree of connection

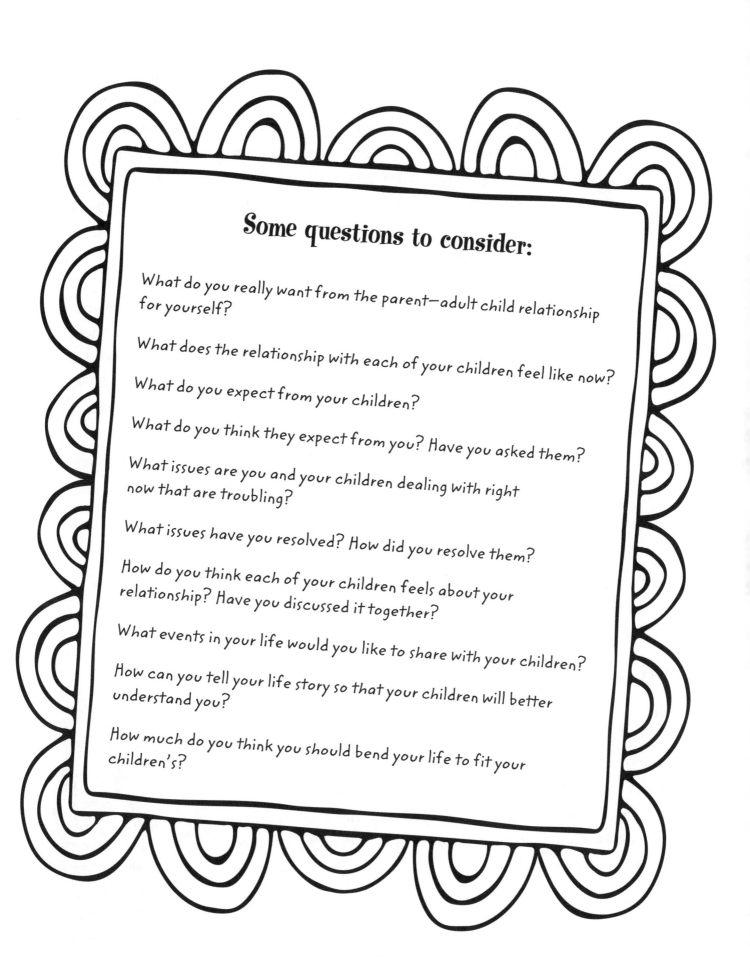

Some questions to consider:

What do you really want from the parent—adult child relationship for yourself?

What does the relationship with each of your children feel like now?

What do you expect from your children?

What do you think they expect from you? Have you asked them?

What issues are you and your children dealing with right now that are troubling?

What issues have you resolved? How did you resolve them?

How do you think each of your children feels about your relationship? Have you discussed it together?

What events in your life would you like to share with your children?

How can you tell your life story so that your children will better understand you?

How much do you think you should bend your life to fit your children's?

that worked for us. Now that they are grown, that metaphorical rope no longer connects us. The challenge is to discover other ways of staying connected that honor our children as competent adults who can share their expertise with us.

- *Don't bite your tongue.* When you are experiencing conflict with your adult children, instead of wasting energy on trying to suppress your feelings and being afraid of the consequences of a conversation, consider what you want to say to them and why you want to say it. Is what you want to tell them necessary and beneficial? Does it come from a place of kindness or a place of judgment? There are different, appropriate ways of sharing what is on your mind, figuring out when to share it, and how—direct conversation, handwritten letter, email, phone, or text. Assess based on each child and each situation. Silence isn't always golden; oftentimes, it is better to make things clear. Other times it is better to leave things unsaid. The clearer you are with yourself about your motivation and the more thoughtful you are about how to share what you are feeling, the more likely it is that speaking or keeping silent will be your choice, not one forced on you out of fear.

- *Say hello to reality.* Deal with what is, not with what you wanted, and appreciate the very best in your children and their partners. Listen instead of judging.

- *Remember that we are all new to this game.* You have never been a parent of this adult child before, and they have never been an adult child before.

Some Common Challenges

While all our situations are different, some common issues emerge as we navigate parenting our adult children.

TO ADVISE OR NOT TO ADVISE

It's okay to give advice, especially when you're asked for it, but don't expect it to be followed. When you do give advice, be sure to explain your reasoning so your adult child can evaluate your ideas. It's easy to get stuck in being the expert or wanting to be the source of all wisdom. You and your child know this is not true. A better strategy is to explain your opinion, based on your own experience, and to suggest that your adult child seek out other opinions as well.

You don't need to weigh in on any of your adult children's decisions. If choices are not inherently dangerous or self-destructive, give your kids the space they need to make their own mistakes. Most decisions are neither right nor wrong. They simply reflect the needs and values of the person making them: loyalty versus opportunity, long term versus short term, choice versus obligation. Their understanding of the variables in modern decision making is probably more current than yours. For example, you may advise your child to stick with the same job for an extended period of time—sound advice 20 years ago but less so in today's economic climate, where many employees switch companies relatively frequently.

TO PAY OR NOT TO PAY

Money can be a means of control, of motivation, or an expression of generosity. However you give money, make the terms clear. Are certain behaviors required for your adult children to continue receiving financial support? Is repayment expected or is this a freebie with no strings attached?

LinkedIn started what is now an annual "Bring in Your Parents Day" after a study showed that one-third of parents don't understand their adult children's jobs. The program has grown beyond tech firms to be embraced by hundreds of companies across the economic spectrum. AARP reports that this does more than foster intergenerational bonding: 65 percent of American workers believe their parents have unshared knowledge that could help them with their careers.

Sometimes parents use money to force their adult children to do what the parents want. You may agree to give money to reinforce a positive behavior, such as going to college or graduate school, or withhold it to prevent a negative behavior, such as substance abuse. While you may get compliance, using money as to exert control often leads to resentment on the part of the adult child. How well you tolerate such resentment will factor into your decision as to whether to use money as a form of control.

Each year, parents spend twice as much on adult children than they contribute to their retirement accounts.

When you give a gift with no strings attached, you may be disappointed with the use of the funds. Think carefully about how you expect the money will be used, considering past experience and current circumstances. If you don't feel that you can deal with the likely outcome, rethink the gift or set terms with which you are comfortable.

As a parent giving a monetary gift, you may not know if you are facilitating constructive behavior or enabling immaturity and irresponsible behavior. Each economic decision you make to support your adult child—giving cash, providing housing, or paying tuition—should be based on a combination of your financial capacity, your view of the child's behavior, and the economics of society. For example, if you decide to support your adult child's graduate schooling, consider the financial obligation, including the possibility that your child might not complete that education. Halfway through earning the degree, your child might receive an offer for a dream job or fail to write her dissertation. If your child does not complete her schooling, for whatever reason, who pays for what was owed in tuition? Will you feel resentful? You may decide to help your child by paying off her student loans and having her pay interest at a lower rate than she would otherwise pay on a loan from the government or bank. While it might feel awkward to take interest from your child, it might actually be a win-win situation for both sides—she gets a lower interest rate and you get the same interest from her that you would get from your bank.

Financial discussions are always difficult. You may not want to share the full extent of your portfolio, or you may not want your adult children to know that you are not as financially well-off as they believe. Even if some of these discussions may have happened years before college, relationships (both financial and personal) shift. It's best to get everyone's emotional and financial expectations out in the open. If you do not discuss your expectations, you may find yourself disappointed when your children do not intuitively meet your needs. The openness you create now will set the stage for future conversations.

TO LET THEM MOVE BACK HOME . . . OR NOT

According to a 2016 NPR report, almost one-third of American young adults live with their parents. Your family must decide whether intergenerational cohabitation is a good idea. Why is your adult child moving home? Is he a victim of high rents and low wages, or are you allowing him to avoid responsibility for his own financial well-being? Does it matter? If you have a partner, you need to discuss this decision, first between yourselves and then with your adult child.

When refilling the nest, make the terms clear:

- Will your child be living with you for the short term or the long term? How long is each of these terms?
- Is your child expected to pay rent? If so, in money or services? Or both?
- Whose space is it anyway? What part of the house is theirs? What part is yours? Or is it all shared space?
- Is your child expected to spend time with you? If so, how often?
- What level of cleanliness is expected in public areas, as well as in her private space? Is your child responsible for doing any household chores? May dirty dishes be left in the sink? May laundry be left unfolded in the dryer? May a coffee cup be left unwashed in the living room?
- Is your child allowed to have friends over?
- Is marijuana or liquor allowed on the premises?
- May a romantic partner sleep over?
- If your child is staying out late or not returning home, what is your expectation of being notified and how?
- How will you each give the other privacy? Are you comfortable being intimate with your partner when your child is in the house?

These are complicated questions. (Oh, for the good old days of easy conversations!) But better to get them out on the table than to sweep them under the rug. Try to discuss these questions before your adult child moves in, and have a method in place for reviewing decisions, such as monthly meetings. You may want to write out a contract or establish a more informal agreement. Only you and your child can decide what is most appropriate. Be sure to modify this plan with time and experience.

If moving back home doesn't seem to be the right decision for you or your child, you may be asked to help cover her rent. According to the *New York Times*, almost half of young adults receive housing support from their parents. Some parents contribute to rent because their child's salary won't cover living independently; others contribute so their child can live without roommates or in a neighborhood they couldn't otherwise afford. If you provide housing support to your adult child, decide whether the money is a loan and, if so, when and how it will be repaid. You might suggest payments in kind, to enhance their sense of filial obligation: This might be something as simple as helping paint your house or doing the weekly grocery shopping.

CREATING FAMILIES OF THEIR OWN

In theory we want for our children what they want for themselves. But this may be harder than it sounds. Your child may have chosen a partner different from one you expected. This person may not look like you, may have a different religion, and may be a different gender from what you anticipated. Stay cool. Get to know the person. You may have questions about whether a particular partner will be a good match for your child, but don't criticize your child's love interest. You might try a gentler approach: "I notice that you're very quiet around X." Be careful about the tone you strike. Remember, if the romance is long term, this new person could be selecting your nursing home.

Many of our children are choosing not to marry, yet are buying homes and having children with a significant other. This may be difficult for you to accept. You can mention it to your child once, letting her know that you still love her, but harping will not serve you well. If your adult child is single, know that times have changed. Single people are no longer the odd person out. They travel with married friends as well as with other single people and can have robust and fulfilling social lives.

IF THEY CHOOSE TO MARRY

We want, of course, our children to support their partner's dreams, not ours. But some of us have been imagining this moment since our kids were little, and it is hard to give up on those visions. Planning a wedding, even the most joyful, often comes with conflict. Everybody's expectations risk being trampled.

One major issue is who pays, and the norms surrounding this are not the same as when you might have married. How much will each family contribute? Are the couple themselves paying for the wedding? Do parents have a say about the budget, the venue, the ceremony, or the guest list? Here it is helpful to have a frank conversation with your adult child, asking him or her to be clear about what is expected from you and the other parents. Remember that the couple is negotiating two families and at least four sets of expectations (their own, plus each of their families).

It is, after all, the couple's wedding. They are creating a new family that you will be connected with but not the focal point. You will need to work with the new family to develop your role in it. Remember, your job once the deal is sealed is to support the couple. If they should divorce, you will need to be in good standing with your son- or daughter-in-law, particularly if you ever hope to see your grandchildren.

BECOMING AN IN-LAW

If your child has decided to marry, you are now the in-law. Ideally, by the time of the wedding you will have established a good connection with your child-in-law by sharing common experiences and by being a supportive presence in the life of the couple. However, this can be difficult if the couple has a conflict and you instinctively side with your own child. It is also problematic at other moments (and you can be sure there will be many) when you are criticized by either your child or their partner.

Giving advice is complicated. Think about timing and remember that your in-law children are more likely to listen to you if they feel listened to. Listen to yourself. Or ask a friend to listen in on your conversation with your children. Might you be offering too many helpful hints? It helps to be positive, to reframe situations in the most optimistic light, and to think of conversations as explorations. Ask questions; oftentimes, your children will have good reasons for doing what they do.

Your in-law children come with parents of their own. Jewish culture has a name for your in-law's parents: *machetunim*. You didn't choose each other, but now you are family. Now every holiday, every future *simchah*, you will likely need to find a way to share these adult children and grandchildren.

From Challenges to Opportunity

The folk saying "Little children, little problems; big children, big problems" echoes in some of these challenges. Solving the problems of our little children was on us. The good news is that we don't have to—and often shouldn't even try to—solve the problems of our adult children. The even better news is that this stage in our lives offers us the opportunity to get to know our children as the adults they have become and to allow them to get to know us as adults as well. What a blessing.

CHAPTER 8

Teaching Your (Children's) Children Well
by Rabbi Laura Geller

Over the years, I have helped hundreds of young teenagers prepare for their bar or bat mitzvah. I often ask them to tell me about someone in their lives who has made a difference to them, someone they think of as a hero. Oftentimes, they share stories about their grandparents: Gabe's grandmother survived the Holocaust by hiding in an attic for two years; Justine's grandfather came to America at the same age she was now with hardly any money and just the name of a relative in New York; Leah's grandfather was the first in his family to go to college, and he couldn't get into the university he wanted to go to because he was Jewish; Aryeh's grandparents left everything they owned in Iran just after the revolution and started all over again without knowing any English; Teva's grandmother was a synagogue president when there were hardly any women leaders in the Jewish community; Ben's grandfather marched in Selma. These stories matter to these young people. Hearing them has helped shape who they will become.

Some of these young people talk about celebrating holidays with their grandparents, turning to their grandparents when they need assurance instead of advice, and learning through their grandparents that family history and connection across the generations really matters. When I meet with couples to be married and they talk about ritual objects they might want to use in their weddings, they often choose a Kiddush cup or a tallit that belonged to a grandparent because that grandparent taught them something powerful about love and commitment.

Grandparents matter. Dr. Karl Pillemer, a researcher from Cornell University, found that the relationship between grandparents and their grandchildren is second in emotional importance only to the relationship between parent and child. Children and grandparents each benefit. Research from Boston College finds that "an emotionally close relationship between grandparent and grandchildren was associated with fewer symptoms of depression for both generations." An American Grandparent Association survey reported that 72 percent of grandparents "think being a grandparent is the single most important and satisfying thing in their life," and 63 percent "say they can do a better job caring for grandchildren than they did with their own [children]."

There are different ways to be a grandparent. For some of us, being a grandparent marks a major transition, and spending lots of time with our grandchildren is a high priority. For others, as lovely as it might be to see our children become parents, having grandchildren doesn't change our lifestyle or our desire to continue to live very independent lives. Some of us live close to our grandchildren; some of us live far away; and some might even live with our grandchildren. Suzanne Macht and her husband, Stephen, are longtime members of my synagogue, who live all three scenarios. Here, Suzanne, a writer and a keen observer of family dynamics, offers insights based on her unique, perhaps unusually involved, experience with different kinds of grandparenting.

The Macht Family *Gantza-Mishpacha*: A Personal Reflection

Having four healthy children and nine healthy grandchildren (and counting) has been the fullness of my life with my husband. But being a grandparent is, in many ways, harder than being a parent. For one thing, the role is indeterminate. Yes, it's great to be loving and accepting, and sneaking a candy or two to the little one while Mommy's not looking. But what about giving your two cents to the parent or child when you think things are going a bit awry? What about when and how to discipline when you think it's necessary? What about having opinions about how the children spend their time? Or how the parents are guiding them? It's a delicate tightrope to walk, knowing when and how to step in or to step out.

As a parent, I said what I thought had to be said— straight out, no diplomatic hedging about what needed to be done or undone. As a grandparent I need to take much more care, not only with the grandchildren but also with their parents. And, of course, it's easier to talk about how the children are

Not everyone has grandchildren, but we can all be surrogate grandparents if we choose. Intergenerational connections, even between unrelated older adults and children, benefit both the children and the adults. (See chapter 26, "Touching the Future through Mentoring.") A University of California, Davis study that looked at children from low-income homes in Hawaii discovered that the children who succeeded (in school) were those who had at least one adult who cared about them. Data from the "Littles" alumni of Big Brothers/Big Sisters found that 77 percent reported doing better in school because of their Big. Sixty-five percent agreed that their Big helped them reach a higher level of education than they thought possible, and 52 percent agreed that their Big kept them from dropping out of high school.

being raised with your own adult children—they'll forgive your trespasses (in time). But with your in-laws, those words may stick, and you have to be extra careful when discussing issues of upbringing.

GRANDPARENTING IN YOUR OWN HOME

One daughter, one son-in-law, and four grandchildren live with us so the kids can go to school in our city. By sharing our home, we share our lives in sometimes the most intimate ways. We continually revise how we interact: how and when it is okay to join the conversation, how and when we allow for real privacy, how and when we schedule our days' activities so as not to interfere with one another's. Talk about a dance!

Forget any kind of formality in our house. We're upstairs, downstairs, sitting on each other's beds, sharing computers, looking at homework papers, visiting with our grandchildren's friends in the kitchen, watching television together. And yet when our bedroom door or office door is closed, our privacy is respected.

We pay our mortgage on the house and our daughter and son-in-law pay their portion of the water bill, the gas bill, the electric bill, the cable bill, and two out of the four times a month the housekeeper comes to clean. We share the cost of household supplies, and they pay for their own food. We try to keep our food separate from theirs, but somehow our half gallon of milk (and Oreos) seem to magically disappear before the end of each day.

I suspect that more and more people will explore this kind of multigenerational housing arrangement in the years ahead, either for financial reasons or as grandparents age. Living together for both sustenance and caregiving makes sense for us. Maybe it will for others, too.

GRANDPARENTING WHEN YOUR GRANDCHILDREN ARE CLOSE BY

Our son's family lives about 15 minutes away from us. With every growing year, those grandchildren are more and more involved in school and after-school activities, and we find ourselves having to make appointments to see each other, which inevitably get canceled or delayed because something else comes up. In sharp contrast to the grandchildren who live with us, we are not there "in the moment."

When we can, we like to take them on outings on the weekends, and we also enjoy attending parent-welcomed school functions, birthday parties, and as many of their soccer games as we can bear. Happily, our son brings his children to our home when he's in the neighborhood—or drops them off when he has some errands to do—and that is always a treat for us. He's very aware that we want to be with them, and he wants his children to be close to us and makes sure they are.

GRANDPARENTING FROM A DISTANCE

Two of our grandchildren live far away. We try to see them every three to four months, and we make every effort to be in touch as often as we can. We FaceTime on the computer, write actual letters to them, and send little gifts periodically. We make sure that whenever we have large family gatherings, they are invited to "sit" *on* the dinner table with everyone else—not in a chair but on our computer screen, where we can all talk back and forth with them.

I occasionally make personalized books for our grandkids, sometimes reminding them of our last visit together. By making a connection through stories and pictures, we form a different kind of bond than the one we have with our grandchildren living close by and those living with us.

BEING A JEWISH ROLE MODEL

As a grandmother who loves being a cultural Jew and who also enjoys throwing parties, Jewish holidays are celebrated in our home with great fanfare. There is an abundance of food, homemade decorations, holiday themes, storytelling, and plays that we write and give to the children to act out in costume for family and friends. Judaism and celebrating our rituals enlivens us and brings happiness and joy to our family, as well as an understanding of our history and the connection we have to Israel and our people.

The Challenges of Grandparenting

While Suzanne's description of her three grandparenting situations—and her efforts to imbue her grandchildren with some Jewish cultural awareness—provides interesting perspective, grandparenting can present a variety of other challenges that require a combination of sensitivity, wisdom, and humor. In particular, issues regarding money, marriage between partners of different faith and cultural backgrounds, and divorce can make the role of grandparent more complicated and more significant in the lives of the grandchildren.

TIME AND MONEY

Some of our generation want a loving but not so hands-on relationship with our grandchildren. Many of us are busy living our own lives—traveling, studying, golfing, volunteering—and we might not want to be obligated to provide child care or help out with our grandkids in other ways. As with all grandparenting, what is most important is clear communication between us and our adult children about expectations and reasonable boundaries.

What is true about time is also true about money. For some of us who have substantial resources, giving gifts to our grandchildren is a total pleasure. When possible, we may help pay for private or religious school tuition or invest in a 529 plan for college. Some of us are not in the financial position to contribute in those ways, or we don't think it is our responsibility to cover those kinds of expenses. Again, it is important for both sides to make their expectations clear.

WHEN YOUR GRANDCHILDREN HAVE PARENTS OF DIFFERENT FAITHS

For many Jewish parents of intermarried children, the question is "But will my grandchildren be Jewish?" Circumstances differ; much depends on the promises the adult children made to each other about raising their children and on whether the non-Jewish partner is actively involved with his or her own faith tradition. Our role as grandparents is not to force Judaism on our grandchildren; that would most likely backfire and prompt resentment from our adult children. Better for us to be models of a joyful Judaism: With the parents' consent, we can read Jewish books with our grandkids; host a kid-friendly Passover seder and invite the whole family; build a sukkah together with our grandchildren, then decorate it, and maybe even sleep over in it. We can make a big deal out of Hanukkah and an even bigger deal out of Shabbat. We can bake challah together and create Jewish memories that connect Jewishness with love, warmth, and joy.

GRANDPARENTING WHEN CHILDREN DIVORCE

The Talmud records that "when a man divorces the wife of his youth, even the altar of God weeps" (*Gittin* 90b). God sheds tears, but that pales in comparison to the tears of the grandparents.

> PJ Library, a program of the Harold Grinspoon Foundation, provides a unique opportunity to share books and stories with your grandchildren. Just sign up and PJ Library will send a Jewish children's book to your grandchildren every month at no cost. As is noted on their website: "Whether they're called Bubbe, Zayde, Savta, Saba, Nana, Papa, Grandma, or Grandpa, there's no denying that grandparents are special. Reading a story with a grandparent builds beautiful memories while also helping develop a child's literacy."

A divorce is a kind of death, but without ritual and clear rules for how to mourn and move forward. This is as true for grandparents as for the divorcing parents and their family.

Grandparents often experience different emotions in the face of divorce. Primary among them are guilt and fear. Guilt: We might ask ourselves whether there was something we could have done to prevent the divorce. Or if we weren't happy about the marriage in the first place, we might wonder if our ambivalence contributed to the tension in the marriage. Fear: Maybe we worry about what will happen to the grandchildren. Where will they live? Who will have custody? How will the divorce affect their economic security? Will our access to the grandchildren be diminished? These are very real concerns, and much of this is beyond our control, but The Spruce, a website offering practical tips on creating a home, offers some suggestions that will make this transition easier:

Stay connected with your adult child. Listen. Don't offer solutions. If your child asks for advice, give it gently and without anger at your child or former in-law.

Avoid taking sides as much as possible. Don't assign blame. You never know what happens in another person's marriage. Taking sides only creates a more difficult situation.

Be careful about your relationship with your child's ex. The better that relationship is, the easier it will be to stay close to your grandchildren. Navigating the wishes of an adult child who wants you to avoid contact with his ex is complicated. In general, it is best to honor that request, at least early in the transition. Sometimes it gets easier over time. If you once had a close relationship, it is probably wise to have a conversation with your former in-law, explaining how painful all this is and hoping she will understand your desire to maintain a connection with your own child and your grandchildren.

Do not manipulate the grandchildren. Never say anything bad about either parent to your grandchildren—it's unhealthy for them. Never try to find out any information from the children about what is going on with their parents. If you need to know something, ask the parents directly.

Provide the grandchildren with a low-stress environment. Don't talk about the divorce unless the grandchildren bring it up. Remind them that the divorce is not their fault and that they are still loved by both parents and all grandparents, no matter what. Continue to do things together, spending time together and having fun.

Be diplomatic with the other grandparents. If you had become close to the other grandparents, the loss of that connection is like another death. Sometimes these friendships actually find a way to continue, but not if you discuss details of the divorce. You will find yourself with them at certain occasions, like graduations or the weddings of your grandkids. Stay cool and cordial.

Be wise about social media. It is not your place to talk about the changes in your adult child's lives. Never share pictures or information on Facebook about your grandchildren unless that has already been shared by the adult children or unless you have explicit permission from both parents.

Be positive about the future. Remember the movie *The Kids Are All Right?* Mostly that turns out to be true, even more often if loving and wise grandparents are in their lives.

GRANDPARENTING WHEN YOU ARE DIVORCED

Complications may arise as a result of our own divorce or blended family, to which we need be sensitive. Split holidays or trips parents make to visit out-of-town grandparents are hard enough without us, the grandparents, laying on the burden of unfinished emotional business about our own divorces. Instead, we can encourage our children to be clear about boundaries with all the grandparents and their partners or step-grandparents. At times when the entire *mishpacha* comes together—for a bar mitzvah or baby naming, for example—have the parents make explicit their expectations for when grandparents come, how long and where everyone stays, and how much those visits overlap. We can try to encourage this clarity and then honor those wishes, leaving at home whatever resentments and jealousy we may still harbor. We can try to remember that the more people in our grandchildren's lives who love them, the better it is for them. That is ultimately more important than our negative feelings about our ex or an ex's partner.

Grandparents Matter

Marc Freedman, a founder of Encore.org and Gen2Gen, observes that "all children need that one adult who is irrationally crazy about them." Who can do that better than a grandparent? As grandparents, we can be mentors, supporters, cheerleaders, teachers, role models, historians, funders, and playful buddies who don't have to worry about daily discipline. We can bring blessing to our grandchildren. In fact, the end of the book of Genesis includes the story of a grandfather, Jacob, blessing his grandsons. And as Psalm 128:6 suggests, the blessing is reciprocal, as a person who lives to see his children's children is indeed blessed.

CHAPTER 9

Rekindling the Flame
by Judith Ansara and Robert Gass

Judith Ansara and Robert Gass are two extraordinary coaches married to each other who conduct an intensive workshop called "Sharing the Path: A Retreat for Couples." We found the experience to be transformative, and we are delighted that they agreed to share some of their wisdom here.

Words of Wisdom

When it comes to sex, the most important six inches are the ones between the ears.

—Dr. Ruth Westheimer

The desire for companionship and intimacy runs deep in our human hearts. We have likely all experienced the blessings as well as the challenges of a committed relationship. Our intimate partnerships are often the source of love, satisfaction, mutual support, sensuality, and simply being in life together—being family. But these relationships can also be challenging and painful. We often enter marriage or partnership with unrealistic expectations. We want our partners to be our best friends, to be great lovers, to share our interests, and to be compatible with our needs and desires on everything from travel to housekeeping.

We have worked with thousands of couples over the last 30 years, and although many of the couples who come to our retreats say they are reasonably happy, we regularly hear things such as:

- "We're comfortable. We're good friends but I want to find the excitement and intimacy we used to experience."
- "We're both so busy and tired. Having time just to be together gets lost in all our responsibilities and the details of life. My partner sometimes feels more like my roommate than my lover."
- "I want to have more fun together."
- "We spend a lot of time together, but somehow we don't really connect. I'm lonely."
- "I don't feel my partner truly listens to me. I repeat the same things over and over again, but I don't feel heard. I sometimes feel, why bother?"
- "Sex—we've lost the spark. We've drifted further from being sexual than either [or one] of us would like."
- "We communicate well, except when we talk about . . . [fill in your favorite/recurring challenging topic]."

The Sacred Third

In committing to a conscious relationship, our shared life becomes
a learning laboratory in which we encounter the most precious
and challenging opportunities to learn about ourselves and
develop our capacity to truly love and be loved. Every relationship
begins with two perspectives: "my" point of view (the "right" one)
and the other's point of view. Most relational challenges arise
when these perspectives diverge or are in conflict. One of the
most important perspectives of a conscious relationship, however,
is that there is a third element present—the relationship itself—
what we refer to as the *Sacred Third.*

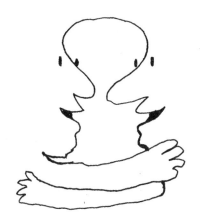

We view the Sacred Third as a living entity of which both partners are guardians, committed
to its flourishing. Relationships suffer from being taken for granted. The relationship itself,
this Sacred Third, needs regular attention, devotion, and creativity; it requires nourishment,
tending, and cultivation in order to mature. In nurturing our Sacred Third, we can:

- Learn practices such as deep listening and self-responsibility
- Address old patterns that choke out trust and love
- Cultivate win-win solutions, rather than power plays
- Learn to ask directly for what we want, rather than withdraw, manipulate, or
  become aggressive
- Share in a commitment to cherish our sacred relationship

Opportunities and Challenges Later in Life

Intimate relationships later in life have their own special opportunities and challenges. On
the plus side, hopefully we are more emotionally mature than in our 20s and 30s. We know
ourselves better. We usually have fewer insecurities, and less self-absorption and emotional
reactivity, that can stand in the way of intimacy. Some of us in second or even third
marriages may have learned important lessons that kept previous relationships from being
truly satisfying. In later life we are often freer from the responsibilities of raising children and
the pressures of work and careers that often exhaust younger couples.

Still, each cycle of life has its own challenges, and aging brings its own unique stresses:

> *The empty nest.* In couples for whom raising a family was a central part of life, the last
> child leaving home signals a profound change. Children in the house take a lot of time

and energy and can interfere with intimate connection between parents. However, the shared commitment to child-rearing can also serve as a kind of glue for couples, providing a sense of shared purpose. When the last child leaves, what's left of the glue? Along with the freedom that comes with the empty nest, couples may be challenged to fill the void or deal with long-ignored relational issues.

Retirement. While many couples welcome retirement, others struggle with the loss of work as a part of their identity and the way to organize way their life and time. We are often not used to being with each other 24/7, and couples may not be sure how to re-create their life and reconcile differing interests and varying levels of energy. One partner may wish to explore the world while the other prefers being close to home. Special challenges may arise if one person retires while the other continues to work.

Aging bodies. If we are fortunate, we live long enough to likely experience increasing physical limitations. But the physical changes associated with aging can put stress on relationships. Our sexuality changes—as hormones diminish, it can affect our libido and responsiveness. Sometimes this occurs more for one partner than the other, bringing its own challenges. Men may experience erectile dysfunction and women vaginal thinning that leads to painful intercourse. These and other conditions often put a damper on physical intimacy. Physical activities that couples used to share and enjoy may become limited or unavailable. A relationship is further complicated when physical limitations occur for one member of the couple, leaving them wondering, "Do I give up the hiking that we used to do together and that I still love when my partner can no longer hike?" And, of course, there's the challenge of the physical, emotional, and sometimes economic stress of being a primary caregiver to one's partner in a more serious situation, such as chronic or debilitating illness, particularly one that will eventually lead to death.

While aging may bring these and other challenges to couples, by choosing to focus on the relationship we make the choice again and again to turn toward these circumstances, rather than complain, withdraw, or fight about them.

> Sexual relations are considered a dimension of Sabbath pleasure.
> —Mishneh Torah, Shabbat 30:14

Practices to Deepen Intimacy

Particular attitudes and practices are good medicine for couples of all ages and sexual orientations. They help us navigate relationship challenges and view them as opportunities for deepening intimacy and partnership.

Deep listening. One of the most common complaints we hear from couples is that one or both partners don't feel heard. The experience of not being heard lowers trust and safety, amplifies other relational issues, and creates a tremendous barrier to intimacy. Simple yet powerful listening practices help create a welcoming and safe space to hear each other's aspirations and concerns and enhance the fabric of a healthy and fulfilling relationship. Deep listening includes a conscious practice of being present, listening reflectively, cultivating curiosity, and learning how to refrain from acting on our own emotional triggers.

Self-responsibility. We spend way too much energy trying to get our partners to change. We are rarely successful. Think about it—what have your blaming and efforts to change your partner yielded? For the most part, your beloved feels criticized and irritated and acts on those feelings by tuning you out or retaliating. You can focus instead on the one person you can really influence—yourself. You can end the blame game by asking, "If I were to take 100 percent responsibility for resolving this issue, what might I do?" You can look at your possible contribution to the creation of challenges, at how you are choosing to respond to your partner, and then try to unpack and reframe the limiting, disempowering stories you have told about yourself, your partner, and the situation.

Authenticity. When we hold back from sharing with our partner what we truly think and feel, it diminishes intimacy in the relationship. This includes not expressing our true wants and desires: saying yes when we don't really mean it, avoiding saying things we fear might upset the other, and not saying no directly. There are lies of commission, lies of omission, and lies we tell ourselves. Sometimes we don't even know what we feel. Many of these patterns have their roots in childhood, where we learned what behaviors earned approval or rejection. Relationships often have dead zones, where both parties collude in denying difficult topics and feelings. By practicing authenticity, you are courageous in choosing, again and again, to bring your heart and voice to your beloved in ways that build connection and nourish the relationship.

Physical intimacy. Over the years we have found that many, if not most couples of all ages experience some challenges regarding sexuality. And it is the rare older couple

Deep Listening Practice: Heart Sharing

Use this deep listening practice to rekindle your relationship on a regular basis. The power of this practice comes from the simple ritual of alternating turns as speaker and listener. This offers you, as the speaker, space to feel and to speak, knowing you won't be interrupted. Then, as the listener, you can focus only on listening, knowing that you too will have your partner's quality attention.

We recommend using a timer, allowing 10–12 minutes for each person to speak without interruption. Some couples also choose to pass an object back and forth—a stone, a piece of jewelry, or anything that is meaningful to the two of you—and only the person holding the object may speak.

The Role of the Listener

The listener's job is to listen. You invite your partner to speak by asking: "[Partner's name], show me your heart."

Other than this, you do not speak. Stay present, open, receptive, curious, attentive. Remember that you really do want to know this person. You want them to experience your interest, compassion, and respect. You want to be present in a way that invites your partner to speak openly from her heart.

If your mind wanders or becomes engaged in reaction to what your partner is saying, breathe. Bring your attention back to your partner and your commitment to your relationship. And listen. Do your very best not to be formulating your mental rebuttal.

You may gently repeat the prompt, "Show me your heart," if there are periods of silence from your partner.

The Role of the Speaker

The speaker's job is to be authentic. Listen to the prompt: "Show me your heart."

Be willing to touch into your felt experience and let yourself be vulnerable with your emotions. You do not need to respond to what your partner has just been talking about.

Share reflections directly related to the relationship—feelings about work, retirement, family, health, your own journey, and so forth. Share any content that would help build connection between the two of you and help you feel seen and known.

Be willing to speak about things that, left unspoken, create distance. Heart sharing is a time to share your love, dreams for the future, celebration of what's going right in your relationship. But don't skip the hard stuff!

When you are not sure what to speak about, share how you feel in that moment.

Important: Heart sharing is about your own experience. Refrain from analyzing something your partner did or didn't do. Emotions often arise during heart sharing, and we do not want to hide these from ourselves or our partner. But if you drift into blame or dumping on your beloved—stop. Come back to your heart. Breathe. Feel and express the vulnerability that lives under the blame or anger.

Heart sharing is best done on a regular basis, to keep things from building up and to ensure ongoing intimate connection. And it's a great practice to use when things occur that are challenging.

who do not have some concerns or questions about sexuality and aging bodies. Some couples begin to avoid sensual contact. We believe that, for the majority of people, physical touch could and should continue to be an important part of intimacy. As we get older, we may need to rediscover new ways of enjoying our sensuality. The two of us are practitioners and teachers of *sacred sexuality*. In this approach to sensual intimacy, we try to release all goal orientation in our encounters, including orgasm. We decide to engage or reengage and learn new skills and practices. Most importantly, we learn to communicate openly and easily with each other about how to better give and receive physical touch and pleasure so that our sensual life, in whatever forms it takes, becomes more consistently pleasurable and a way to connect with each other physically, emotionally, and spiritually.

Commitment and renewal. In long-term relationships, commitment is not a one-time or static thing. Rather than thinking of relationship as a noun—a thing or a possession— consider relationship as a verb, something alive and dynamic. A key to maintaining a healthy relationship while navigating the changes of aging is to revisit and renew why you are together and envision the shared life you want to create. Explore your values, first independently and then together as a couple. For the next cycle of your lives, what will be the new mutually satisfying weaving of family, home, creative expression, service, spirituality, and play?

Some years ago we created new vows and held a recommitment ceremony. We found this so meaningful that we now encourage and support couples to consciously undertake their own process of recommitment and renewal. (For ideas about how to do this, see chapter 2, "Cooking Up New Rituals.")

Your partner gives you the greatest gift of your adult life: the choice to be your companion and to walk with you through all of life's fluctuations. Every day, remember to thank each other and to offer at least one appreciation. This very simple act will infuse your shared life with positive energy and a generosity of spirit for the journey ahead.

CHAPTER 10   Acquiring for Yourself a Friend

by Helen Dennis

The soundtrack of our youth was filled with songs about friendship. The Beatles' "With a Little Help from Our Friends," Carole King's "You've Got a Friend," the Jackson Five's "I'll Be There," Bill Withers's "Lean on Me," and James Taylor's "Fire and Rain." For many of us, each song evokes a face, a memory, a connection. Some of those people are still in our lives. Many are likely not.

Some of us are lucky to have lifelong friendships, but friendships often fall by the wayside because of differing interests, circumstances, and priorities. Many of our friends when our children were young have drifted away. It used to be so easy to see them because we shared common activities—sitting together as our kids played sports, volunteering in our kids' classrooms, coaching their Little League teams. But as the kids grew and became more independent, those occasions became less frequent. Work friends often fall out of our lives when we or they change jobs or leave the workforce, and even occasional visits become less appealing because we have less in common . . . and fewer people in common to talk about.

As we get older, our social networks tend to shrink, and we need to become more intentional about cultivating, deepening, and nurturing those friendships that are still part of our lives, as well as finding and making new friends. Friendships are not one-size-fits-all; there are many varieties. Maimonides, the renowned 12th-century Jewish philosopher and physician, reflects this in his description of three kinds of friendship:

Laura first met Helen Dennis at a retirement seminar for rabbis where Helen facilitated a session about the challenge of preparing for retirement by imagining a fulfilling encore career, in addition to financial planning. That insight led to the NextStage Initiative, which Laura spearheaded at her congregation. Since then, Helen has become a friend and colleague, and we have consulted with her frequently about the many issues addressed in this book.

Words of Wisdom

"Acquire for yourself a friend" (Pirkei Avot 1:6). How so? This teaches that a person should get a companion to eat with, drink with, study with, sleep with, and reveal secrets, the secrets of the Torah and the secrets of worldly things.

—Avot d'Rabbi Natan 8:3

1. Friendships of utility or mutual benefit
2. Friendships of pleasure and trust
3. Friendships of virtue, where each partner feels responsible for helping the other grow in self-understanding (Commentary on Avot 1:10)

Cultivating New Friendships

To find new friends, seek out those who like to do similar things and have similar values and circumstances. As an example, I am a widow and enjoy theater but had no one willing to commute with me to downtown Los Angeles. I sat next to a woman at a foreign film and introduced myself. Turns out she was the widow of my former internist, and I asked if she would be interested in attending theater productions in Los Angeles. She has become my theater buddy.

If you meet someone you like, call him or her and set up a date. Take the initiative. People usually are flattered by the attention. As a sixty-five-year-old woman who participated in Project Renewment, a discussion group for career women in later life, said, "I never thought I would make a new best friend at this age." Well, it can happen, but not by being passive.

How long does it take to make a new friend? Shasta Nelson, author of *Friendships Don't Just Happen*, notes that it usually takes six to eight meaningful interactions before women feel comfortable calling someone a friend. It may take a year or two before a person becomes someone in whom you confide. The same may not be true for men. According to Geoffrey Greif, author of *Buddy System: Understanding Male Friendships*, studies indicate that it is harder for men than for women to make friends, since women often are more comfortable reaching out to others.

One strategy for getting good at getting older is to intentionally cultivate younger friends. Besides the pleasure of intergenerational connections, having younger people in our lives makes getting older a bit easier, especially if they will still be part of our lives as we need more help. One friend revealed that he and his wife informally "interview" prospective younger friends by inviting them over for Shabbat dinner or lunch. If they feel a spark, they continue to cultivate the connection. And the prospective friends never suspect they are being auditioned.

Deepening Friendships

One of my friends tells a story about a colleague he knew from their common social circles. They decided to get to know each other better by studying a Jewish text together. Each week or so they met at one or the other's apartment, read a little of the text, and talked about their lives in relation to the issues raised. Though they no longer live on the same coast, the friendship continues in a deep and profound way. Now they study texts over the phone.

Developing friendships like this requires intention, desire, and action. Consider some of these ideas for deepening existing friendships:

> If you're not into studying Jewish texts, you could choose a book of short stories or a collection of poetry. Meet face-to-face, on the phone, or over Skype, Zoom, or FaceTime. Let the conversations deepen your friendship. (See chapter 3, "Putting the Life in Lifelong Learning.")

- Set aside time for meaningful conversations. Talk about what's important in your lives, changes that you've gone through, your aspirations and dreams for the next chapter of life. Try to go beyond the weather, traffic, and kids.

- Do something physical together and leave the electronics at home. Consider walking, hiking, biking, taking a yoga class, or camping.

- Work on a project you both care about, such as a fund-raiser for an organization you support, a literacy project, or even coauthoring an article for a newsletter.

- Do something nice for the other person. When you see something he might like, buy it for him, even if it's not his birthday.

> In Jewish tradition, when you see a friend you haven't seen for more than a month, you say a blessing: "Holy One of Blessing, whose Presence fills creation, who has given us life, sustained us, and brought us to this moment." When you see a friend you haven't seen for more than a year, you say a different blessing: "Holy One of Blessing, whose Presence fills creation, who revives the dead."

- Be authentic. Be willing to take risks. Sharing feelings of joy, grief, anticipation, or disappointment can bring you closer.

- Play a game together. Whether it's racquetball or a board game, doing the crossword puzzle together or playing poker, just having a good time is good for your attitude and your friendship.

- Go to cultural events together. Have lunch at a hot new restaurant or go to hear one of your favorite bands. Take in a special exhibition or an afternoon movie.

Male and Female Friendships

In the classic film *When Harry Met Sally*, Harry says that men and women cannot be friends because the sex part always gets in the way. Can men and women just be friends? The answer: It depends who you ask and what you read. Conventional wisdom suggests that non-romantic friendships between men and women are possible and common. Lots of men and women work together or live near each other and don't sleep with one another. Yet some believe this platonic coexistence is just a façade that conceals sexual impulses below the surface.

In any case, opposite-sex friendships have unique challenges. Here are some tips that might be useful in negotiating friendships between men and women:

> More and more, psychologists have found that for older persons, loneliness is not necessarily linked to the death of a spouse or to how infrequently they see their children or grandchildren, but to the absence of personal relationships with peers, friends of their own age or any age who share their interests and with whom they sustain their roots of shared experience.
> —Betty Friedan, *The Fountain of Age*

- Understand that your goals may be different. One of you may want companionship or resources, while the other may want sex or a commitment.
- Discuss your intentions. Be honest about what you want out of the relationship, and realize that goals may change. Platonic relationships can evolve into romantic ones.
- End the friendship if there is a mismatch in goals. For example, you are only looking for friendship and he wants marriage. Sometimes these intentions take time to materialize.

Ending Friendships

Ending a friendship is a complicated and often painful process throughout our lifetime, but particularly when we are older. Some long-term relationships are just no longer satisfying, and considering that time is so very precious, we may feel it isn't worthwhile to continue investing in them. Other relationships may be not only unsatisfying but also toxic.

Here are some signs that a friendship may be toxic. If someone:

- Tries to control and be manipulative
- Ignores boundaries and thrives on the violation
- Is dishonest and exaggerates, telling white lies with repeated patterns of dishonesty
- Loves to be the victim and intentionally finds ways to feel oppressed
- Blames other individuals and situations
- Does not take responsibility for his actions
- Takes without giving and will take as long as the person is willing to give

These characteristics may go unnoticed for years. It's easy to adapt to a toxic friendship until one day you step back and assess what's not working.

To resolve such a relationship, consider distancing yourself gradually or what's now called "ghosting." Stop initiating conversations, either by phone or text, and try to avoid running into the person. If you have to miss an event to avoid her, consider doing so. Assuming that you meet this person by chance, keep the conversation light. Decline invitations and say, "No, but thank you for thinking of me."

Friendships and Social Media

Baby boomers are increasingly adapting to internet communications and social media, which provide millions of middle-age and older adults with the opportunity to connect with others despite barriers of distance, physical immobility, or other circumstances that would lead to social isolation. One study shows that 81 percent of older adults who use the internet interact with online friends on a daily basis.

Casual relationships also may occur among those engaged in online games. For example, the AARP website hosts games such as poker, solitaire, sudoku, backgammon, and mah jongg. See also scrabble.com for online game sites.

Technology has modified the meaning of friendship. With the click of a button, we can add a so-called friend. Having hundreds of online friends is not the same as having a close friend you see face-to-face. Online friends cannot give you a hug in tough times, visit you when you are sick, or laugh and smile with you to celebrate happy occasions. Although such expressions can be conveyed online, the digital experience is different and less personal. Still, social media provides isolated people and others of any age with outlets for connection. The value in terms of social capital is undeniable.

Can friendships originate through social media? Yes, casual ones. But some are safe and others are unsafe. You can maximize safety by "meeting" a new person first via videoconferencing. Even so, you still have no idea of the person's intention. Experts in social media suggest using websites where you actually meet the person, such as www.meetup.com or Stitch (www.stitch.net), and the websites vet each individual.

Predators and scam artists prowl chat rooms, so be discriminating and cautious. Face-to-face interaction is the safest. Check out www.wikihow.com/Be-Safe-in-the-Chat-Rooms for safety tips.

Chat rooms, in particular, encourage social engagement through online discussion about a particular subject. Everyone who is logged in sees what everyone else is typing, although two people can decide to break off and have a private chat. Topics might include religion, politics, abortion, or drugs. On the lighter side, chat rooms might address dream vacations, photo sharing, or what's on your desktop.

Why Social Media in My Maturing Years

Many people feel that time spent on the computer is time that could be better spent. For me, I find that keeping in touch with my friends and family gives me continued spirit and strength to live my daily life.

Do I want to share all of my trials and tribulations, triumphs and joys on Facebook for everyone to see? Not really. I use Facebook selectively for things I want the whole world to know . . . particularly my politics. However, I use WhatsApp and group texts for private communications where only the people invited are allowed to participate.

In WhatsApp, I have two groups: Noni's Girls and Our Family Chat. Noni's Girls are my seven closest girlfriends who want to and do know everything going on in my life. When someone is sick, we bring each other meals; when someone is celebrating, we gather for lunch and share a gift; when a relative has a baby or has some highs or lows, we are there for each other on a day-to-day basis. I find this very comforting.

Our Family Chat includes all members of our immediate family, including grandchildren. We all know who has finals, who has boyfriends, who has girlfriends, who is coming for dinner, who is selling Girl Scout cookies and needs buyers. You name it, we share it, with one simple message that goes to all of us.

Group texts are a bit more specific:

- All family adults only. *No kids.*
- All committee members working on the same project.
- Trying to put together a group dinner date and coordinating available times.

Some think that the main reason people use digital communication is to combat loneliness. I thrive on face-to-face interactions, but with everyone's time obligations, not to mention traffic, the internet can be a great way to keep those close to you—CLOSE—and yes, it also keeps you from feeling lonely.

—Toni Corwin, Beverly Hills

Finding or Creating a Community
by Richard Siegel and Rabbi Laura Geller

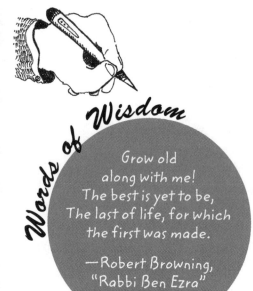

Words of Wisdom

Grow old
along with me!
The best is yet to be,
The last of life, for which
the first was made.

—Robert Browning,
"Rabbi Ben Ezra"

There is a legend in the Talmud about Honi, a miracle worker famous for his ability to bring rain. Honi and an old man are planting a carob tree, which takes about 70 years to bear fruit. Honi asks, "Why do you plant it? You won't be around in 70 years." The man responds, "When I came into the world I found carob trees planted by my ancestors. I plant these for my descendants."

Although this is a well-known story, few people read to the end. Honi falls asleep and stays asleep for 70 years. When he wakes up, no one recognizes him. He feels isolated and invisible. His overwhelming loneliness leads him to pray for death, and he dies. The Talmudic sage Raba comments, "Hence the saying: either companionship or death."

Our legacy is enriched by what we plant for future generations, but our lives depend on the community we create here and now. Current research suggests that almost one out of three older adults in the United States reports feeling lonely, with damaging effects comparable to smoking 15 cigarettes a day. Dr. Carla M. Perissinotto, a geriatrician at the University of California, San Francisco, notes that "the profound effects of loneliness on health and independence are a critical public health problem. It is no longer medically or ethically acceptable to ignore older adults who feel lonely and marginalized."

Choosing companionship over loneliness raises these questions: With whom do we want to grow old, and where? One-fifth of the total U.S. population—about 88 million people—will be 65 or older by 2050. Most of us in this age group say that we want to age in place, and we're asking what kinds of changes we need

WE COOL—

to make in our current homes and neighborhoods to make that possible. Others of us want to move to retirement or continuing-care communities so we can be confident that our future physical and health needs will be covered. Still others want to create a new kind of living arrangement.

Staying in Your Home

For the overwhelming majority of us who want to stay in our homes as we get older, the easiest (although not necessarily the cheapest) solution is to "senior-ize" our house or apartment. Home-improvement (aka "adaptive reuse") service providers can help with everything from installing grab bars in showers to building ramps to accommodate wheelchairs, downsizing and decluttering closets and shelves, and enhancing interior and

For information on avoiding home improvement fraud, check out:

- AARP, "Home Improvement Contractors"
- US News & World Report, "How to Spot a Home-Contractor Scam"
- MSN Real Estate, "10 Ways to Avoid Contractor Scams"
- FEMA, "Avoiding Loan Scams after a Natural Disaster"
- University of Illinois Cooperative Extension Service, "Home Repair Fraud"

exterior lighting. Ride-share services have already made it possible to get around without owning a car. Food and meal delivery services have made grocery shopping more convenient. As physical and medical challenges arise, and if we have the means, we can hire additional services, such as a handyperson to change the battery in a beeping smoke detector or an aide to help while we're recuperating from a hip replacement. The options will continue to improve as new technologies emerge.

NATURALLY OCCURRING RETIREMENT COMMUNITIES (NORC)

After Richard's parents sold the house he and his brothers grew up in, they moved to an apartment building in the neighborhood—upper floors were residential; ground floors, commercial. Over a number of years, it slowly turned into a naturally occurring retirement community, or NORC. All their neighbors grew old together, and even after Richard's mom was widowed, she wasn't lonely—so many friends were right there as neighbors. Because the building was convenient for public transportation, she could easily get to the local museum to volunteer, take yoga classes at the JCC, and attend services at her synagogue. After a while, social service agencies moved into the ground floor of her building, so she had pretty much everything she needed to stay active and engaged until she died.

The term *naturally occurring retirement community* refers to a housing development or apartment house, not originally built for seniors, where 40 percent of the population is over age 60. In the mid-1980s, UJA-Federation of Jewish Philanthropies of New York pioneered a partnership of federal, state, and local governments, housing developers, philanthropic organizations, and local businesses, as well as the residents themselves, to offer social services, such as adult day care, health-care management, home safety advice, and other resources. Because the model enables people to age in place, it turns out to be a much more cost-effective strategy than many alternatives.

Unfortunately, today there is significantly less governmental financial support for such housing situations. Economic and political challenges have forced cutbacks in some federal supports for aging-in-place initiatives. Still, it might be worth checking out. If you live in a building or housing development that you think could qualify as an NORC, check with your local Jewish Family Services or Department of Aging, which continue to support these housing environments in some communities.

THE VILLAGE MOVEMENT

The majority of boomers want to stay in their homes as long as possible, and they often do, until they can no longer climb a ladder to change a light bulb. But what if they had help? How many people would it take to change that bulb? Maybe a village. The village movement began in 2002, in Beacon Hill in Boston, when neighbors got together to figure out how they could age in the homes they loved. There are now more than 200 villages around the country and 150 more in formation.

A village is a membership-driven, self-governing, grassroots "virtual" community. Potential members determine its boundaries by drawing a circle around a geographical area as wide as any of them would drive to bring food to someone who is sick. It is a not a social service agency; nobody moves to a different facility. It is the embodiment of a radical old idea of neighbors helping neighbors through services such as walking the dog when someone is out of town, helping the transition when a neighbor comes home from the hospital, bringing meals when someone is sick, bringing the trash cans up a steep driveway, providing transportation to medical appointments, or assisting with technology.

Many villages are formed through word-of-mouth or social networks, some even by signs posted on trees inviting neighbors to get together and discuss their needs. Although some villages are entirely run by volunteers, most often there is an annual membership fee that funds a professional to manage the requests for services and to work with the volunteer leadership team. As important as these services are, however, many villages are finding that social programs are even more valuable to their members in helping them continue to build social capital.

Village programs create opportunities for us to use our talents and expertise to benefit the entire community, to give back to others, and to continue to be seen and valued as individuals with gifts to share. The activities and the services that individuals offer each other are an important antidote to the loneliness so many people feel as they grow older.

Village to Village Network (www.vtvnetwork.org), a national organization, provides a variety of tools to people who want to organize such living environments. It also offers a directory of existing villages around the country.

When You Need or Want to Move

For a variety of reasons, we may not be able or want to continue living in our homes as we age. We may want to move closer to our kids. We may not want to maintain a house anymore.

We may want fewer stairs. We may want a warmer, more rural, or an urban living environment. We may want to move where the cost of living is lower. That may mean buying or renting a house or apartment in a neighborhood that meets our particular criteria or choosing one of an increasing number of housing options that have built-in community engagement opportunities.

COHOUSING: INTENTIONAL COMMUNITY

For those of us who are nostalgic for communal living arrangements popular in the sixties and seventies, cohousing may be an attractive, age-appropriate option. Cohousing communities are intentional neighborhoods organized collaboratively, where residents have their own private spaces but come together to share meals and facilities, plan activities, and look out for each other. Similar to the Israeli model of a *moshav,* many of the over 160 established cohousing communities in the United States are multigenerational, with anywhere from 5 to 56 households. Can you imagine a group of boomer friends buying and renovating a small apartment complex?

Common facilities may include a dining hall, kitchen, indoor or outdoor recreation space, lounge, community garden, children's playroom, guest rooms, art or exercise studio, workshop, laundry, office space, and vehicles. Buildings are purposefully designed to support and promote community among residents. Individual homes are typically (though not necessarily) owned privately, with all the amenities characteristic of private homes, including full kitchens. Oftentimes, residents share resources, such as tools and other equipment, as well as three or four meals together each week. They also share a commitment to community, a respect for privacy, and the reward of daily connection and being a part of each other's lives.

Particularly for seniors, cohousing has many advantages over standard housing arrangements, especially if it is intentionally intergenerational including:

Community. Cohousing reduces social isolation, fosters a sense of togetherness and belonging, and promotes emotional and physical well-being.

Safety and support. Cohousing encourages residents to keep an eye out for one another. You have immediate neighbors to easily call on when needs arise.

ChaiVillageLA is the first synagogue-based village in the country. Its philosophy is in part: "By coming together as a community, we can grow not just older, but bolder." This cutting-edge partnership of two Reform synagogues challenges their congregants to rethink aging and empower them to use their accumulated experience, skills, wisdom, and creativity to build a community based on values that emerge out of the Jewish experience, including a commitment to volunteer.

"ChaiVillageLA came into my life at just the right time. I had recently retired from my practice as a psychotherapist and a teacher. The people I met and the friends I made were bright, interesting, and full of life. It is rare at this stage of life to have an opportunity to expand my friendship circle with such ease and fun. I am endlessly grateful."

—Sandy Silas

"We are not retired but have supported ChaiVillage from the beginning. The motto 'independent — together' has inspired us to think about our future—both financial and social. We are making the village and its members an integral part of our present and future, knowing that when we do retire the transition will be a smooth flow rather than an abrupt stop and start."

—Caroline Bloxsom and Samuel Kolstad

Sustainability. Cohousing allows residents to pool efforts and share resources, thereby increasing efficiency, reducing waste, and saving money.

Collaboration. Cohousing fosters collaboration among people who share similar interests.

ACTIVE RETIREMENT COMMUNITIES

One of the fastest-growing areas of the housing market is age-restricted communities, usually age 55 and up. While once regarded as "elderly islands," cut off from the surrounding areas, today these communities are increasingly designed for "active adults," including those who are still working, allowing people to live independently while providing access to a variety of amenities, including clubhouses, restaurants, athletic facilities, fitness centers, interest groups, classes, and excursions. As reported in a 2017 *Los Angeles Times* article, "Developers are particularly bullish on multigenerational communities which provide senior-only neighborhoods in an otherwise family-oriented master plan . . . often located in metropolitan areas rather than far-flung resort towns."

CONTINUING-CARE RETIREMENT COMMUNITIES

An article in the *Atlantic,* "Living, and Dying, at Home," describes a pizza delivery worker who grew concerned when she hadn't heard from a regular customer for several days. She drove to the customer's home and discovered that the customer had fallen and couldn't reach the phone for help.

While that story had a happy ending, it points to an important fear that many of us will experience as we grow older: What if I need help and no one is there?

That fear may prompt us to move to a senior facility of some sort, often a continuing-care retirement community (CCRC), where we can start out in an independent setting and move to assisted living or skilled nursing as our situation requires. A CCRC is generally an expensive option. Some CCRCs require monthly payments, as well as a down payment, a significant portion of which may be refunded to our heirs after our death, as well as regular monthly payments.

We need to explore a number of issues with our families as we consider choosing a CCRC. In her book *Facing the Finish,* life transitions expert Sheri Samotin lays out some strategies:

- *Scout ahead of time:* Options for senior living are many. . . . It can be overwhelming to figure out what you need and what you want. So start the process sooner rather than later, even if you can't imagine that you'll ever choose to move.
- *Understand the math:* Money *does* matter. Your resources as an older adult will determine the range of available options. Crunch the numbers ahead of time to figure out how much you can spend each month and what is included. Most communities provide a worksheet that will help you make this calculation.
- *Visit each locale* and take photos to help you remember each individual place. Discuss the pros and cons of each place while the memory of the visit is still fresh. Try the "Six S" method:

> **Size:** Will you be more comfortable in a larger community with many residents or a smaller, more intimate setting? Can you still get around reasonably well or will a large campus become frustrating? Will you take advantage of the facilities that might be available in a larger community or will these amenities likely go unused? Will the size of the living unit work for your needs?

> **Sights:** The classic line you hear from people exploring senior living options is this: "Everyone here is old!" Sometimes that's true. Some communities cater to an older crowd with more physical limitations, and you'll see lots of walkers and wheelchairs. Other communities attract younger, more physically active residents. . . . Some have a homey feel, while others look like an upscale hotel or even a cruise ship. Still others give a more clinical or medical impression. Ask yourself whether you can see yourself in a particular community. Take the time to notice the details, especially in the public spaces.

> **Sounds:** When you first enter the community, do you hear a hush or a loud television set? Or perhaps you hear ringing phones and beepers, much as you would in a hospital. Do you get the impression that the residents are socializing, gathering, and participating in activities? Is music playing?

> **Smells:** Try to visit about half an hour before mealtime, and notice the smell. Is it appealing? When you are in the living areas, do they look and smell clean? Does there seem to be a strong air freshener odor everywhere that might be masking less than optimal cleaning? Your sense of smell is a fabulous clue to what's really going on.

Services: You'll want to check out the services available to help with activities of daily living, transportation, physical therapy, etc. Take a close look at the social calendar, since interaction with others is one of the huge benefits of community living. Ask to review meal plans and menus and ask to have a meal in the dining room. That will not only give you a hint of the quality of the food served, but will allow you to see some of the residents.

Similarities: You are looking for a place where the residents are as similar to you as possible in terms of age, activity level, mental acuity, hobbies and interests, and socioeconomic factors. Ask about the demographics of the place you visit.

Before you decide that a particular community is on your short list, be sure to ask for and check a few references. Ask for permission to talk with the family members of two or three residents, in addition to the residents themselves. When you have these conversations, don't be shy about asking tough questions. Ask to meet some of the staff as well—not just the marketing staff, but the servers, aides, nurses, even the director of the place. Make a list of things you want to know and literally interview them.

Other Housing Options

We baby boomers are creating myriad new living and housing arrangements. For instance, some of us are opting for purpose-built communities—niche or affinity communities where we share a common interest or identity, such as sexual orientation, ethnicity, profession, or religion. These include organic farming communities, artists' colonies, and even an astrology village in Florida.

Escapees CARE (Continuing Assistance for Retired Escapees) Center in Livingston, Texas, serves a unique niche: recreational vehicle (RV) enthusiasts who can no longer hit the road but whose only home is the one on wheels. As residents of this community, they can remain in their RV, with affordable services on site. The bumper sticker of choice: WE'RE SPENDING OUR CHILDREN'S INHERITANCE.

Bridge Meadows in Portland, Oregon, is a particularly creative approach to multigenerational and affordable housing. This intentional living community provides affordable housing for foster care youth and their foster parents, as well as older adults in a common development with some shared meals and activities. The seniors volunteer their time with the children, providing emotional support to the foster parents and serving as surrogate grandparents to the children.

As another example, one Dutch nursing home offers rent-free housing to university students if they spend 30 hours a month acting as "good neighbors."

Some singles, on the other hand, opt for house sharing. Think *The Golden Girls* or *Grace and Frankie*. According to the National Shared Housing Resource Center, "Home sharing is a simple idea: A homeowner offers accommodation to a homesharer in exchange for an agreed level of support in the form of financial exchange, assistance with household tasks, or both. Shared living makes efficient use of existing housing stock, helps preserve the fabric of the neighborhood, and, in certain cases, helps to lessen the need for costly chore/care services and long-term institutional care."

With so many options available, the choice is really up to us. As Melissa Stanton advises in an article on creative housing options in *AARP Livable Communities*:

> The best community for you is one where you feel you can make a real contribution, have a sense of shared control over decisions that affect you, and have a choice of compatible companions. It is where you can enjoy as much or as little social interaction as you determine, where you can have your own front door, and a sense of being in your own home. It is ideally an environment that is physically designed for you to grow older in so that you don't have to move out later. There are such communities. Where they don't exist, they can be developed. Go for it!

Tools and Resources

General All-Around Great Information Resource

Next Avenue (http://www.nextavenue.org/about-us). Public media's national journalism service for America's baby boomers and beyond offers news, ideas, and perspectives on all sorts of issues. Well worth a visit.

Chapter 6: Honoring Your Father and Mother

Check out AARP caregiving resources as well as your local Jewish Family Service for lower-cost strategies. Another helpful resource is www.discover.com/online-banking/banking-topics/7-resources-caring-for-elderly-parents/.

Samotin, Sheri. *Facing the Finish: A Road Map for Aging Parents and Adult Children*. Minneapolis: Publish Green, 2013. Samotin, a life transitions coach, offers wisdom, stories, and tools to enable dialogue between adult children and older parents about the issues and decisions that emerge as parents grow older.

Sobel, Eliezer. *L'Chaim! Pictures to Evoke Memories of Jewish Life*. Rainbow Ridge Books, 2016. This book is specifically written for the person with dementia to read and enjoy. Sobel is a blogger for PsychologyToday.com and the former publisher and editor of *Wild Heart Journal*.

There are many online resources that can help in the challenge of caring for increasingly frail parents. Among them is www.AgingCare.com, which gives families navigational tools. Its caregiver's resource library offers downloadable guides.

Chapter 7: Caring for (and Feeding) Adult Children

Grown & Flown (www.grownandflown.com/). A great site by and for parents of children in high school through the early stages of adulthood.

Isay, Jane. *Walking on Eggshells: Navigating the Delicate Relationship between Adult Children and Parents*. New York: Broadway Books/Flying Dolphin Press, 2007. Through stories uncovered by extensive interviews, Isay offers insights about many of the complicated issues that arise between adult children and their parents.

Nemzoff, Ruth. *Don't Bite Your Tongue: How to Foster Rewarding Relationships with Your Adult Children*. New York: St. Martin's Press, 2008. Offers specific tools for navigating the challenges and blessings of being a parent of adult children.

Chapter 8: Teaching Your (Children's) Children Well

Grandparents for Social Action (www.grandparentsforsocialaction.org). Founded by Jewish educator Sharon Morton, with this mission: "Educating and engaging seniors to do social action; empowering the youth to be lifelong philanthropists and social activists; and creating a legacy from one generation to another."

The Jewish Grandparents Network (www.jewishgrandparentsnetwork.org) sees grandparents as essential family members who can make unique contributions to future generations. Its mission is to support different kinds of families, including multifaith, LGBTQ, single-parent, and grandparents, and to help mitigate the challenges of geographical distance.

Stahl, Lesley. *Becoming Grandma: The Joys and Science of the New Grandparenting*. New York: Blue Rider Press, 2016. The well-known broadcast journalist shares the transformational effect becoming a grandmother has had on her through a combination of personal stories, interviews with friends and colleagues, and research.

Witkovsky, Jerry. *The Grandest Love: Inspiring the Grandparent-Grandchild Connection*. New York: Xlibris, 2013. Social work professional and nonprofit leader turned grandparenting activist, Witkovsky shares stories of diverse and multigenerational families and puts forth a number of creative and practical strategies to foster a family "teaching and learning culture." Visit www.thegrandestlove.com.

Chapter 9: Rekindling the Flame

Couples workshops, such as those offered by Judith Ansara and Robert Gass (www.sacredunion.com) in venues around North and Central America, can be amazing experiences.

Grushcow, Lisa, ed. *The Sacred Encounter: Jewish Perspectives on Sexuality*. New York: CCAR Press, 2014. An extensive anthology, including interpretations of traditional Jewish texts, theological reflections, cultural explorations, and personal reflections about many different issues related to sexuality from a progressive perspective.

Among the books worth taking a look at are Harville Hendrix and Helen LaKelly Hunt's *Getting the Love You Want: A Guide for Couples* (New York: St. Martin's Press, 2007). Also check out the DVDs available on the website of these two therapists-speakers-authors (www.harvilleandhelen.com).

Chapter 10: Acquiring for Yourself a Friend

Pogrebin, Letty Cottin. *Among Friends: Who We Like, Why We Like Them, and What We Do with Them*. New York: McGraw-Hill, 1987. A now-classic book about friendship.

Chapter 11: Finding and Creating a Community

There are many resources on cohousing, house sharing, and retirement communities on aarp.org/livable, and *Housing Options for Older Adults: A Guide for Making Housing Decisions*, produced by the National Association of Area Agencies on Aging (www.n4a.org).

ChaiVillageLA (www.chaivillagela.org) is the first synagogue-based village in the United States.

National Shared Housing Resource Center (www.nationalsharedhousing.org) is a clearinghouse of information about all things related to home sharing, in which a homeowner offers living space to a home sharer in exchange for an agreed level of support, monetary or otherwise.

Project Renewment® (www.renewment.org) is a mini-movement for career women who are exploring their next chapter in life after their primary career. Groups of 8–10 women typically meet monthly in someone's home.

ROMEOs: Retired Old Men Eating Out (www.romeoclub.com). These are clubs of men having a good time who are retired or semi-retired. No membership required.

Silvernest (www.silvernest.com) is an online service designed for boomers and empty nesters who want to home-share. Silvernest's service pairs homeowners who have extra space in their homes with long-term housemates.

Stitch (www.stitch.net/) is a community that helps anyone over 50 find companionship. Stitch focuses on those who want friendship, companionship, romance, or anything in between.

The Village to Village Network (http://www.vtvnetwork.org) is a national grassroots nonprofit membership organization that offers resources to help villages get established and flourish. Over 200 villages have been established in the United States.

Urban Moshav's initial projects are in Berkeley and in Boston. Visit www.urbanmoshav.org for more information.

PART
3
Getting Good at Getting Better

Three older guys are out walking.

First one says, "Windy, isn't it?"

Second one says, "No, it's Thursday!"

Third one says, "So am I. Let's go grab a beer."

The search for the Fountain of Youth never ends. Magazine ads tout "anti-aging" creams. Doctors promote minor—in some cases, major—surgery to achieve a younger appearance. Some smart—and super-rich—folks in Silicon Valley are even trying to find a way to eliminate death. The truth, however, is that while we may not like the changes, our bodies inevitably wear out as we age, and we don't yet have replacement parts. We aren't as strong, flexible, or trim as we once were. Our physical tolerance for late-night parties is seriously diminished. Our hair is receding and/or turning gray. Our hearing gets more selective.

OLD GUYS OUT WALKING.

Aging is out of your control. How you handle it, though, is in your hands.

—Diane Von Furstenberg

Don't take it personally. Although we probably could have done or still can do things to make the changes less severe, entropy is simply part of the plan, a law of nature. Food spoils. Bodies get slower. Life is irreversible.

We can ignore or deny the changes, but they will happen anyway. We can be angry, depressed, or defiant, but our joints will still ache. We can choose to just give up, curl up into a fetal position, and do nothing as we slip into decrepitude, or we can choose to "get better," to become as strong, flexible, and fit as we can—not as we once were but plenty impressive nonetheless. "Getting good at getting better" means we stop pretending that 70 is the new 50. Instead, we embrace 70 as the new 70 and challenge ourselves to adapt creatively.

We all know the basic recipe: Exercise more, consume fewer calories, eat better foods. There's no magic here or, if there is magic, it's the body's constantly surprising ability to renew, restore, and repair itself to the extent that it does. The chapters in part 3 explore contemporary wisdom and best practices for taking care of our physical, psychological, and emotional well-being, all of which include shifting our perspective to one of acceptance.

Of course, "getting better" takes on even greater significance when we are sick. A lot of us will develop a serious illness, whether acute or chronic, at some point in our lives. We offer tips for navigating the territory of illness when we ourselves are sick, as well as advice for what to say or how to act around someone who is ill. We also explore responses to dealing with the loss of people we love.

Four residents of a retirement home are discussing their respective ailments. "My cataracts are so bad that I'm close to blind," says one man. "I'm having a terrible time with my hearing," a woman chimes in. "My blood pressure pills make me dizzy," says another. "Well," says the fourth, "I guess that's the price we pay for getting old. But let's count our blessings. At least we can all still drive."

The trick to getting good at getting better is to find new ways to count our blessings.

CHAPTER 12

Staying Fit Is a Mitzvah

by William Novak

Richard met William (Bill) Novak in 1970 when they became part of the third-year class of Havurat Shalom. Along with having been a ghostwriter for celebrity autobiographies, Bill coedited *The Big Book of Jewish Humor* and marked his approaching geezerhood with the compendium *Die Laughing: Killer Jokes for Newly Old Folks.*

Words of Wisdom

THE 2,000-YEAR-OLD MAN'S SECRETS OF LONGEVITY: 1. Don't run for a bus—there'll always be another. 2. Never, ever touch fried food. 3. Stay out of a Ferrari or any other small Italian car. 4. Eat fruit—a nectarine—even a rotten plum is good.

—Mel Brooks

A few months before I turned 60, a member of my congregation called to ask if I would give the teaching just before the concluding service on Yom Kippur, which was still months away.

"Me?" I asked in astonishment. Although I think of myself as a pretty good speaker, the prospect of addressing the community during the holiest, most dramatic hours of the religious calendar lay well beyond my comfort zone. Moreover, it didn't seem fair to the congregation.

"No, no, you don't want *me*," I said. "At a time like that you want somebody more learned, more religiously sensitive, more *spiritual*. You should ask someone who can talk about the theology and meaning of that special hour, who can discuss the meaning and symbolism of the closing of the gates and things like that. At the very least you want someone who can be inspiring."

She wasn't dissuaded. "I think you could do it," she said. "Please consider it."

"I'm totally the wrong person," I said again. And then, because I was reading a powerful and inspiring book, rather ambitiously titled *Younger Next Year: Live Strong, Fit, and Sexy—Until You're 80 and Beyond*, I blurted out, "I'm just sitting here thinking about life and death."

For some reason she took that as a yes.

Younger Next Year, a collaboration between a lawyer and his doctor, described by the *Hartford Courant* as "a near cult item among some baby boomers," tells us that what most of us believe about growing older and the inevitable decline of our bodies is wrong. Or, as the authors put it, "decay is optional."

Of course, it's not quite that simple. Decay is optional only up to a point, they write, and only if you follow their one simple rule, which the authors lay out with no equivocation or ambiguity: "Exercise six days a week for the rest of your life," they write. "Sorry, but that's it. No negotiations. No give. No excuses. Six days, serious exercise, until you die."

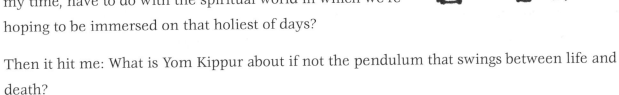

How could I talk about *that* on Yom Kippur? What did the secular, mundane, physical world, where I spend almost all my time, have to do with the spiritual world in which we're hoping to be immersed on that holiest of days?

Then it hit me: What is Yom Kippur about if not the pendulum that swings between life and death?

Throughout Yom Kippur services, Jews pray to be inscribed in the Book of Life. Sometimes we say these words as if the whole matter had little to do with us, or at least little to do with our behavior beyond the moral realm. But as moderns who have reached a certain age, we might want to expand the traditional message of Yom Kippur with a little more—let's call it *agency*. We might acknowledge that, although matters of life and death aren't *totally* in our hands, we can do a great deal to increase the odds of living another year. As Torah tells us, we can "choose life!" If there's a more important two-word phrase in Judaism, I can't imagine what it is.

Yet on Yom Kippur we rarely ask ourselves what *we* can do to choose life, how *we* can make death a little less likely to occur in the coming year. We may ask that question in ethical, moral, or spiritual terms, but we rarely ask it in physical terms. Until I read *Younger Next Year*, neither did I.

We've been around long enough to know that life offers no guarantees. Incidents and accidents may catch us by surprise; life may give us trials, troubles, tumors, or other unfortunate events over which we have little or no control. So, yes, a lot is beyond our power. But what about all the things that we *can* control?

A joke comes to mind: A poor Jew prays every Shabbat that he'll win the lottery. Finally, after years of continuing poverty, he cries out in frustration: "*Ribono shel olam* [Master of the universe], for 30 years I've been asking you for help with the lottery, and all you do is ignore me!"

Whereupon a voice calls out from the heavens, "*Nu*, meet Me halfway. Buy a ticket!"

For those of us who are praying—or hoping—that we'll win the lottery of life again this year, doesn't it take chutzpah to make that request without even buying a ticket?

Again, no guarantees, but we can still do everything possible to try to stay healthy.

What does it mean to buy a ticket for the lottery of life? To me, it boils down to taking three fundamental steps: eating smart, being more active, and pursuing happiness.

Step One: Eat Smart

Hundreds of thousands of pages have been written on the art of eating wisely. We can do worse than to follow the oft-quoted, seven-word wisdom of author Michael Pollan, who famously advised, "Eat food. Not too much. Mostly plants."

That's easy to say, of course, but hard to do, even if we agree with Pollan—and not everyone does. Change is difficult, and so far I've had the most success with the first two words of Pollan's prescription. I'm still making progress on the rest of that wisdom.

As Jews, we have a great deal of experience with careful eating—and I mean *careful*, which isn't always the same as *healthful*—and plenty of practice with various restrictions on our intake of food. Whether or not we are religiously observant, we as a people have centuries of cultural history to build on.

To state the obvious, we all know that being overweight often causes serious health problems. We also know, although we often forget, that restrictive diets don't work, but consuming fewer calories often does.

Step Two: Be More Active

Inactivity is a fairly new problem in human society. For thousands of years we had no need for extracurricular exercise, and nobody had to be told to get moving. The lives of our ancestors included plenty of movement and exertion; at one time human survival depended on it. Our bodies had to be capable of running toward certain animals—the ones we hoped to eat—and away from those that hoped to eat us. Each of us is alive today because our ancestors managed to survive at least until adolescence, and each generation passed on at least some strength and resilience to the next one.

The good news is that inactivity is so new in human history that we can overcome it remarkably quickly. In the 1950s it didn't take long for the Israelis to reverse generations of European shtetl life and turn themselves into a new and much stronger nation. Some of those newer, stronger Jews had even survived the Holocaust. In other words, it's never too late to be more active. If we set our minds to it, we can see dramatic changes within a few months or even weeks.

*Eat food.
Not too much.
Mostly plants.
— Michael Pollan*

In 2017, Politico published details of Supreme Court Justice Ruth Bader Ginsburg's twice-weekly 90-minute workout, which was devised by her personal trainer, Bryant Johnson, a former Army Reserves sergeant. Ginsburg was nearing 84 at the time. "I'm no athlete, but I'm young and reasonably fit. I thought the workout would be pattycake, but it was much harder than I expected," Politico staffer Ben Schreckinger wrote.

Early in Genesis God tells Adam, "By the sweat of your brow you shall eat bread," making clear the connection between sweat and sustenance. It's as if God handed the first human a sign to carry: Will Work for Food. Ever since the Industrial Revolution, however, we in the West have found ways to circumvent that age-old connection, since much sweat-inducing labor has disappeared (or soon will) from the earth and sedentary activities, such as media consumption, fill our days.

But our bodies still respond to the traditional connection between exertion and eating, between expending calories and consuming them. To stay fit, our bodies *need* to sweat, and our hearts *need* an opportunity to work harder. So we've come up with a pretty good substitute for physical labor: exercise.

Maybe what God told Adam about the connection between sweating and eating wasn't a curse or a punishment but rather a mitzvah, a commandment.

The Ruth Bader Ginsburg Workout

(All exercises include three sets of 10—13 repetitions)

- 5 minutes on the elliptical

- Stretches

- Machine bench press
  (Ginsburg, who is 5-foot-1 and thin, presses 70 pounds)

- Leg curl machine

- Leg press machine

- Chest fly machine

- Lat pull-down machine

- Seated rows

- Standing rows

- One-legged squats

- Sideways planks
  (30 seconds on each side)

- Push-ups
  (Ginsburg started doing them against the wall but progressed to doing them on her knees and then with straight legs)

- Hip abduction exercises

- Squats against exercise ball and wall

- Dumbbell curls against exercise ball and wall

- Platform step-ups

- Squats on an upside-down balance trainer

- Medicine ball tosses while standing up off a bench and sitting back down

I know, I know. All of this is so much easier to talk or write about than to put into action. I was urging a friend to join a gym when he stopped me and said, "Look, I'm not the kind of person who joins a gym."

"Then change!" I wanted to say. "Become that person!" We are the kind of people who read newspapers, magazines, and books, or their digital equivalent. We are the kind of people who watch TV and, in some cases, who read magazines or computer screens *while* watching TV. Most of the people I know have spent their working years analyzing, teaching, diagnosing, communicating, going to meetings, and tending to the needs of others. These are valuable activities, but they're mostly sedentary. The least we can do is perform more of them standing up, and more and more people are doing that.

> Belonging to a gym or health club has advantages, such as access to equipment, trainers, and classes, but there are a lot of ways to fit more exercise into your everyday life that don't involve gym fees. Take the stairs whenever you can, park in an outer parking space and walk to the store, join or form a walking group. (Walking is one of the most effective, safest, and accessible forms of exercise for people over age 60.) Take a yoga or dance class. Walk the greens instead of riding in the golf cart. Clear a space at home and download some senior-specific motivational exercise programs so you can go at your own pace.

Not the kind of person who exercises? If my friend had said that he had a serious health problem, it wouldn't occur to him to protest that he's not the kind of person who goes to the hospital or visits a physical therapist. We do what we must, and what is inactivity if not a health problem?

Most of us need at least a little motivational help to keep us on a healthy track. For some, it's exercising with a trainer, partner, or group. For others, it's setting goals, such as getting the buzz of achievement after hitting 10,000 steps a day on an exercise tracker. A rule that works for me: No breakfast until I have exercised (except on Shabbat). And there's no way I'm going to miss breakfast!

I take motivation wherever I can find it. Lately I've been finding it in the classic compendium of Jewish wisdom Pirkei Avot, in which Rabbi Eliezer says, "Repent the day before your death." Many commentators have stated the obvious: Because we don't know the day of our death, we should therefore repent today. In other words, although it's never too late, don't delay any longer. Shouldn't we say the same about exercise?

Elsewhere in Pirkei Avot we are advised to "establish your daily study at a fixed time." Why? So we'll be sure to do it. Exercise is similar: It's a lot easier if it becomes routine and habitual, if we do it at the same time every day. I get it done early, before I'm fully awake; otherwise I might come up with reasons not to exercise—there are always reasons not to do something.

Also in Pirkei Avot, Hillel famously says, "Don't tell yourself that you'll study when you have the time, because you may never have the time." In my translation, when Hillel says *study*, he also means exercise.

And finally, when Pirkei Avot advises us to "find yourself a teacher and acquire for yourself a friend," I read it as "Get yourself a trainer, at least until you know what you're doing, and keep working with that trainer if he or she supplies the motivation you require. Otherwise exercise with a friend," which gives you another reason to show up.

Weekly Walking Group
from ChaiVillageLA

Weed: From the '60s to Our 60s

In the '60s some of us smoked it to get high. Now, in our 60s, many of us are smoking, eating, massaging, or spraying it under our tongue to feel better. We are talking with our medical doctors about THC and CBD, and we are visiting other medical practitioners who have developed expertise in medical marijuana as potentially palliative and even curative remedies for many different kinds of ailments. The research is not conclusive. But there is no question that a revolution is unfolding. While the federal government continues to outlaw marijuana, it is legally available both for medicinal and recreational purposes in a growing number of states and Canada as well. Many resources online can connect you with providers, advisors, and experts who can help you determine if marijuana could be a part of your toolkit for getting good at getting better. Ask your own friends if they use it. You might be surprised to discover how many already do. Check out nextavenue.org for useful articles about cannabis and boomers.

AGING HIPPIE.

YO DUDE.

DOOBIE DEANGELO.
CELEBRATING 45 YEARS OF UNEMPLOYMENT.

IRV....DID WE LEAVE OURSELVES GO?

YES WE DID BERNICE; YES WE DID.

Step Three: Pursue Happiness

The third and final component of buying a ticket to the lottery of a longer life—of being wholly fit—is the passionate pursuit of happiness. Happiness isn't always easy to define, but many of us have a pretty good idea of what its absence feels like.

For some of us, being happy doesn't come easily or naturally, any more than eating healthy or staying physically fit does. We live in a world of tragedy and violence, and we could argue that being depressed is an appropriate response to that reality. Maybe so, but it's not a healthy or a useful response. If happiness doesn't come to us naturally, we have to work at it.

If we need help, we live in a country that offers it in many flavors. Exercising is one of them; in fact, there's plenty of research that shows the link between physical fitness and mental health. But exercise by itself may not be enough. Another thing that helps our emotional health is belonging, feeling connected to others, being part of a congregation or a community.

As you may have guessed, I ended up giving that talk on Yom Kippur. Ten years later I still hear an occasional comment from somebody who heard that talk and responded to it.

That, of course, was what I was hoping for. But I received another benefit that hadn't occurred to me at the time. By going public with my commitment to exercise, I was making it even more likely that I would uphold my end of the bargain.

Of course, there's no need to wait until next Yom Kippur to improve our health, happiness, and fitness. We can start tomorrow, maybe even before breakfast.

CHAPTER 13

Taking Care of Your (Emotional) Self

by Ben Pomerantz

Most of us already know what being physically, mentally, and emotionally fit entails: being proactive about getting plenty of exercise, keeping our weight at a moderate level, eating lots of fruits and veggies, getting enough sleep, managing stress, having friends and a social community. In short, relating to ourselves in a healthy way. The problem is actually implementing these behaviors.

Each of us, with more or less success, is obliged each day to care for ourselves. Thankfully, our bodies do most of this for us automatically. We don't need to think about how to breathe, how to make our heart beat, how to digest our food, and so forth. Other types of health maintenance, however, demand our conscious involvement—an active, persistent, and wise partnership with our body and mind.

We might hope that simply deciding to give top priority to our physical and mental needs would be sufficient. JUST DO IT, as the Nike ads remind us. Sadly, for most of us, this doesn't work. Oftentimes, our partnership with our bodies devolves into an ongoing internal struggle, and our fitness and peace of mind suffer. Generally, we don't engage in the full range of healthful activities for intrinsic, pleasurable, self-reinforcing reasons. We may wonder whether it is even possible to pursue healthy behaviors cheerfully, gratefully.

To change this scenario, we might benefit from adopting the "tend and befriend" motivational system, a relatively new perspective on self-care that is strongly supported by recent psychological research. This approach opens up a range of new behavioral ideas and choices and gives an emotional and

Ben Pomerantz is a clinical social worker and educator living in Los Angeles. He and Richard share a love of gardens and were part of the ChaiVillageLA backyard gardening group. As a child of Holocaust survivors, he has explored many therapeutic approaches, such as self-compassion, both personally and professionally.

Words of Wisdom

My own good heart, out of compassion, takes care of me. It all happens when I am able to say to myself (I honestly do use these very words), "Sweetheart, you are in pain. Relax. Take a breath. Let's pay attention to what is happening. Then we'll figure out what to do."

—Sylvia Boorstein, PhD

practical boost to our fitness goals. Best of all, it actually extends ways of being that we already know well.

"Tend and befriend" refers to the deep part of our nature that wishes to care for ourselves and others. As a motivational system, it quite simply guides us to treat ourselves in caring, compassionate, and kind ways, as we often do with others. The great sage Hillel mentions it in the first line of his famous saying: "If I am not for myself, who will be for me? If I am only for myself, what am I? And if not now, when?"

We start by "being for ourselves"—actively, regularly, wholeheartedly, skillfully, and kindly caring for our body, mind, and social and spiritual well-being. We include ourselves in our compassionate circle of caring, of appreciating ourselves in the full sense of the word *appreciate*: We become aware of who we are, recognize our full worth, feel gratitude for ourselves, and by so doing increase our intrinsic value.

This may sound daunting, but we can learn to foster and cultivate these behaviors. A substantial amount of recent literature in the social sciences about self-compassion skill training, including the work of Kristin Neff and Brené Brown, describes positive outcomes, improved emotional health, lower levels of anxiety and depression, less shame and self-criticism, fewer physical ailments, better immune-system functioning, better heart rate variability (which measures how quickly we recover from stress), lower rates of post-traumatic stress disorder in combat vets, and improved health behaviors in older adults.

When I was young, I admired clever people. Now that I'm old, I admire kind people.
—Rabbi Abraham Joshua Heschel, in conversation with Carl Stern of NBC News

According to Neff, "Self-compassion involves treating oneself with care and concern when confronted with personal inadequacies, mistakes, failures, and painful life situations." It has three elements:

1. *Self-kindness*, meaning that we are gentle and understanding with ourselves, rather than harshly critical and judgmental.

2. Recognition of our *common humanity*, feeling connected with others in the experience of life, rather than feeling isolated and alienated by our suffering.

3. *Mindfulness*, holding our experience in balanced awareness, rather than ignoring our pain or exaggerating it.

Self-Kindness

Moving from self-criticism to self-kindness is evolutionary. Biologically, self-criticism is associated with our fight-or-flight response, which is an activation of our sympathetic nervous system. Our bodies go on rapid alert in anticipation of danger. We get uptight; we get ready for action. This very primitive biological response is useful when our concern is survival. But we don't need to get so aroused every time we notice our stomach bulging over our belts or realize how long it's been since we last exercised. And that certainly won't improve our fitness behavior.

Brené Brown, a research professor of social work at the University of Houston, studies courage, vulnerability, shame, and empathy. Her TED Talk on vulnerability has been seen by more than 30 million people. Kristin Neff, an associate professor in the University of Texas at Austin's Department of Educational Psychology, has been credited with conducting the first academic studies into self-compassion.

As mammals, we've evolved beyond simple survival reactions and acquired more nuanced behaviors that encourage emotional attachments between parents and children, among friends, and so on. These caring attachments naturally engender warm, tender feelings in both caregiver and receiver. Neff notes that when we treat ourselves in these same caring ways, we "feel safe as we respond to painful experiences. . . . Once we let go of insecurity, we can pursue our dreams with the confidence needed to actually achieve them." When we grow beyond insecurities and self-blame, we can relate to ourselves not as problems to be solved but as individuals deserving of care and encouragement. Not surprisingly, as we learn from research, this works much better than self-criticism and other fear-based motivators.

Recognizing Our Common Humanity

The second element of self-compassion is recognizing our common humanity. When faced with life's hardships, we have a choice: Take them personally or adopt a broader perspective and see them as part of the universal experience.

It's been said that our mind is a scary place to visit, and it's best to avoid visiting alone. One reason may be that habitual self-criticism leads to feeling isolated and alienated from others.

Stretching Our Self-Kindness Muscles

This exercise can help us connect with our potential for self-kindness. Pause for a bit between each step and notice what's happening—sensations, emotions, thoughts—before proceeding. Look for feelings of openness or spaciousness as signs of increasing self-kindness and well-being.

1. Sit or lie down.

2. Take three deep breaths.

3. Put the palm of your hand over your heart or, if you prefer, gently touch your forehead or cheek.

4. Put a smile on your face.

5. Remember a time when you were distressed and then comforted; savor the feelings.

6. Imagine calming and comforting someone you care about (a friend, relative, pet) who is distressed.

7. Imagine calming and comforting yourself: Acknowledge the reality of being distressed, comfort yourself with tender touch, say soothing words, make soothing sounds, be patient with the process.

For best results, start by carving out a few minutes of distraction-free time in a private, quiet space. As you get more comfortable with the exercise, you can do it almost any time or place with no one knowing. It's not necessary to complete all the steps each time.

This often results in obsessive, unfavorable comparisons of ourselves to others who seem happier, richer, more attractive, fitter; others who almost never disappoint themselves or act badly; others who invariably seem to have fewer, mostly trivial problems compared to our own. This tightly contracted state of mind is all too familiar; it is the scary place we'd like to avoid.

Neff offers "common humanity" as an alternative, expansive, realistic perspective that is available to us when we're feeling bad about ourselves, when we're disappointed in our progress and prospects, when we're confronted with genuinely hard times. It is a place in our minds where we are not alone by any stretch of the imagination. From the perspective of common humanity, Neff points out, we're able to see that everyone is subject to periods of self-doubt, self-reproach, hardships of all kinds, loss, failure to reach goals, and, eventually, the death of loved ones and oneself. Neff explains:

> Hiding our true selves from others . . . makes us feel even more alone. That's why it's so important to transform our relationship with ourselves by recognizing our inherent interconnectedness. If we can compassionately remind ourselves in moments of falling down that failure is part of the shared human experience, then that moment becomes one of togetherness rather than isolation.

Of course, we are unique, just like everyone else. Our disappointments, frustrations, and failures feel unique to us, very personal. This is true for everyone else, too. Remembering the universality of our common humanity helps dispel the torments of self-isolation and provides symbolic and practical comforts and opportunities for transcendence.

Mindfulness

The third element of self-compassion is mindfulness, which is the simple awareness and nonjudgmental acceptance of what's happening in the present moment, in and around us. Neuroscientists are finding that mindfulness facilitates critical-thinking performance. Slow, mindful awareness permits us to respond consciously to thoughts, emotions, and situations, rather than reflexively or habitually reacting to them. No longer tied to old, conditioned habits, we are now able to more wisely assess our self-critical and self-isolating behaviors. The balanced awareness of mindfulness increases our emotional, cognitive, and behavioral choices. (For more on mindfulness as a spiritual practice, see chapter 1, "Changing Your Life for [the] Good.")

All of the above might suggest that "being for yourself" will only lengthen your emotional fitness to-do list. It doesn't have to. Neff greatly simplifies things by envisioning the

Stop, Look Both Ways, Go

Here's another exercise to feel more connected with others.

1. Stop for a moment and take a deep breath, or three or four, resting your attention on each breath in and each breath out.

2. Look both ways:

   First way (feeling bad about things and yourself): You find yourself feeling and saying things such as "Something's wrong. Things should be going better in my life. This shouldn't be happening to me. Why do things like this always happen to me? What did I do to deserve this? I should have seen this coming sooner so I could have prevented it. I'm ashamed of myself for being in this mess. I hope other people don't find out this has happened. My plans for success have been dashed. What's wrong with me? When will stuff like this stop happening to me?"

   Second way (consciously try to move past these feelings by remembering that you are connected to others): Say things such as "I know that stuff happens to everybody. It's my turn now. How bad is the situation, really? I would like to move past all this as soon as possible. This too shall pass. Would getting upset at myself or fate or the universe help any? What can I do to make it better? Who or what could help?"

3. Go. Now that you've looked both ways, make your choice: to feel sorry for yourself or to recognize your interconnectedness and common humanity with everyone. Take a few more mindful breaths, choose, then go.

essence of self-compassion in three words: *loving* (self-kindness), *connected* (common humanity), and *presence* (mindfulness). Emotional fitness that targets loving, connected presence is a good place to start.

Haim Ginott, a renowned Israeli psychologist and author, suggests that when a child spills the milk, parents should say, "The milk spilled. Please get a sponge" in a calm, friendly, and matter-of-fact tone of voice. No threats, no punishments, no recriminations. Simply, here's a problem; please do something sensible now to correct it.

We can apply this same message to ourselves as we develop self-compassion, to help us evolve from fight-or-flight agitation to self-kindness and self-appreciation. Going forward, we can skip the self-blame altogether and go directly to loving, connected presence. You can't go wrong that way.

CHAPTER 14

Visiting Someone Who's Sick
by Rabbi William Cutter

William (Bill) Cutter taught Laura when she was a rabbinical student at HUC-JIR in Los Angeles in the early '70s. Over the course of a long career as a teacher and scholar, Bill founded both the Rhea Hirsch School of Education and, particularly relevant to this article, the Kalsman Institute of Judaism and Health at HUC-JIR.

Words of Wisdom

Here are seven lines sick people say they do want to hear: "I'm so sorry this happened to you." "Tell me how I can help." "I'm here if you want to talk." "Just give me my marching orders." "That sounds awful. I can't even imagine the pain." "I'm bringing dinner." "You must be desperate for some quiet time. I'll take your kids on Saturday."

—Letty Cottin Pogrebin, *How to Be a Friend to a Friend Who Is Sick*

It is a mitzvah to visit the sick. Near relatives and friends should come immediately, and others more distant should come after three days. But if the illness is sudden and acute, both groups of people may come immediately.

—From *The Prepared Table* (*Shulchan Aruch*), 15th–16th century

The most prominent code of Jewish law, the *Shulchan Aruch*, begins its chapter on the healing responsibility of friends and family by saying it is a mitzvah to visit the sick. For our forebears, visiting the sick and praying on behalf of someone's health had direct physical benefit. For most modern people, the word *mitzvah* has been transformed to mean a "good deed," rather than an obligation. Either way, as an obligation or a good deed, with a prayer or without, out of theology or out of kindness, visiting the sick is an important component of a compassionate life. Visiting is not complicated, nor does it need to be a burden, but there are a number of things to keep in mind in today's environment in order to make it a healing experience.

Telling sick friends or family members that we are thinking about them, that we will do whatever is needed to ease their anxiety and pain, is an important part of the healing process. But it seems that nothing is easy these days. Some folks don't like to be the subject of too much attention; but everyone— even someone with a broken toe—is likely to appreciate an email or a phone call. On the other hand, if an illness is chronic and people are "living with" it rather than in danger of "dying from" it, friends and family might want to exercise a different sensibility when it comes to visiting or even checking in. And always examine the nature of your relationship—because we want to avoid a presumptuous intimacy as well as excessive restraint.

How Should We Attend to Sick Friends in the Hospital?

We can't just pop in on sick people in the hospital. Hospital protocols often tire patients out. In addition, the patient may be out of her room for extended periods. First of all, it is considerate to call ahead or, at the very least, ask the ill friend's closest relative or friend—there may be a designated or implied gatekeeper in the patient's social or family circle—for appropriate times to visit. Second, try to find out how the patient's special circumstances might influence the duration of your visit. And finally, take a few moments to center yourself and reflect on this particular ill person with this particular illness. Some may think of this as a practice of mindfulness; whatever you call it, take the time to be conscious of all that you are doing when you call on a sick person.

The *Shulchan Aruch* spells out an argument for determining the best time to visit: If you visit early in the day, the patient may be feeling too well, so you might not be inclined to pray; and if you visit at the end of the day, the patient may be so tired that you might despair over the efficacy of prayer. Today we can draw on a more practical version of this concern: Choose the time that is most comfortable for the patient.

WHAT SHOULD WE TALK ABOUT? HOW SHOULD WE ACT?

We want to visit people who are sick, yet we're afraid of troubling them. If we're in a friend's hospital room, how do we know whether to talk about his illness or whether that's a taboo subject? Let your sick friend be the guide. If he wants to talk about his medical or hospital experience, it's important to welcome that conversation and not be impatient. On the other hand, it's best not to press a sick friend to talk about his illness just because we think it would be therapeutic for him. A relaxed and welcoming presence on your part is your best protection against appearing to snoop or pry. It will also convey to your friend that you are prepared to be on his journey with him.

If illness is not to be the subject, talk about your shared interests. Let your sick friend guide you as to just what topics will remove a touch of the illness from the room. Find activities that you can enjoy together, whether reading a magazine article out loud or doing a crossword puzzle. If he is mostly alert and shows signs of keeping up with the times, talk about current events or news from your shared community. Remember: If you have a caring relationship with this person, your mere presence means a great deal.

For longer stays, a radio might be a welcome gift or a loan. Some patients feel "dosed out" on television. Show the latest picture of your grandchild (if that's not a sensitive topic), and be sure to let her share back whatever pictures she wants to show you. Sometimes singing a little melody (or *niggun*) together can be comforting. You don't want to pretend that her illness isn't serious business, but you also must empower her in her healing. Whatever you do, *empower*.

Pay attention to how you position yourself in relation to your sick friend. The ancient code urged visitors not to stand while the patient is lying down, but the reason is surprising. It was believed that God's presence was hovering at the patient's head, and it was considered inappropriate to have one's head above God's. Whether or not we share that belief, how we position ourselves *is* important: It can be uncomfortable for a patient to keep turning his head to make eye contact or to be looking up the nose of person who is visiting.

Thoughtful doctors usually sit down when visiting a patient. Are you allowed to sit on the bed? Sometimes that kind of intimacy is just what the patient needs; at other times it can be imposing or even embarrassing; or it may be prohibited for medical reasons. So as not to be presumptuous, you might ask, "Where would you like me to sit?" or just wait until you are invited to sit in a chair or on the bed.

SHOULD YOU BRING GIFTS?

Bringing a gift to your sick friend can be a nice idea, but these days hospital stays are often brief, and loading up the patient with gifts adds to the baggage she has to take home. And some gifts are a bad idea anyway. Food is generally not a good gift, even if your friend says she would really like a corned beef sandwich. One patient I worked with felt ignored by staff because she kept asking for a Coca-Cola. It seemed like an easy thing to provide, so one of the

The Challenges of Dementia

Visiting patients with Alzheimer's disease or other forms of dementia has unique challenges that can be lessened with creativity and a heightened sensitivity to the patients' circumstances A 2015 article in *AMA Wire* describes how the actors Karen Stobbe and Mondy Carter use techniques from improv to reach people with Alzheimer's:

Accepting the reality given to you. Instead of following a prescribed script or trying to predict every moment, improv actors are encouraged to fluidly accept and act on the ideas, plot twists, and characters their fellow actors propose onstage. Communicating with people who have dementia requires a similar break from reality. "Accepting their reality means letting go of ours. . . . Stepping into their world provides a launching pad that is positive instead of negative. It provides a connection that you can talk about—[you can] have a conversation."

Listening fully. "Going with the flow is really the crux of improv. . . . That's exactly the same for being with a person who has Alzheimer's. Be spontaneous and accepting of whatever comes your way."

Making an extra effort to say "yes and . . ." "It's crucial to commit to practicing saying 'yes and . . .' and not 'yes but . . .' when performing. . . . 'Yes and . . .' provides agreement. It provides validation—even empathy. Persons with Alzheimer's receive 'no's' all the time. That's why, for a person living with Alzheimer's, hearing the word 'yes' can feel really good."

hospital chaplains went to the concession machine and purchased a Coke for this "neglected" patient. Unfortunately, the patient had been on diabetic watch, so soda was hardly what the doctor ordered. If you have an impulse to bring food, check with someone who knows what's going on, so that your gift is beneficial and not an unsuspected poison.

Sometimes patients like to give their visitors gifts, whether it's a magazine they've just finished reading or a piece of candy or fruit. Try to accept this act of "reverse giving" graciously because it helps an ill person feel like a mensch.

PAY ATTENTION TO SIGNS

Hospitals are getting much better about alerting patients, family members, and friends to certain practices: safely helping people walk, observing posted visitors' hours, avoiding visits

Traditional versions of prayer for healing include: "May the One who blessed our ancestors, Abraham, Isaac, and Jacob, Sarah, Rebecca, Rachel, and Leah, bless and heal those who are ill [name them]. May the Holy One of Blessing give them strength and comfort, and those who care for them wisdom and compassion. We hope and pray for the renewal of body and spirit. Amen." A contemporary version is the prayer composed in 1987 by Debbie Friedman (of blessed memory) and Drorah Setel, which has become almost ubiquitous in liberal congregations:

Mi shebeirach avoteinu, m'kor hab'rachah l'imoteinu,

May the Source of strength who blessed the ones before us, help us find the courage to make our lives a blessing.

And let us say, Amen.

Mi shebeirach imoteinu, m'kor hab'rachah l'avoteinu,

Bless those in need of healing with r'fuah sh'leimah, the renewal of body, the renewal of spirit.

And let us say, Amen.

with too many other people, and, above all, *keeping your hands clean*. Wash your hands or use hand sanitizer when you enter and leave the room.

Stay alert for signs or signals from the patient herself. This person you are visiting may have had some tough medical moments that she may not want to share with you—moments of embarrassment, failed steps, problems getting her body to work. Be sensitive to those signs as well, no matter how subtly they are expressed.

PRAYERS UP AND PRAYERS ACROSS

Our ancestors believed in the power of prayer to change God's "actions." We can still believe in the power of prayer. Many of us have adapted the idea of prayer to ground our visit in Jewish tradition and to preserve an ancient link that has us aspiring to a higher power. A prayer, however we interpret its effect, assures our sick friend or family member that his life is precious and merits the attention of the community to which he belongs. If he's Jewish, you might think of simple ways to make any Sabbaths or special days of observance Jewishly meaningful for your sick friend. For example, during your visit, share a short prayer over some wine, a challah (if medically appropriate), or a special biblical reading. (Most hospitals will not allow fire in a room, so candles are out of the question.)

Prayer, and especially prayer from the Jewish tradition, is a perfect intersection between our longings upward and our attachment to the community in which we live. The traditional formula for prayer at the bedside permits ample opportunity for improvisation—a few words or sentences about the special place of this person in your life or in the community to which she belongs. For those so inclined, a poem can be a meaningful alternative to a prayer.

Visiting at Home

Visiting a sick friend at home is an entirely different matter. But it still begins with washing your hands. The hospital is like a republic with multiple governments, where the patient has little control over his schedule. At home there are fewer rules and regulations, but you still have to check with the responsible members of your friend's family before visiting.

When coping with illness at home, your friend is in the privacy of her own space, and you shouldn't just drop in anytime you want. In the hospital, if the patient is tired, there are ways to urge visitors to leave; at home, patients may feel as if they have to play the host. Take the patient's personal boundaries into consideration, and don't be insulted if you are not welcomed on a certain day. On the other hand, don't be surprised if your friend wonders where you have been if you don't at least try to stop by. Some people with illnesses are especially sensitive about being abandoned. Calling first or texting might give you a sense of whether and when a visit will be welcome.

Remember the Person You Are Visiting . . . and Why

Visiting the sick is a compassionate act that can improve your emotional and mental well-being.

While you will certainly feel better from having paid a visit to your sick friend, your visit is about her, not about you. Remember to check your needs at the door, wash your hands, meditate on what you are about to do, and enter with a pleasant countenance. A cheerful attitude can mean the world to people. Light laughter can be combined with serious expressions of concern.

There is an important distinction between "curing" and "healing." Visits might not cure someone who is ill, but the comfort and connection of a visit bring healing to the spirit, if not the body. Perhaps that is why rabbinic tradition interprets a Talmudic passage as follows: "Whoever visits the sick removes one-sixtieth of the sick person's suffering" (BT *Bava M'tzia* 30b).

CHAPTER 15

Living in the Land of the Sick
by Richard Siegel

I had assumed that health and sickness were separate, distinct terrains. I've since learned that those boundaries do not really exist. Instead, the world is composed of the sick and the not-yet-sick. —Paul Cowan

Paul Cowan—a celebrated investigative journalist with the *Village Voice*, an activist in the Jewish Renewal movement on New York's Upper West Side, and a friend—wrote these words in May 1988, five months after being diagnosed with leukemia. He was 47. In his article, "In the Land of the Sick: Letter to a Potential Patient," he wrote about serving as an advance scout or, to use his metaphor, a foreign correspondent, reporting on the front lines of a battle he was fighting at the time, and that many of us would join over the next decades.

During the past five months, I've learned there is a land of the sick. When you receive a passport—an unwelcome diagnosis—you learn that the land has its own language (medical terminology), its own geography (hospitals, outpatient clinics, blood testing labs, doctors' offices), its own citizens (other sick people), its own pantheon of heroes and authority figures (doctors, medical researchers, hospital administrators), its own calendar (dictated by the changes in one's body or by the results of medical tests), and—most of all—its own emotional demands. —Paul Cowan

As we get older, most of us will get sick at some point in our lives, in spite of our best efforts to remain physically fit, watch what we eat, meditate, and cultivate positive character traits and attitudes. We are all susceptible to illness and injury, whether something temporary, such as the flu; or chronic, such as

Words of Wisdom

From this narrow constricted place I cry out for expansiveness.

—Psalm 118

arthritis; or life-threatening, such as leukemia. It is not uncommon for friends of a certain age to begin their visits with an organ recital, filling each other in on their particular ailments and infirmities.

How Do You Know If You Are Sick?

In retrospect, I realize that I denied the first manifestations of leukemia when I experienced them on a vacation last summer. In early August, I noticed several bruises on my legs, but I've always been a clumsy person, so I assumed I had been bumping into furniture without noticing the minor pain. —Paul Cowan

Our bodies are magnificent organisms—intricate, finely tuned, self-repairing. The wonder of our physical being is captured in the Jewish prayer for the body (Asher Yatzar), traditionally said every morning as well as every time we use the bathroom:

Holy One of Blessing, whose Presence fills creation, shaping the human being with wisdom, creating within us all the openings and vessels of the body. It is revealed and known before You that if one of these is open and not closed, or blocked and not open, we could not stand before You. Holy One of Blessing, who heals all flesh and acts wondrously.

It is sobering, humanizing, and exhilarating to stop every once in a while and remind ourselves of the simple, improbable miracle of being alive, day after day, year after year. Our heart continues to beat, pumping blood throughout our body through an intricate network of veins and arteries; our lungs inhale oxygen and exhale carbon dioxide; our digestive system extracts nutrients from the food we eat and discards the waste. Miraculous!

Unfortunately, too often we're only aware of our wondrous body when one of our systems malfunctions. Sometimes the symptoms are obvious. If you have a sharp pain in your stomach, if you pass out, or if your arm goes numb, you call your doctor and/or go to the emergency room.

The problem is that many symptoms are subtle and easily dismissed. Some bruises on your leg? "I must have bumped into something." Out of breath walking up the stairs to your house? "Wow, I'm really out of shape." Many of us have a powerful denial mechanism that leads us to minimize our symptoms. "It's just a little blood in the urine. Nothing worth mentioning." But it *is* worth mentioning; what might seem insignificant might be a key indicator of something serious. The earlier we get it looked at, the better our chances of recovering from it.

Even if you choose not to run immediately to a doctor for these seemingly minor health conditions, remember to at least schedule an annual physical examination and report all the health incidences and changes to the doctor then. The simplest way to remember this is to schedule the exam around a birthday. Medicare doesn't currently cover routine physicals; however, even a wellness checkup, which is covered, can give us an opportunity to discuss our physical and psychological condition with a primary care physician, who can then decide whether to order more tests or make referrals to specialists.

What If You Are Diagnosed with a Serious Illness?

> I couldn't accept the idea that there was a single set of guidelines to the kind of behavior that enables patients to cope with illness or prolong their life. Each patient— each person—is unique. They can't change their personalities when they get sick. They can only try to strengthen the strongest part of themselves. That was what I had to do. —Paul Cowan

That is what we all have to do. Each of our experiences of illness is unique, and we need to assemble the tools and resources that work best for us, that best fit our personalities.

There is no "correct" response on learning that you have a serious, possibly life-threatening illness. Fear, grief, anger, sadness, guilt, embarrassment, stunned silence—they're all possible and appropriate. In all probability, you'll be too shocked to ask coherent questions or hear the answers. This will come later, after you've had some time to absorb the reality that you have now entered the land of the sick.

What follows will be a "new normal"—taking tests, visiting specialists, analyzing results, doing research, learning information, considering options, discussing (and sometimes arguing) with loved ones about courses of treatment.

After receiving a diagnosis, some people want to know everything about their condition, every option and alternative treatment available, and every contingency down the line. Others only want to deal with the next step ahead. Regardless of where you are on the continuum, the first source of information is your doctor.

The doctor-patient consultation can be a fraught situation. Your doctor will want to be thorough and efficient when providing information to you, but you may be too overwhelmed or distracted by your fears and anxieties to absorb it. A little preparation will make the conversation easier and more productive:

- Whether it's with your primary doctor or a specialist, prepare for your visit. Record all your symptoms or changes in your condition. Write down all your questions and concerns.

- Most doctors will want you to be well informed so you can make good decisions about your care. You are not imposing on them by asking questions or asking them to repeat what they've said. If you feel that you are not getting answers to your questions, consider seeing a different doctor, if possible.

- Take another person with you and make sure that she has a copy of your questions. Hearing details about your condition and treatment options can be stressful and scary, and you might not be able to pay attention or remember what was said. Your companion will be able to listen, take notes, and ask questions you may have forgotten or that might arise during the appointment.

- Before you leave, ask for any written material about your condition or what websites the doctor recommends for more information.

You might also benefit from talking with others who have or, even better, *had* your condition. They can help demystify the process, answer questions you may not have felt comfortable asking your doctor, and give you a sense about the future. Ask your doctor to put you in touch with former patients, check with local support groups, or ask friends if they know of someone who has had a similar diagnosis.

Whom Do You Want to Tell What and How?

One question was at the forefront of my mind: "What should I tell my children?" Should I gloss over the truth or present it in an unvarnished form? My doctor answered, simply, that when a family member is sick, no one is helped by a lie.

—Paul Cowan

On first learning of your diagnosis, you need to decide whom you want to tell. Most people will want to tell the people they love, even if these are the hardest conversations, particularly with children of any age. Again, there's no right way to do it. In person is good. By telephone is fine. Trust that your loved ones will be able to absorb the news. You did.

Beyond your family and closest friends, however, who you want to let know about your condition is a personal choice. You may want to keep the information within a small group of intimates, either because you are private by nature or because you do not want to attract undue attention.

Sharing information about your condition can be a double-edged sword. On the one hand,

hearing words of support from family, friends, colleagues, and acquaintances can be an important part of the healing process. On the other hand, constantly repeating your saga with one person after another can be exhausting. CaringBridge, a web-based personal health journal, can be a helpful resource in this regard, as it allows you to provide updates as often as you like. People in your networks can access your site to get the latest information on your condition and leave messages of support and concern for you, without any expectation for you to respond.

How Do You Want to Deal with Expressions of Concern from Other People?

Expressions of support and concern can be comforting and help in the healing process, but you can easily become overwhelmed by the attention and the feeling that you need to respond to every call, email, or text.

It will be helpful to people who care about you and stress-reducing for you to set some ground rules based on your wants and needs:

- Do you want people to visit you, either in the hospital or when you are convalescing at home? Would you rather limit visits to relatives and close friends? Do you want visitors to call first or visit during certain hours?
- Do you mind people calling on the phone to talk to you?
- Do you (and your family) want people to bring meals?
- Are there chores that you (and your family) need taken care of—grocery shopping, walking the dog, or putting out the garbage cans? People will ask if they can help. Don't hesitate to make them aware of simple tasks they can do.
- Do you want people to pray for you? In Jewish tradition there is a prayer for healing, called the *Mi Shebeirach*, that can be said either in English or in Hebrew. If you want your name included in Hebrew, traditionally, you are referred to as [your name], son/daughter of [mother's name].

Try to articulate your preferences and post them on CaringBridge or as an automatic email response. Designate someone—a spouse, an adult child, a relative, or a friend—to field calls and inquiries and keep people updated so you are not exhausted by dozens of repeat conversations.

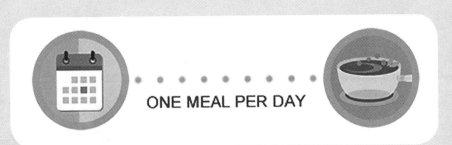

ONE MEAL PER DAY

Mealtrain.com, a free online tool, is a convenient way to organize meal delivery. Typically organized by a family member or friend who has knowledge of the recipient's meal preferences, calendar, and network, Meal Train provides an online sign-up calendar for when meals are needed. The organizer then contacts friends of the recipient to invite them to provide meals, whether homemade or purchased, hand-delivered or sent by a restaurant or delivery service.

You don't need to respond personally to every call, email, text, or message. A general acknowledgment on CaringBridge or even Facebook of your appreciation for the concern should suffice.

Keeping One Foot in the Land of the Well

During my first weekend in the hospital, I began to learn how important it was to retain my ties to the land of the well—to see myself as an exile who would return one day. . . . I wanted to retain a sense of myself. . . . Over time, I would be able to use the room to create my own little island in the midst of the hospital. —Paul Cowan

So much of what goes on when you are sick is foreign and disorienting. Particularly in the hospital, you wear different clothes, eat at different times, answer to different people. Much of this you have no control over, such as being awakened at 3 a.m. to take medication. However, you can do a number of things to make this a more familiar environment:

- If you are going to be in the hospital for an extended stay, ask to wear your own pajamas or nightgown.
- Bring in pictures or objects that will remind you of people and places you love.
- If your diet allows, have food brought in from outside.
- Sit in a chair, rather than lying in bed.
- When people visit, walk around with them or sit in the lounge.

If you are convalescing at home, try to reestablish some of your routine as quickly as possible. Nothing is more reassuring than returning to some semblance of normalcy:

- Go to sleep at your regular bedtime.
- Wake up when you normally wake up.
- Brush your teeth.
- Shave.
- Shower.
- Meditate.
- Wear fresh clothes.
- Eat at regular times.
- Go for walks in the neighborhood.
- Work on a project, whether something related to your regular business or something special, such as sorting photographs, knitting a sweater, researching investment ideas, or writing a book.

Staying Positive—Morning, Noon, and Night

I try to maintain hope—or at least the memory of hope—when I am consumed with fear or despair. I believe that hope is part of the will to live: It allows people to choose forms of treatment that are painful, risky, and promising; it enables people to fight fear with enthusiasm for family and friends, for books and ideas.

—Paul Cowan

Being sick can be depressing and overwhelming, but it can also give you a new appreciation of life, gratitude, wonder—and hope. When your body isn't working right, you realize how much you have been taking this everyday miracle for granted.

Every tradition offers spiritual techniques that enable us to keep our focus on the healing potential within us. The following meditations may acquire new meaning when we're living in the land of the sick.

The traditional Jewish prayer on waking up in the morning:

I am grateful before You, the Living and Eternal Spirit, who has compassionately restored my soul. Great is Your faithfulness.

The Bedtime Sh'ma includes reciting the Sh'ma ("Hear, O Israel, God is our God, God is One") and a number of other biblical, rabbinic, and mystical passages. Two, in particular, provide some comfort and perspective when you are sick:

1. Lying in bed, imagine yourself surrounded by angels, enfolded in an embrace of protection and grace, and recite:

   In the name of the Holy One of Blessing: Michael (the Archangel) be at my right hand, Gabriel (the Angel of Strength) at my left; in front of me is Uriel (the Angel of Light), behind me, Raphael (the Angel of Healing); and above me is Shechinat-El (Your Presence).

2. This more elaborate passage both offers and requests forgiveness, a reassuring way of settling up your accounts every night before you go to sleep:

   Source of Forgiveness, I hereby forgive anyone who angered or antagonized me or who sinned against me—whether against my body, my property, my honor, or against anything of mine; whether accidentally, willfully, carelessly, or purposely; whether through speech, deed, thought, or notion; whether in this transmigration or another transmigration. May no one be punished on my account.

   As I forgive and pardon fully those who have done me wrong, may those whom I have harmed forgive and pardon me, whether I acted deliberately or by accident, whether by word or deed. Wipe away my sins with Your great mercy. May I not repeat the wrongs I have committed.

   May the words of my mouth and the meditations of my heart be acceptable to You, my Rock and my Redeemer.

Also consider the Metta meditation from the Buddhist tradition. Sitting or lying in a comfortable position with your eyes closed, recite and repeat these phrases:

   May I feel safe.
   May I feel happy.
   May I feel strong.
   May I live with ease.

Deceptively simple. At the very time when you might not be feeling safe, happy, strong, or at ease, you offer up a wish, a hope, an intention that you feel otherwise. The meditation itself is a window into another reality—the land of the well—where you feel safe, happy, and strong and you live with ease.

Fair Trade Judaica has designed a banner of five healing flags made in Nepal. Each flag is imprinted with a hamsa with the words Body, Heart, Mind, and Spirit, and the central one saying R'fuah ("Healing") and El Na R'fah Na La ("O God, Please, Heal Her"). The flags can be hung over a bed or across a doorway.

This meditation has extensions you might want to add when you are strong enough. First, instead of saying "I," think of a loved one and say, "May X feel safe; may X feel happy; may X feel strong; may X live with ease." Do this with other loved ones as well. Then think about your doctors, nurses, and other medical professionals with whom you interact and on whom you depend, and recite the meditation with their names or just with their roles, for example, "May my anesthesiologists feel safe. . . ."

This may be enough for you. The practice continues by adding other people with whom you have more casual interactions, then people with whom you have difficulties, and then expanding out to all humanity.

Leaving the Land of the Sick

In most cases, we will get better or we will reach a "new normal." At what point do you want to acknowledge that you are no longer in the land of the sick, that you have returned to the land of the well? When you go back to work? When you complete your final treatment and are now on a quarterly checkup schedule? When you're down to consulting with one doctor instead of four?

Three decision points—they may come together or separately—you might want to consider:

When we are ill, we are particularly reliant on the skill and compassion of medical professionals— doctors, surgeons, nurses, hospitalists, technicians, and others. In addition to including them in your meditation, consider sending a note of appreciation to hospital staff who were particularly kind or helpful to you.

1. When do you stop updating your CaringBridge site? When do you post your final update and what do you say in it?
2. When do you ask people to stop praying for you?
3. When do you make a public acknowledgment of your return to the land of the well?

The last one is particularly tricky. In the Jewish tradition, we recite the Birkat Ha'Gomel (Prayer of Redemption) after surviving a dangerous situation—for example, returning from an overseas trip, after having a life-threatening experience, such as a car accident, or after having recovered from a serious illness.

When are you ready to make such a public declaration? Maybe it is after every surgery that involves general anesthesia or upon completion of a full course of treatment. If you have a chronic condition, you may choose not to say it at all. Although short and nondescriptive, standing up in public and acknowledging that you have survived a difficult ordeal can be cleansing and sobering, a recognition that, even though you are back in society, your life has changed—you have changed.

The Prayer of Redemption is normally said during the Torah reading, but can be said during any service. The one who is making the blessing says:

Holy One of Blessing, whose Presence fills creation, who shows goodness to us beyond our merits, upon the undeserving, and has bestowed kindness upon me.

Those who hear the blessing respond "Amen," followed by:

May the One who has bestowed goodness upon you continue to favor you with all that is good.

For ideas about creating a ritual to mark your return to health, see chapter 2, "Cooking Up New Rituals."

> I've learned that I can need love and be self-reliant at the same time. I've learned that I can keep loving and laughing and working in the face of relentless fear. I've learned a more important lesson, one I hope stays with me. Dreading death, I've discovered I can still affirm life. —Paul Cowan

Mourning and Moving On

Unfortunately, another dimension of getting older is losing people we love. All of us, if we are lucky, will eventually become orphans. The death of a parent is a predictable death, and when it happens after a long life, it is often one for which we can prepare. But other losses, which accompany getting older—the death of a sibling, of an adult child, of a partner or a friend—are often much harder. Jewish tradition doesn't even recognize a friend as a mourner. But we do.

Kaddish: Grief Is Praise

by Rabbi Laura Geller

Jewish tradition identifies a mourner as one who recently lost a parent, a spouse, a sibling, or a child. An (adult) child is supposed to say Kaddish (the Mourner's Prayer) every day for a year after the death of a parent, but for all other categories of mourners we say Kaddish daily only for one month. Why? These rules were instituted a long time ago, when infant mortality was rampant, when a person had many siblings, when spouses died very young. The intention was for the mourner to reenter the world as soon as possible, have more children, marry again, fully participate in the life of the community. The death of a parent was a different kind of death—and the year of mourning would offer time to work through unfinished business carried with us from childhood throughout our lives. In addition, saying Kaddish every day for a year was viewed as a way to fulfill the commandment to honor your mother and father. Another view is that Kaddish enables the soul of the parent to rise up to heaven and while, theoretically, that ascent takes a year, for the righteous 11 months is sufficient. Most people mourning a parent in this traditional way stop reciting daily Kaddish after 11

Words of Wisdom

Give your grief all of its due but only its due.

—Etty Hillesum

months. There are many wonderful resources that deal with the death of a parent (see Part 4 Tools and Resources). However, few deal with the death of other people we love.

On Mourning a Beloved

Over my career as a rabbi I have read "We Remember Them" (Sylvan Kamens and Rabbi Jack Riemer) about a thousand times—at funerals, at homes of shiva, at services, or with a grieving survivor. I have always found it comforting.

At the rising sun and at its going down;
We remember them.
At the blowing of the wind and in the chill of winter;
We remember them.
At the opening of the buds and in the rebirth of spring;
We remember them.
At the blueness of the skies and in the warmth of summer;
We remember them.
At the rustling of the leaves and in the beauty of the autumn;
We remember them.
At the beginning of the year and when it ends;
We remember them.
As long as we live, they too will live, for they are now
a part of us, as we remember them.

When we are weary and in need of strength;
We remember them.
When we are lost and sick at heart;
We remember them.
When we have decisions that are difficult to make;
We remember them.
When we have joy we crave to share;
We remember them.
When we have achievements that are based on theirs;
We remember them.
For as long as we live, they too will live,
for they are now a part of us,
as we remember them.

Every great loss demands that we choose life again. Grieving is not about forgetting. Grieving allows us to heal, to remember with love instead of with pain. It's a sorting process. . . . One by one you let go of the things that are gone and mourn them. One by one you take hold of the things which have become a part of who you are and build again.

—Rachel Naomi Remen

But now, as I mourn my husband Rich, it's not so comforting. It feels too easy . . . because it doesn't tell us how we remember, what we do in order to remember . . . or what we do when we don't want to remember. It doesn't help us figure out how those we loved are a part of us, even though they are physically gone.

Mourning Rich has elicited so many different feelings. Panic: Am I going to be okay? Numbness: Hard to think clearly, or to make routine decisions. Denial: This can't really be happening. Anger: How could you die and leave me alone? Depression: What's the point? Irritation: The complicated feelings that arise when people ask, "How are you doing?" I know they mean well, but I don't know the answer. "I am still alive. I got up this morning. I know I am going to be all right. But I am very sad."

I thought I was prepared. I am very grateful that as we worked on this book we took our own suggestions for getting ready (see Part 4). We spent hours debating between cremation and burial; we filled out advance directives for health care, and we talked to our children about our choices; we gathered all our passwords and business information into one document; we wrote versions of our ethical wills.

I am still surprised at how much I wasn't prepared for. Like merging our frequent-flier miles; closing his Geek Squad account; changing the names on our joint checking account; canceling his AAA membership, and so on. I was surprised at how little I could prepare for when I burst out in tears (or when I wouldn't) on a phone call about health insurance or previously scheduled appointments or in a conversation with our gardener or handyman. I was surprised by how much work there was, even though I was prepared.

I wasn't prepared for all the "firsts" that come along. Like the first time I was called "widow." Or the first time I had to decide where to sit at our dining room table when I invited guests for dinner. The first Sukkot. The first Thanksgiving. Other firsts: going out to dinner with a couple and noticing the awkwardness about who pays. My instincts to say yes to every invitation because I worry that if I say no I will no longer be invited.

I have asked for help, particularly from other widows. I invited myself to dinner with two much older friends who have been widows for years. They picked me up and I got in the car's back seat, behind the passenger. The woman in the front passenger seat turned around and said, "Here is the first rule for being a widow. Never sit behind the passenger seat. If you sit there, the passenger in the front seat can't

> Grief is praise because it is the natural way love honors what it misses. —Martin Prechtel from The Smell of Rain on Dust

turn around to talk to you, and you don't want the driver to turn around. Get out and sit behind the driver. Then I can talk to you." I must admit that it gave me comfort to get such concrete advice . . . and to be with women who have survived the death of their partners and gone on to full lives. One friend told me that the years since her partner died have been a continual path to deeper self-awareness, compassion, love, and forgiveness for her. And then she added, "But I also know that while this is a universal experience, it is so very unique to each one of us that nothing can really 'prepare' us for our loss except, perhaps, the knowledge that it is inevitable if we are lucky enough to find and have love in our lives."

For me, there is comfort in Jewish traditions. For example, the Kaddish, the Mourner's Prayer, which says nothing about death but only about praise, reminds me that hope can surface, even in the face of sadness. By embracing the sadness, rather than being frightened by it, we can touch the capacity we have for love. I went to a daily minyan to say Kaddish every day during *sh'loshim*, that first month after a loss. While I will still say Kaddish on Shabbat and holy days, I am no longer a mourner in that sense. And so I am slowly rejoining the world of the living. Part of that is recognizing the gratitude I feel to the community that has reached out to me as I mourn. Community really does make a difference. And I know that as long as I remember him, he too will live, because he is now a part of me.

During your lifetime, be sure to work with financial advisors or trusted friends who can help you organize your financial affairs and guide you through the administrative process after a death. This includes estate planning and administration, accounting/tax returns, financial planning and investment management, and life and disability insurance. The process is overwhelming, extremely emotional, cumbersome, frustrating, and time-consuming. Even though you may have an attorney and accountant, there are numerous administrative tasks that must be handled by the fiduciary for the decedent. It is important to have someone who can help you understand the big picture. Then family members can grieve without the hassle of handling detail work related to administration of the estate.
—Craig Farkas, CFP, VP Harold Davidson & Associates, Inc.

Climbing Out of the Pit

There is a certain need to examine this thing called "grief"—something between curiosity and compulsion. I take it out and hold it in my hands, like a trinket. I turn it over, rub my fingers along its sharp contours, knowing that inside, it is as nebulous as shadows at dusk. Perhaps, I think, if I look at it closely and long enough, I will gain some understanding of its substance and be able to conquer it over time.

It is uncomfortable to examine grief in this way, as if I am a voyeur looking at the mangled car and bodies of an accident I witnessed. But not looking at it doesn't feel right either, as if somehow, in not looking, I do dishonor to my husband Ray. And so I concede that I am drawn to my grief as a way of being in relationship with the man I loved. But it is not the only way to remain close and I am grateful to know this as well.

I find great comfort in writing. My journal naturally takes the form of letters to Ray which I write before I go to sleep. It replaces what I miss: the whispered sharing of daily events as we lie in bed together, the give and take of dealing with life and its complexities.

At first, my need to write to Ray feels almost religious, like a ritual I shouldn't change. I want and need to honor him, to connect to "us" in a specific way. But over time, I find that I am writing less and only do so when I have something I want to remember—like a dream I had or a bit of wisdom that has helped me. As time passes, I become aware that I have internalized our relationship; the external giving way to the internal because he is a part of me now.

A friend, who lost her husband years ago, wrote a card to me after Ray died. The words, which helped her in her grief, gave me perspective and a sense of optimism: "There will always be a big hole in your life but at some point, you will stop falling into it."

I know I am not falling anymore. I am slowing inching my way through my grief, peering into the hole but no longer finding myself at the bottom of the pit. Deep down I know that it is essential to examine my grief in order to accept it. And in doing so, I am certain that both grief and I will change.

—Amy Lederman

On Mourning a Friend
by Rabbi Naamah Kelman

When we lose a friend in his young adult years, it is a shattering experience. It's not supposed to happen. We can spend decades wondering, what if? Who would he have been? I remember the sting when my son turned the same age as my friend who was killed in an Israeli Air Force accident. When this friend died, so did our sense of a carefree young adulthood. And yet we lived, and to this day he will always be 23.

As we enter our last decades, the loss of dear and lifelong friends is painful in other ways. The years of shared experiences, ups and downs, life's losses and blessings, create a bedrock of security and comfort. Who knows us better than that friend from our youth, or that one from college, or that parent I met at our kids' preschool, or that fellow student who has become a lifelong colleague and friend. Research keeps telling us that deep friendships have the most positive effect on quality of life and even longevity. Our oldest friends are the great sources of our history, folly, and triumph. We know each other in ways that even our siblings, spouses, and children do not, and yet we often do not have a role in their funeral or any obligation for mourning.

Richard met Naamah Kelman when she was in high school. She is the sister of his friend Rabbi Levi Weiman-Kelman, and the daughter of one of his mentors, Rabbi Wolfe Kelman. Over the years, Naamah, now a rabbi herself and dean of the HUC-JIR Jerusalem campus, has become our friend, colleague, and teacher.

ALWAYS IN MY HEART

Once a week there's some sort of bad news. Once a month there's a funeral. You lose close friends and discover one of the worst truths of old age: they're irreplaceable.
—Nora Ephron,
I Remember Nothing:
And Other Reflections

But grieve and mourn we do and must.

When someone dies without children and little family, friends sometimes step in to oversee the funeral, even sit a symbolic shiva, and gather once a year for the *yahrtzeit*. Here, friends act like family, and their grief is the

> When the much-beloved Rabbi Rachel Cowan died, friends organized a virtual Kaddish for her. A calendar went out over social media, and friends signed up for specific days to say Kaddish in her memory. This continued throughout the first year after her death.

public expression of this person's death. But in most situations, where the family handles all arrangements, how can we participate in the roles and rites when our beloved friends leave us? How do we comfort ourselves when we find ourselves losing more and more friends to infirmity—mental and physical? And what happens when children move their parents far away from their close friends so the adult children can take care of them?

It behooves us to consider a number of rituals or acts of memorializing lost friends. Friendships are stories to be told, to be celebrated. When my young friend died, we friends spent an evening telling stories about him. We recorded those stories and gave the recording to the family. When my father passed away too early, his colleagues who were his friends put together a booklet of eulogies and reminisces for us, his children, for posterity. Most friends will support the immediate family in their mourning, but not necessarily have the space, time, or rituals to mourn the death themselves. We need to make the space.

In liberal Jewish traditions, Kaddish (the Mourner's Prayer) can be said by friends as well as family. Or you can stand for Kaddish without saying it aloud as a way to mark the week, month, or year following the death. And just as the family has its own private mourning, a group of friends could certainly create some mourning time as well. The eulogy that you did not give at the funeral could be written and shared with other common friends, as well as family.

When people share friends, they can gather perhaps for an evening of stories. How about an annual gathering of closest friends over lunch at that friend's favorite restaurant? Maybe visiting some place you all loved, or listening to music you all enjoyed, or watching that movie you all laughed so hard at or cried through together.

But what if you did not share friends? One of my dearest friends lost one of her dearest friends whom I only knew casually. I knew my friend would need comforting; I knew she would need something to mark the loss. I treated her as if she were mourning a close relative.

As we move into our later 60s, 70s, and even into our 80s, we can actually use this time to reclaim friendship. With children grown up and even grandchildren independent, we can turn back to dear and beloved friends, travel with them, dine with them, take in cultural events with them. It is a period to really savor friendships; this is how we bring meaning and comfort to our lives. Investing in friends at this time in our lives paradoxically eases the pain of loss. By creating new memories, relishing the past, and hoping for the future together, we are not alone.

When we lose a life partner, siblings, or, God forbid, children, these are terrible losses; a part of us has been taken. Friends are different. We have hopefully worked out our "issues" and enjoyed their company and counsel. It is a loss but also a recognition of that wonderful aspect of ourselves that this particular friend was so able to help us see and know. In the death of our loved ones, we die a little bit. With friends, we are reminded of how we lived and formed our lives.

Friendships are unique; there's that bird-watching friend, or that crazy childhood friend, or that colleague who seemed so different; or that woman whom you saved after her divorce and you became soul sisters. Friends reflect different aspects of ourselves and different biographies and periods in our lives. We need to figure out how we might mourn, let go, and ultimately celebrate what sustained us.

This is an invitation to do so . . .

Regarding My Body

by Nessa Rapoport

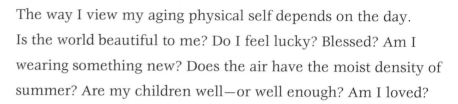

Nessa Rapoport, a friend of Richard, is a writer whose work explores the realms of Jewish vision and imagination, including a novel, *Preparing for Sabbath*, a collection of her prose poems, *A Woman's Book of Grieving*, and a memoir, *House on the River: A Summer Journey*.

Words of Wisdom

There's a crack, a crack in everything. That's how the light gets in.

—Leonard Cohen

The way I view my aging physical self depends on the day. Is the world beautiful to me? Do I feel lucky? Blessed? Am I wearing something new? Does the air have the moist density of summer? Are my children well—or well enough? Am I loved?

On other days, the view is darker. Am I ill? Is someone I love in a desperate predicament? Did I just finish reading an article that described (why didn't I stop at the headline?) the torture of children? Is the news out of Washington or Jerusalem calamitous? Am I afraid?

My body is a story I tell and retell myself, variations in a grateful or grieving key. In the permanently unstable relationship between body and being, here are some of the improvisations.

I grow softer

It is no longer possible, whether I exercise maniacally or not (I choose not), to have the taut flesh of my youth. All the interventions in the world result in a look that has become ubiquitous in a certain social class of women: Done. But still not young.

For a long time, two decades after my teens, I would look in the mirror and feel "the same." My body rose and fell with pregnancy, but I seemed to myself unaging. I noticed older women, and noticed the difference, but—like many in my baby-boom generation—I did not believe that what had happened to those women's bodies and faces would happen to mine.

Now, when I look in the mirror, I find my genealogy. The creases on my forehead are my father's, and they do not disappear, even after (rare) good sleep. I see my great-aunt Bella in my face. Words I never used—pucker, wither—come more readily to mind.

The antidote?

I summon the silk of my grandmother's cheek when I kissed her. The fineness of her skin was incomparable. The older she got, the more I adored her. Should I not be as lovable to myself as she was to me?

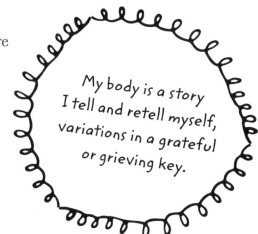

My body is a story I tell and retell myself, variations in a grateful or grieving key.

Or I tell myself: My dead friends, of whom I have too many, would give anything, *anything*, to look in the mirror and mark the signs of aging.

Everything is heading down, trying to return

My body knows where it's going—and nothing I do will reverse its descent. Slacken and fall: From dust I came, and to dust . . .

The grave calleth. What folly to try to reverse gravity. Better to try to reverse injustice, to look heavenward and remember what matters.

Perhaps the point of the inevitable parting of one's self from one's youthful surface is to begin to distinguish the soul from absolute identification with the body, to understand, in the flesh: It is time to rededicate ourselves to the pursuit of goodness.

The essential role of vanity

When I was in my thirties, a friend told me that she could not wait until she was old enough to "let herself go."

Turns out that's a poor idea—and even she, now close to sixty, has forsaken it.

MAKING PEACE WITH THE MIRROR.

Among the many extraordinary very old people I have known was my husband's grandfather, a cultured, worldly, observant Jew who gave half his time (and half his office space) to *chesed*, deeds of loving-kindness. He was also unfailingly elegant. Even in his final illness, he wore a silk dressing gown, a pristine white handkerchief in his breast pocket.

I am convinced his vanity contributed to a long life. From him, I learned that to care for the body—he swam in his nineties—is to respect the Creator's image. One of his favorite words was sumptuous. Life was the banquet to which he was invited every day. He intended to be a graceful guest.

The girl I was is within me

Sometimes I feel as if centuries have elapsed between the summer I turned sixteen, when a human being first stepped onto the moon; the summer I turned seventeen, when I first fell in love; and the digital era in which I live, married for more than thirty years, with three emerging adult children. But then a song comes on the radio and I'm back, time collapsing, no longer the mid-age woman with my share of abundance and trouble, but the ardent, gold girl who was hungry for everything.

I know each note of this song. In the midst of my life, I am awake, immediate. I am who she was, vitality coursing through me, restoring me to a life I can savor not because time has passed, but because I know myself to be continuous, in harmony, vanquishing relentless chronology, the arrow pointed in only one direction.

What a joy to admit her return, to recognize and welcome her. When she and I are one, I cannot be old.

It's their turn

As I walk along the streets of the city, almost everyone is younger than I am. So much awaits them that I have already completed. So many of those who laugh and chat and play with their phones are obliviously beautiful. I register their unlined skin, shining hair past their shoulders, bare legs gleaming.

Then I recall the phrase a friend used long ago about the beauty of young women: It's their turn.

I will continue to care for my face and body—but I am not under the illusion that such care will restore me to their state. No one stays young; it's how we perpetuate the species.

But the years of youth are hard. My friends and I gaze with astonishment at images of ourselves in our twenties. We were beautiful, but we felt repulsive. We ate breakfast in twenty-four-hour diners after dancing all night. Then we cried about how we would never fall in love or get revenge on abusive bosses in our glamorous entry-level jobs.

I am so much happier now.

Hair versus charity

I believe that when I meet my Creator, I will be greeted with these words: "Some months you spent more money on your hair than you did on tzedakah."

Last year, I decided to do the math. The results were not reassuring.

Since I am unwilling to compromise on my hair, I am increasing the balance in my moral bank account by giving away more. Because the most urgent calculation is one I can do in my head: There are far fewer years ahead of me than behind.

The body ailing

When I stride across the park, elated by motion, by my body's capacity to do what I ask, when I take the stairs and beat the escalator beside me, I am the incarnation of thanksgiving. All my bones declare, "Lord, who is like You?"

But when I am ill, I cannot identify with my body at all. Lodged in a present of pain, I feel eviscerated, my self sacked by frailty. I know, absolutely, that no one can help me. My body is an encumbrance I am lugging around, as if I am wearing a sign that says, "Separate from the human condition." My soul, too, has shriveled. I have lost my receptors to glory.

I try to summon the wisdom I've acquired for just these circumstances, but it feels rehearsed. In its stead, an agonizing solitude, terrible, breath-stealing.

"The world is full of broken hearts," a friend reminds me. At the instant of suffering, we are in communion with all those who suffer alongside us.

A voice inside me, so small I can scarcely hear it, begins its chant of solace: Not alone, not alone, not alone.

The big D

Only once have I traveled within, led by a healer's chime through a sequence of dawns I'd lived; and then through a wresting of my childhood self from recalled terror to tenderness and freedom. The journey ended beneath an infinite night sky, darkness a benevolent embrace, without fear, intimate and comforting and protective. Above me was the galaxy, an endless wonder of stars.

No, the journey answered my tormented questions, life is not a speeding diminishment from birth to the end. Everything is immanent. All is light, all is ever dawn. And when the consoling darkness descends, we will join the boundless world, part of creation forever.

Creation, revelation, redemption, return. And then: Creation.

The psalm of my generation proclaims that we are stardust. Our bodies may change form while we live, shrink, protrude, lose parts, become mottled or even mutilated.

"Glory be to God for dappled things," says Gerard Manley Hopkins.

We are made of eternity, our bodies the vessels that make love possible.

Aspirational stance

My aunt, who has always looked much younger than she is, relays her summer of infirmities.

"When you feel pain you never had," I say, "or notice what you can't do, what's your attitude?"

She thinks.

"Bemused."

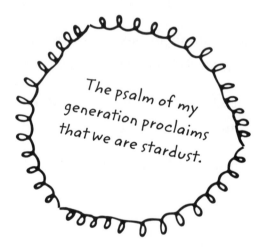

The psalm of my generation proclaims that we are stardust.

Tools and Resources

Chapter 12: Staying Fit Is a Mitzvah

TO ESTABLISH A WALKING REGIMEN:

Visit *KCET City Walk* (www.kcet.org/shows/city-walk), a series of 30-minute episodes exploring pedestrian life in Los Angeles, Portland, Boston, Atlanta, Washington, DC, and New York that explores how walking is "reconnecting us to our bodies, our civic values, and public space."

An interesting video to watch is "The Transformative Power of Walking" by Vancouver, BC, city planner Sandra James at TEDxCarsonCity (www.youtube.com/watch?v = 2-8ams9yG98).

WANT TO DROP A FEW POUNDS, EAT HEALTHIER, OR GET MORE EXERCISE? THERE ARE APPS FOR THAT.

For counting calories and logging exercise: Lose It! (https://www.loseit.com/). Free.

Map My Walk (https://www.mapmywalk.com/us/). Uses the GPS in your phone to map out walking routes, record details of your workout, and calculate the number of calories you've burned. (If you're a runner or a cyclist, try Map My Run or Map My Ride.)

My Fitness Pal (https://www.myfitnesspal.com/). A free one-stop shop for setting your weight-loss goals, recording what you eat, and tracking your activities. With a food database of more than 5 million items and a bar code scanner, you can make the best choices at home, in the supermarket, and in restaurants.

OTHER TYPES OF EXERCISE:

Dance of all kinds is good for the soul and the body.

The Feldenkrais Method (https://www.feldenkrais.com/) applies gentle, mindful movement in basic positions, such as sitting or lying on the floor, standing, or sitting in a chair to help a person develop new alternatives to habitual patterns of movement.

Pilates workouts (https://www.mayoclinic.org/healthy-lifestyle/fitness/in-depth/pilates-for-beginners/art-20047673) build strength in your core muscles for better posture, balance, and flexibility.

You can find the RBG Workout here: https://rbgworkout.com/.

YOGA VIDEOS/DVDS:

Aerobic Yoga: The Flow Series with Tracey Rich and Ganga White. Based on a flow series, linked by sun salutations, this is suitable for experienced students who want to cultivate strength, endurance, and flexibility.

Power & Precision: Power Yoga for Beginners with Baron Baptiste. An offshoot of the popular Pattabhi Jois–based Ashtanga system.

Yoga: Alignment and Form with John Friend. Friend's teaching blends Iyengar-style physical precision with his distinctive brand of psychological and spiritual insight. A marvelous instructional recording for all levels of students.

Yoga at Home: Beginners Level 2; Intermediate Level 1; Intermediate Level 2; Advanced Level 1 with Yogi Hari. Four recordings of gradually increasing levels.

Yoga Workout Series for Beginners with Lilias Folan. Four very mild, 30-minute sessions, culled from Lillias's popular PBS series.

Chapter 13: Taking Care of Your (Emotional) Self

APPS FOR MEDITATION

Learn to meditate in 10 days with Headspace (www.headspace.com).

Time your meditation sessions with Insight Timer (www.insighttimer.com).

ONLINE

Brown, Brené. (June 2010). "The Power of Vulnerability," TED Talk. www.ted.com/talks/brene_brown_on_vulnerability

Stanford Forgiveness Projects (www.learningtoforgive.com). An ongoing series of workshops and research projects that apply forgiveness therapy with people in war-torn areas as well as in corporate, medical, legal, and religious settings.

READINGS

Dess, Nancy K. "Tend and Befriend." *Psychology Today*, September 1, 2000. https://www.psychologytoday.com/articles/200009/tend-and-befriend.

Gogarty, Jim. *The Mandala Coloring Book or Stress Less Coloring.* Boston: Adams Media, 2016.

Rubin, Gretchen. *The Happiness Project.* New York: HarperCollins, 2015. Witty and wise account of an entire year the author devoted to cultivating happiness.

Chapter 14: Visiting Someone Who's Sick

THOUGHTFUL GIFTS TO BRING TO YOUR VISIT:

Nothing shows how much you are thinking about someone than making her a mixtape. Today's version of that would be a Spotify playlist (www.spotify.com).

A deck of playing cards, or a game of Scrabble.

A favorite book of yours that the person might derive some joy from reading.

READING

Pogrebin, Letty Cottin. *How to Be Friends to a Friend Who Is Sick.* New York: Public Affairs, 2013. An extremely useful book that helps the reader navigate this difficult terrain and to be present when it counts.

Chapter 15: Living in the Land of the Sick

It is imperative to have a sense of humor, so get yours in shape!

READINGS

Bowleer, Kate. "What to Say When You Meet the Angel of Death at a Party." *New York Times,* January 28, 2018. https://www.nytimes.com/2018/01/26/opinion/sunday/cancer-what-to-say.html. A *must-read* op-ed piece.

Ostaseski, Frank, with a foreword by Rachel Naomi Remen, MD. *The Five Invitations: Discovering What Death Can Teach Us about Living Fully.* New York: Flatiron Books, 2017. A book about what death can teach you, from a Buddhist perspective.

Pantilat, Steven Z., MD. *Life after the Diagnosis.* New York: DaCapo Press, 2017. A book about living with illness.

Tip: If you want to know more, there are myriad sources accessible on the internet. Some are more reputable, responsible, and well-written than others. Check first with sites from major medical or research institutions, such as the National Institutes of Health, the National Cancer Center, or organizations for the disease or condition you are investigating.

Chapter 16: Mourning and Moving On

Brener, Rabbi Anne. *Mourning and Mitzvah: A Guided Journal for Walking the Mourner's Path through Grief and Healing.* Woodstock, VT: Jewish Lights, 2017. Combines Jewish wisdom with psychotherapeutic exercises.

Caldwell, Gail. *Let's Take the Long Way Home: A Memoir of Friendship.* New York: Penguin Random House, 2010. Caldwell, a Pulitzer Prize winner and former chief book critic for the *Boston Globe*, writes of a profound friendship that transformed her life.

Greenberg, Blu. "Contemporary Reflection." In *The Torah: A Women's Commentary.* New York: WRJ/URJ Press, 2008, pp. 632–633. A short powerful reflection on silence and mourning the death of adult children.

Lamm, Rabbi Maurice. *The Jewish Way in Death and Mourning.* Middle Village, NY: Jonathan David Publishers, 1969. This now-classic guide from a traditional perspective takes the reader from the moment of death through each step of mourning until the end of the first year.

Rapoport, Nessa. *A Woman's Book of Grieving.* New York: William Morrow, 1994.
A slender volume of moving reflections and poetry about loss and grief.

Shiva.com (www.shiva.com). A site entirely devoted to learning and practical resources having to do with Jewish mourning—practices, customs, even help with ordering sympathy gifts.

PART

4

Getting Good at Getting Ready

We live in Los Angeles—earthquake country. Everyone knows that a big earthquake is coming. It's just a matter of time. Yet almost no one is prepared. Preparations aren't hard, but they take time and a certain amount of effort—gathering supplies, organizing emergency stockpiles, planning communication strategies, and checking and updating everything on a regular basis. Maybe we don't want to think about something so unpleasant, we don't feel that we can do anything about it, or we don't want to exhaust ourselves with making lists of everything that needs to be done. Whatever stops us from preparing now, our biggest impediment is denial. And when the "Big One" happens, we'll be kicking ourselves—or worse—that we didn't spend the time and effort when we had the chance.

Dying is like a California earthquake in one respect: It's inevitable. We don't know when it's going to happen, but it's a certainty. We can do lots of things to prepare for this eventuality and yet almost none of us is prepared. Because, just like that earthquake, we're in denial, reluctant to imagine that the fate of all flesh is our fate as well.

Perhaps we think that the consequences of not planning won't make much of a difference to us. We'll be dead, after all. But for our families and friends, the consequences of not planning are enormous. Confusion about what kind of end-of-life care we want . . . or don't want. Panic about not knowing how to find key documents and valuables. Sudden expenditures and decisions that must be made in the chaos of the moment. Arguments between siblings, spouses, and children about how and where and whether we are to be buried. All of these are avoidable if we just take the time and make the effort to write down our preferences, make a list of critical information, and communicate our plans to our loved ones.

Part 4 is about preparing—getting organized and getting ready—to facilitate our life completion and to help those who will live on after us. Whether it's organizing our personal affairs—estate planning,

If you believe you can accomplish everything by "cramming" at the 11th hour, by all means, don't lift a finger now. But you may think twice about beginning to build your ark once it has already started raining.

—Max Brooks, The Zombie Survival Guide: Complete Protection from the Living Dead

preparing an advance health-care directive—or preplanning our funeral, the choices and documentation we make and share now will help ease the anxiety, confusion, and stress of our loved ones and allow them more room to grieve and heal.

Lack of planning also has consequences for ourselves as well. We miss the opportunity to reflect on our lives. In his germinal book From *Age-ing to Sage-ing*, Rabbi Zalman Schachter-Shalomi encourages us to think about this stage as the October, November, and December of our lives and to do the work he calls "harvesting." "By harvesting, I mean gathering in the fruits of a lifetime's experience and enjoying them in old age," he writes. "The more we embrace our mortality, not as an aberration of God and nature but as an agent urging us on to life completion, the more our anxiety transforms into feelings of awe, thanksgiving, and appreciation."

Getting Your Stuff Together
by Leah M. Bishop

Leah M. Bishop, a partner at Loeb & Loeb LLP in Los Angeles, is a friend and congregant of Laura's. Named 2018 Best Lawyer of the Year for Trusts and Estates (Los Angeles), she lectures widely on charitable giving and estate planning.

Words of Wisdom

Rabbi Eliezer would say: "Prepare for your death one day before your death." His disciples asked: "Does a person know on which day they will die?" Said he to them: "This being the case, you should prepare today, for perhaps tomorrow you will die."
—Pirkei Avot 2:10

I once had a client who could not access any of her bank accounts after her husband died because he did all their banking online, and she didn't know the passwords. Another client carefully put all her important papers in a safe deposit box, but only she had access to the box. As an estate planning attorney, I have witnessed innumerable times when critical information has been unavailable to family members because it was known only to the person who died or became incapacitated. Stressful emotional times become even more difficult if important information isn't accessible. In February 2014 I sat down with my 91-year-old mother to complete a personal affairs organizer I developed to compile vital information so it would be readily available when needed. Three months later, my mother had a stroke that left her unable to communicate essential information. Having her personal affairs organizer was invaluable to me in handling her affairs.

One of the greatest acts of love is to be organized, so that our family and friends can grieve without the distraction and stress of trying to find essential information or figure out who is in charge of decisions.

Components of the Personal Affairs Organizer

Several predesigned personal affairs organizers are available online (see Part 4 Tools and Resources). (You can access the template I developed at www.behrmanhouse.com/ggago.) Here are the basic categories any organizer must have:

- Personal Information, Family, and Other Important Contacts
- Medical/Health Information
- Financial Information

- House and Car Information
- Digital Account Numbers, Passwords, and Answers to Security Questions
- Funeral Arrangements
- Death Certificate Information
- Location of Important Papers

Tip: Review the document twice a year, when the clocks change, like smoke alarm batteries.

Keep in mind that your personal affairs organizer needs to be updated as your life changes—for example, your doctor retires, you change passwords, or you consolidate accounts—and this requires a level of discipline that most of us lack. When you are discouraged by this, imagine your family members trying to sort through all of this without you.

Keeping It Safe and Accessible

Because of the amount of information required, completing a personal affairs organizer can be a daunting task. Figuring out where to store it and who should know about it are equally challenging. If the document is on your computer and others have access to your computer, you may want to password-protect it. But if you do so, be sure that someone you trust knows where to find the document and has the password. You may want to print it, put it in a sealed envelope, and hide it in your house, but be sure someone knows where it's hidden. Protecting the privacy of confidential information—and ensuring that the right person will be able to find it when it's needed—is a delicate balance.

Make sure your spouse or partner and grown children (if any) know about the document and where you keep it. Or designate a close friend or trusted colleague as your agent under a power of attorney, and make sure she knows where to find the document.

The Personal Affairs Organizer Is Not Enough

No one should have to guess what we wanted to do with our estate, and we should not allow state law, rather than our wishes, govern how our property is divided up, which will happen if we die without a will or trust (known as "intestacy"). We all should have our wishes specified in a will or a revocable trust, which is a legal document set up to dispose of personal assets.

Both a written will and a revocable trust allow you to determine how your assets are distributed and to whom, but in most states a trust allows you to avoid probate of your estate. Depending on where you live, probate can take months or years to complete. On the other hand, a revocable trust generally involves higher legal fees. Keep in mind that any estate taxes that may be due are a separate issue and are not affected by whether your estate passes under a will or a trust.

ACCiDENTS MAY CATCH US BY SURPRISE.

THiS MAN WAS HiT BY A LOW-FLYiNG BLiMP.

A lawyer experienced in trusts and estates can help you understand these complicated legal matters and draw up the will or trust for you. She will be able to answer your questions as you go through the process of thinking about what you want to accomplish and how best to do it. Some other things to consider:

- If you sign a trust, make sure to place all your transferable assets, such as bank accounts, brokerage accounts, or real estate, into the trust in order to complete the estate planning process.

- Make sure that beneficiary designations—for example, for life insurance, retirement assets, annuities—are accurate and kept up-to-date.

- While you are healthy, take the time to fill out an advance directive for health care (also known as a durable power of attorney for health care, a health-care proxy, or a medical directive) that directs who makes medical decisions if you cannot and what you would want those medical decisions to be. (See chapter 19, "Planning for What You Don't Want to Plan For.")

- Authorize one or more people you trust—a spouse, an adult child, or a close friend—to receive confidential medical information so they can help you make intelligent and compassionate health-care decisions if you are incapacitated. Make sure to sign a financial or asset

> Your estate includes all your property, such as your financial assets, real estate holdings, jewelry, artwork, and heirlooms.

durable power of attorney, which is a document that authorizes other individuals to handle your financial matters if you become unable to do so. This is important because even if you have a revocable trust, not all your assets can be transferred into it—for example, life insurance, retirement accounts, Social Security, credit cards, medical benefits, or other assets your attorney will tell you about.

Estate planning and completing a personal affairs organizer are not fun projects. But completing a personal affairs organizer will give you a great sense of accomplishment and might even earn you the eternal gratitude of your family. Remember: The biggest impediment to planning for death or incapacity is denial. Many of my clients begin the discussion of all these matters with "If I die . . ." I stop them and tell them that death is not a possibility, but a certainty—the only question is when.

Probate is a court proceeding in which the court determines, based on your will, who your beneficiaries are and the creditors who need to be paid before your estate can be distributed.

Do not store your personal affairs organizer in a safe deposit box. Your family may not be able to access it if they don't know where the box is or can't find the key.

Planning for What You Don't Want to Plan For

by Rabbi Elliot N. Dorff

Elliot N. Dorff, a leading expert in bioethics, is a colleague of Laura and Richard. As the chairman of the Rabbinical Assembly's (Conservative movement) Committee on Jewish Law and Standards, he has written many opinions and legal rulings on various aspects of Jewish law and ethics. An award-winning author, he has written 13 books and is editor or coeditor of another 14.

Words of Wisdom

It is important that we realize there is no "date with destiny." Destiny doesn't just appear on our calendar waiting for us at the nearest Starbucks. ... Destiny equals the creative response to the impermanence of life.

— Rabbi Dina London

Medical care has changed dramatically in the last century. Until recently, doctors could do little to cure diseases or postpone death. Now doctors have at their disposal medications and machines that can literally stop us from dying and return us to life. I am one of the beneficiaries of those advances. I inherited from my father's side of the family a weakness in my bronchial tubes. My uncle died of bronchitis that turned into pneumonia in his early 20s in the 1920s. Pneumonia used to be "a dying person's best friend" because it brought on death sooner and less painfully than living through the course of other diseases. I was lucky enough to be born after the discovery of penicillin, however, and so I have had bronchitis 15 or 20 times in my life and am alive and well in my 70s.

Antibiotics, though, can cure one thing while leaving us suffering from a host of other problems. Now we have to consider carefully whether the use of an antibiotic is advisable or not in a particular situation. If this is true of antibiotics, it is all the more so of recently introduced procedures that may be invasive, complicated, or involve multiple internal systems, such as organ transplants or cancer treatments.

With these advances in medicine come modern-day quandaries: Should we do something just because we can? A particular medical procedure may prolong our life but may diminish our quality of life, or what is involved may conflict with our personal ethics. So the question becomes "Do I want that for me?"

In Western countries, such as the United States, where individual autonomy and rights are sacred, these questions are not only for health-care personnel but for all of us. The advance directive for health care (ADHC) is a legal document developed in the last several decades to help us consider and communicate the medical interventions that we do and do not want done to us as part of the dying process.

What Is an Advance Directive?

An advance directive for health care consists of two parts:

1. *A durable power of attorney for health care.* The ADHC identifies the person you want to make health-care decisions for you when you cannot make them for yourself. Unlike other powers of attorney, which generally govern financial matters and expire when you become incapacitated, a durable power of attorney for health care takes effect only when you can no longer make health-care decisions on your own. Usually the document includes your name, an assertion that you are of sound mind, and the name and contact information of the person you want to make decisions for you—your surrogate decision maker. The document should also include the names and contact information of a second and third person, in case the previous designee is unable or unwilling to serve in this capacity. Depending on the civil law in your jurisdiction, the document then must be signed, witnessed, and/or notarized.

2. *A "living will."* This part of the ADHC expresses your desires and preferences about your future medical care under various circumstances and situations. None of us knows how we will die or the questions that will arise in that process, but a living will asks us to respond to health-care questions that commonly arise when someone is dying. So, for example, you may be in an irreversible coma or a vegetative state; you may survive with medical interventions but end up with permanent mental or physical disability; you may be mentally awake and aware but suffer immense pain that can be controlled only by making you unconscious; you may have dementia. In these and other situations, the living will expresses your wishes: To stay alive

> Whom should you choose to be your health-care agent? The most important factor is trust that the person will make the decisions you would make and not be intimidated by the wishes or judgments of other people, including other family members. This is made easier if you have had "the conversation" with all the people who will be there at the end of your life so everyone is clear about what matters to you.

no matter what your physical or mental condition? To attempt to find a cure but continually reevaluate? To limit treatment to less-invasive interventions? To provide comfort care only? The ADHC also specifies which medical interventions you want or do not want: Cardiopulmonary resuscitation? Major surgery? Mechanical breathing? Dialysis? Blood transfusions? Artificial nutrition and hydration? Antibiotics?

Why Fill Out an Advance Directive?

In 1973, California was the first state in the United States to pass living will legislation, and subsequently every American state and many other nations have adopted such legislation. The reason for doing so goes back to Western Enlightenment convictions that we all have individual rights, including the right to determine our own health care in advance so that doctors and family members, or other surrogate decision makers, know what we want and follow those wishes.

The problem is that if you are mentally incapacitated, your doctors are going to ask your family members what to do and will generally follow their instructions, no matter what you wrote in your living will. The reason for that is simple: You will not sue your doctors after you die, but your family members might. Furthermore, even if the doctors and hospitals that follow an explicit advance directive win in court, they do not want to spend the time and incur the expense involved in litigating their decisions. So the advance directive works to determine care under one of these three conditions:

1. Your surrogate decision maker agrees to follow your wishes.
2. You have no family members or surrogates willing to make medical decisions for you.
3. There is a dispute among family members as to the end-of-life care you should receive.

THE SUDDEN DEATH OF THEODORE PEPPER DEL POE.

The real reason to fill out an advance directive, then, is so that your adult children, partner, siblings, or close friends can avoid a situation in which your dying process becomes a bone of contention among them. As a longtime member of the Ethics Committee of UCLA Medical Center, and in consultation with families elsewhere as well, I have unfortunately witnessed more than a few situations where what to tell the doctors to do in treating Mom or Dad has become the source of very tense family arguments and frayed relationships. I actually have heard one adult child say, "Mom and I did not get along very well during her life, but in the end I was there for her and you guys killed her."

We all want to avoid that kind of family dynamic, and an advance directive can be an important tool in doing so. In filling out your ADHC, get help from your doctor or someone who knows what the various medical interventions entail. I was that person for my mother-in-law. When it came time to fill out her ADHC, she first told me, "I want everything." I said, "Okay, let's go through the various interventions so you see what you want." I then told her that if she wanted cardiopulmonary resuscitation, that often includes breaking her bones. She said, "Oh, no, I would not want that." We then went on to the next intervention, and when she understood what it entailed, she did not want that either. It turned out that she wanted nothing but to be kept comfortable. When she said "I want everything," she did not understand the medical realities and consequences of the possible interventions. Furthermore, she really meant that she was afraid of being abandoned by her doctors, a fear that I understand but one that should not result in taking medical actions that might conflict with her personal wishes.

So ask your doctor, another medical professional you trust, or perhaps your rabbi for help in filling out your advance directive. Then get it signed, witnessed, and/or notarized, as your civil jurisdiction requires, and give copies to your primary care physician, your lawyer, and the person who holds your durable power of attorney for health care.

Finally, call a meeting of your family and hand out copies of your advance directive to each adult member. None of us likes to contemplate, let alone discuss, our own death or that of a loved one, but the document provides a convenient focus. The ADHC can help everyone get over the reticence to talk about dying and death, and face the issues involved. Review the document with everyone present. That way, if one of your children serves as your surrogate decision maker, he or she can plausibly say to the others, "Look, we were all there when Dad gave us the advance directive and described what he wanted and did not want. I personally may make different decisions for myself, but I am simply carrying out Dad's wishes." This will not guarantee good relationships among your children after you die, but at least your dying process is less likely to be a cause of friction among them.

How Different Jewish Denominations View the Directives

A variety of medical associations and hospitals offer advance health-care directives (see Part 4 Tools and Resources), and so do the largest religious movements in North American Judaism, with each template reflecting that movement's ideology. Each denomination's approach is described below.

ORTHODOX

The advance directive endorsed by the Modern Orthodox Rabbinical Council of America states that the person filling it out is an Orthodox Jew and wants his or her health-care decisions to be determined by Jewish law as the Orthodox understand it. It then identifies the person's rabbi with his contact information, and that's the end of it.

There is a range of opinions among all the movements about end-of-life situations. For example, Rabbi J. David Bleich, a professor at Yeshiva University and an authority on bioethics, maintains that everything should be done to keep a person alive, regardless of that person's mental or physical state. Rabbi Moshe Tendler, a biology professor at Yeshiva University, does not require initiating medical procedures to keep a person alive, but, once initiated, he maintains that they cannot be withdrawn. Rabbi Immanuel Jakobovits, who wrote the first comprehensive book in English on Jewish medical ethics, instructs physicians that if they are using a heart-lung machine to enable a patient to recover and it becomes clear that the patient will not recover, they may turn it off. The use of a timer to do this has become the accepted method to deal with medical interventions involving machines in certain Orthodox circles, particularly in Israel.

CONSERVATIVE

The Conservative movement's advance directive is similar to the Orthodox in that it is guided by Jewish law.

The prevailing opinion is to withhold and withdraw machines and medications from patients for whom they are not helpful in preserving the health or life of the patient. However, there are two opinions about artificial nutrition and hydration. One sees it as the equivalent of the food and liquids we all need throughout our lives because it functions

The case of Terri Schiavo, a woman in an irreversible, persistent vegetative state from 1990 to 2005, brought on by cardiac arrest, illustrates the differing opinions among clergy, as well as bioethicists. One opinion is that the patient's artificial nutrition and hydration should not have been removed throughout the full 15 years of her end-of-life treatment, while another would maintain that it should have been removed one year after she entered a persistent vegetative state. Why? Because by then it was clear that despite the various forms of therapy that had been tried, she could not regain consciousness, and her husband attested that she would not want to live in an unconscious state, supported by machines.

in place of those nutrients when a patient cannot ingest them on her own. Therefore, artificial nutrition and hydration must be given whenever a patient needs it and may not be withdrawn until the patient dies. In contrast, the other opinion views artificial nutrition as the equivalent of medicine because it lacks many of the characteristics of food, such as taste, temperature, or texture, and it comes into the body through tubes, rather than the usual way food and liquids are ingested by mouth. This means that artificial nutrition can be withheld or withdrawn under the same conditions that medicines may be—namely, when they are not in the best interests of the patient, as defined by the patient's advance directive (or surrogate decision maker) and based on the patient's medical condition.

REFORM

The Reform movement does not have an advance directive officially adopted by either its rabbinic or synagogue organizations. Rabbi Richard Address, however, the former director of the Department of Jewish Family Concerns at the Union of Reform Judaism and the founding director of Jewish Sacred Aging, has created an advance directive that reflects the Reform emphasis on individual autonomy. Examples of that guidance, together with the guidance provided by the other movements, are listed in the Part 4 Tools and Resources section.

In most jurisdictions, if you or someone on your behalf calls 911, the emergency personnel must do everything possible to keep you alive, regardless of what you indicated in your advance directive. However, you can complete a document called a POLST (Physician Orders for Life Sustaining Treatment) that spells out the limits of emergency care and is valid in almost every state, thus enabling chronically ill, terminally ill, and elderly individuals to have more control over their end-of-life care. It is meant to complement an ADHC and requires a conversation between you (or your health-care agent) and your physician, who each must sign the form. Keep it in a place that is quickly accessible to emergency-care personnel. A best practice is to attach it to the door of your refrigerator.

IS ORGAN DONATION PERMISSIBLE?

Most religious authorities, regardless of denomination, allow us to provide in an advance directive that our organs and tissues may be used for transplant into another person before burial. Organ and tissue donation must take place immediately after death for the organs to be viable, so the funeral will not be postponed. Because Jewish burial rites use a closed casket, nobody will see our sewn-up body. Thousands of lives are lost each year for lack of an organ transplant.

Advance Directives for Teenagers?

My admittedly unusual idea is that as soon as a teenager gets a driver's license, she or he should fill out an advance directive. In other words, this should be an activity for juniors and seniors in high school and certainly for college students. While such documents filled out by minors would not have legal force, the very process of filling one out would impress on young drivers the responsibility they are undertaking in driving a car. Furthermore, many of the hardest legal cases about end-of-life care—for example, those involving Karen Ann Quinlan, Nancy Cruzan, and Terri Schiavo—were about young people in their 20s, when people presume that they will live forever and never even consider, let alone communicate, what kind of care they would want if they suffered some catastrophic event that undermined their ability to decide for themselves.

Don't Wait

Without an advance directive, loved ones face real dilemmas in knowing what you would want in terms of medical care if you were no longer able to make your own medical decisions. Even in the most closely knit families, that can lead to tension and hard feelings. It also can lead to your family deciding in a way that you yourself would never want.

So fill out an advance directive for health care, and encourage your loved ones to do so now, regardless of their age.

CHAPTER 20

Having the Last Word in Funeral Planning

by Richard Siegel and Rabbi Laura Geller

Words of Wisdom

If Shaw and Einstein couldn't beat death, what chance have I got? Practically none.

—Mel Brooks

We plan for every major life event. That planning is often fun and filled with joy.

When expecting a baby, we may visit the hospital where the birth will occur, take childbirth classes, furnish a nursery, attend to the details of a *brit* (if it's a boy) or a naming ceremony (if it's a girl), and read reams of information about pregnancy and parenting.

Planning for a bar or bat mitzvah can take several years: enrolling our child in religious school, finding an open Saturday around the time of our child's birthday on the synagogue calendar, deciding whether to have a Kiddush lunch or a kids' party or both, shopping for a tallit, hiring a tutor, helping our teen write the speech (or not).

A wedding, whether our own or our child's, entails endless details and decisions: choosing an officiant, picking the date, finding the right venue, mapping out the ceremony, giving roles to family and friends, drawing up the guest list, writing a marriage contract (*ketubah*), selecting the menu, hiring the band, choosing the music. And so on.

No one questions our need and responsibility to plan these major life transitions. No one questions the time it takes to plan them thoughtfully and carefully, because planning is essential to their success. We wouldn't leave such planning entirely to other people or start thinking about it the day before.

Yet most of us don't plan for the biggest event of our adult lives—our death.

We are all a bit like a comedian who once quipped, "I'm not

afraid of death; I just don't want to be there when it happens." Many of us are reluctant to think about it, and even those of us who do often don't plan for it. But avoiding the subject does not make it go away. It just means that we—and others—won't be ready when it happens. We lose out on the gratification of participating in our last act, as unpleasant as the planning may seem initially.

URN FILLED WITH ASHES OF GRANDPA TUBBS.

← THERE MIGHT BE A LITTLE OF GRANNY IN THERE TOO.

Planning Your Funeral

Preparing for our final moments involves creating instructions about our funeral to help those we will be leaving behind. By not planning, we leave it to family members or friends to make major decisions at the last minute, at a time when they are vulnerable and often confused or in conflict with one another about what we might have wanted. Some planning is a gift to those we leave behind, who will be relieved to know that the choices they make are the ones we wanted.

Because we don't know when we will die, we must plan for it sooner rather than later, because later could be too late. Preplanning a funeral can be done at any time, and decisions that we make are not (yet) set in stone. (See "Components of the Personal Affairs Organizer," in chapter 18, "Getting Your Stuff Together", and chapter 21 "Talking about Life and Death.")

DO YOU WANT TO BE BURIED OR CREMATED?

Either choice has advantages and disadvantages.

What about Tradition?

Traditional Jewish law makes it clear that the dead must be buried in the earth. Genesis 3:19 tells us, "For dust you are and to dust you will return"; Deuteronomy 21:23 specifies that in the case of the body of a convicted criminal, "you shall surely bury him." Later rabbinic teachings, such as the Talmud (*Sanhedrin* 46b), Maimonides's *Sefer Hamitzvot*, and the *Shulchan Aruch* emphasize that the dead are to be buried. Other reasons for burial include the mystical tradition's view that the soul doesn't immediately leave the body, so burial provides the opportunity for a gradual separation. Another is the belief that our body belongs to God—it's only lent to us—and we need to return it intact. Since humans are understood to be created in the image of God, cremation has been seen as a desecration of God's own image. Jewish tradition also includes a belief in the resurrection of the dead when the Messiah comes, which Maimonides, the great medieval philosopher and codifier of Jewish law, publicly declared to be among the 13 fundamental principles of faith. Choosing cremation suggests otherwise.

THiS TRee WAS FORMERLY MiNDY Jo FEiGENBUSH

For all these reasons, until very recently cremated remains were not buried or placed in a mausoleum in a Jewish cemetery. (This proscription does not apply to those who were cremated against their will, including victims of the Holocaust.) What's more, even if a person requested cremation, the next of kin were not expected to honor the request.

For many of us, these are no longer compelling reasons to avoid cremation. Many of us do not believe in a messiah or the resurrection of the dead. Some of us believe that if God can resurrect from bones, God can surely also resurrect from ashes.

What about the Environment?

The same biblical story that tells of the creation of the first human out of dust continues with a description of that human placed in the garden "to till and to guard it." From this and many other sources comes the Jewish imperative to protect the environment. It is hard to determine whether burial or cremation is more environmentally friendly.

Cremation requires the same amount of energy—natural gas and electricity—that a typical American uses in six days. On the other hand, a traditional burial usually involves a coffin made from wood that needs to be manufactured and often shipped from another location, and many cemeteries require coffins to be encased in concrete vaults to prevent the ground from collapsing. Burials also have fossil fuel costs connected to maintaining cemetery grounds. So neither has a light carbon footprint.

For people concerned about the environment who want a traditional in-ground burial, many cemeteries now offer "green burials," where preservation of the natural habitat takes precedence over manicured lawns. Graves in the green burial sections are separated from the rest of the cemetery and don't have chiseled tombstones or headstones. The graves are either unmarked or marked by natural rocks. The deceased are buried either in biodegradable caskets or simple shrouds without caskets, which is a traditional Jewish custom and the preferred custom in Israel.

Burial vs. Cremation

- The expected and customary religious traditions

- Funeral does not have to be delayed

- Bodies can be exhumed and relocated, if necessary

- Comfort in accompanying the deceased to the final resting place

- Environmentally conscious options are available

- Higher cost than cremation

- Body decomposes in the ground

- Subject to the rules of the cemetery

- Usually less expensive than burial

- Remains can be scattered, buried, or kept

- Perceived as more environmentally friendly than burial

- Memorial service usually occurs without the body present, so more flexibility about timing of memorial service

- Waiting for the final disposition of the body or ashes is often emotionally complicated

- Takes several days for the cremation to take place

- Scattered remains often means no permanent memorial

- Considered by some to be contrary to Jewish tradition

Cremation urns come in a variety of forms, including the *Poetree*, designed for those with an ecological bent.

According to the designer, Margaux Ruyant of DSK International School of Design, "Poetree is a funeral urn that evolves over time. . . . The ashes are placed in the urn, covered with soil, and a tree sapling is planted in the soil. When the tree is big enough, the urn can be planted in a garden or a park. Eventually the urn, which is made of a biodegradable material, will disappear and only the tree and the ceramic ring will remain."

Other Questions to Consider

Do you want to choose what your parents or grandparents chose? Or is your decision an aesthetic or emotional one? For some of us, watching a casket being lowered into the ground is a powerful experience. So too with the tradition of mourners shoveling earth on the casket and, in many cases, actually filling up the grave with dirt. The thud of the earth upon the casket can be both heartbreaking and cathartic at the same time, reinforcing the finality of death. While cremated remains can be buried, even in many Jewish cemeteries, the remains of a cremated human body fill up a container just a little bigger than a shoebox. Placing earth over such a small container may not produce the same emotional jolt. Will your loved ones want to visit a physical place in a cemetery or another setting where ashes might be scattered?

IF YOU CHOOSE A CEMETERY, WHICH ONE AND WHERE?

Many of us will choose to be buried near where we live. However, we might want to be buried with our ancestors in the place we were born or even in Israel. Different cemeteries and mortuaries offer different packages, and the costs and aesthetics can vary considerably. A Jewish cemetery, mortuary, or funeral home will be knowledgeable about Jewish customs, such as having earth available to shovel on the casket. You may find it helpful to visit several and talk with the advisors about their services, options, and costs.

A mortuary or funeral home prepares the body for burial, arranges for the casket or urn, and handles the funeral service, death certificate, and other funeral-related items. The cemetery takes care of everything related to the actual interment, including the burial site, opening and closing the grave, the gravestone or marker, and perpetual care of the site. Cemeteries often offer mortuary services as well, so it can be a one-stop service; otherwise, these are handled by separate businesses.

It's an ancient Jewish custom to purchase a gravesite during one's lifetime and own it outright prior to burial. The Torah states explicitly that Abraham bought a grave for Sarah, where other biblical matriarchs and patriarchs were eventually buried, and that Joseph was buried in a family plot acquired by his father, Jacob. Even in more modern times, it was common for people to buy plots through the burial society of a fraternal or religious organization. Today we can also buy plots directly from a cemetery, whether in a Jewish cemetery or a multifaith cemetery or a community cemetery. Jewish cemeteries used to bar the burial of non-Jews and even non-Jewish spouses of Jews. That has changed as the Jewish community has become much more inclusive, accepting, and welcoming of marriage between partners of different faith backgrounds.

Buried in the Ground or in a Wall?

According to traditional Jewish practice, burial in the ground is preferable to burial in a wall, but there is also a long tradition of burial in a crypt or mausoleum. The very burial plot that Abraham bought for Sarah is, in fact, a cave, called the Cave of Machpelah. Biblical stories suggest that Moses and Aaron were interred on mountainsides. And Isaiah 22:16 refers to the practice of "digging a grave on high and carving out in the rock an abode." At different times in Jewish history aboveground burial was practiced in Italy, Tunisia, Libya, Asia Minor, and Egypt. In Israel, examples of aboveground interment include the ancient archaeological sites of Sanhedria and Beit She'arim. Ultimately, we decide based on aesthetics as well as personal beliefs, family history, and more.

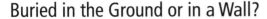

WHAT DOES A FUNERAL COST?

Long before Sam and Doris died, they went with their adult children to the cemetery to make all their decisions. First, they all met with a funeral planning counselor, who answered their questions about costs and options. Then they visited the showroom with the different caskets. They might have been tempted by the ones with the lavish interior but in the end decided that wasn't worth the money because, no matter what, they were intending to rest in peace, if not in silk. The only conflict came when they toured the grounds to choose the site. Doris wanted side-by-side plots; Sam was more interested in two plots, one on top of the other, because it cost less money. Doris turned to her daughter and whispered, "He's been on top of me for all these years; I don't want it for eternity!"

Won't You Be My Neighbor—for Eternity?

Pete and Diane married later in life, after the death of Pete's wife and Diane's divorce. Pete always assumed that the plot next to his late wife would be his. That is what his children expect as well. But now, after 30 years of marriage, Pete and Diane want to be buried next to each other. In this case, the easy answer is to buy an additional plot on the other side of what will become Pete's, but such space may or may not available. There is no right or wrong answer in situations like this. Discuss it as a couple and share your considerations with family members. Decisions like this should never be left to the last minute (and probably not left to adult children!).

Planning ahead, making decisions about our burial or cremation and funeral, as well as making financial arrangements to cover our funeral costs, relieves a burden from our loved ones at a time of considerable stress for them. Even if we leave sufficient funds to cover the costs, our survivors might have trouble accessing them, especially on short notice. Buying a cemetery plot or paying in advance for elements of our funeral locks in today's prices. If costs are intimidating, there are always installment—or should we say, "layaway"—plans.

When it comes to cemetery property, like other real estate decisions, "location, location, location" is a major factor in the cost. Some people want a spot with a beautiful view or near a tree. Others don't care because they'll be dead. Loved ones, however, might care about where they visit a grave. According to funeral directors we consulted in Los Angeles, the cost of a plot can range from a few thousand dollars to more than $30,000, depending on the cemetery.

After the burial plot, the casket is one of the most expensive elements of a funeral, ranging from $700 to $1000 for a plain wooden casket up to $30,000 for a more elaborate or ornate coffin. Choosing a casket can be an emotional experience. Jewish tradition specifies a plain wooden casket or simple shrouds to remind us that we are all equal in death, and since traditional Jewish funeral services don't include a public viewing of the body, the inside aesthetics of the casket don't matter. Still, there are many choices of materials, interior linings, commemorative panels, and internal hardware and designs.

When you purchase in advance, the decisions are up to you. Ask to see a complete list of prices before you see the caskets, in case some of them are not displayed in the showroom. While most of us will buy our casket from a funeral home, we can also buy one online or even build it ourselves.

Instructions for making the simple pine casket, preferred in Jewish burials, can be found with an internet search. The estimated cost of materials is around $300. If you make your own, you and your loved ones could decorate the outside of the casket in advance of your death.

Most of the other funeral costs are set by the funeral home or cemetery without any leeway for negotiation or alternatives. Since services and prices vary considerably from one facility to another, it really pays to shop around.

The Federal Trade Commission's Funeral Rule gives you the right to see a complete price list before viewing any caskets.

ANYTHING FOR GRANDMA.

SHE WILL LOVE THE CORINTHIAN LEATHER INTERIOR SIDING.

WHAT ARE THE OPTIONS FOR YOUR FUNERAL SERVICE?

Jewish funerals are brief (or used to be before it became common for multiple family members and friends to give eulogies) and intended to honor the memory of the deceased. A traditional funeral consists of a psalm or two, often the familiar Psalm 23, and, for a woman, the last chapter of the book of Proverbs, "A Woman of Valor" (Eishet Chayil); a eulogy (or two or three); and the memorial prayer "God of Abundant Mercy" (El Malei Rachamim), in which we ask that the soul of the deceased be "bound up in the bond of eternal life." This prayer is typically offered in both Hebrew and English, so you will need to include your Hebrew name on the instructions you leave for those planning your funeral. If you don't know your Hebrew name, your English name could be substituted. Or you could choose a Hebrew name now!

It's often a good idea to have a rabbi at a funeral service because he or she can do things that your friends or loved ones wouldn't know how to do. If you want a rabbi to provide a eulogy, include that in your instructions, and the rabbi will prepare it after a conversation with family members. That conversation is as much a therapy session for the family as it is a way for the rabbi to learn about you and your legacy.

Note to self: I do not want the DANCING KNISHBERGS at my funeral.

Sometimes family members and friends also want to offer eulogies. You decide if you want them to. If you do, determine how many and by whom, and let them know in advance. While eulogies may be cathartic for the mourner, too many can be repetitious and tiring for those in attendance unless the eulogies are thought out and written down. Consider having different people talk about different aspects of your life: a sibling to talk about your family relationships, a friend to talk about your personal qualities, a colleague to talk about your career. You might also want to specify who you don't want to speak.

GRAMMY FESTOON MADE GREAT BORSCHT. SHE IS FOREVER "THE BORSCHT QUEEN."

BERNIE REALLY KNEW HOW TO DANCE AT BAR MITZVAHS

Funerals often include poems or songs that capture the spirit of the deceased. You might want to suggest readings or particular music to be part of your service. Is it "My Way," the Frank Sinatra anthem? Leonard Cohen's "Hallelujah"? James Taylor's "Fire and Rain"? Best not to pick all three, however.

Although flowers were part of a funeral in ancient times, most likely to counter the smell of decay, traditional Jews view flowers as a non-Jewish funeral custom and therefore avoid them because flowers fade. However, it is up to you whether to include them or not. Instead of flowers (or in addition to them), you might want to designate a particular charity to which contributions can be made in your memory, as a lasting part of your legacy.

As technology has changed, funeral practices have changed as well. Some mortuaries now offer the option of live-streaming a service or presenting a (short) video celebrating the life of the deceased. If that is something you'd like as part of your funeral, you might want to create it in your lifetime.

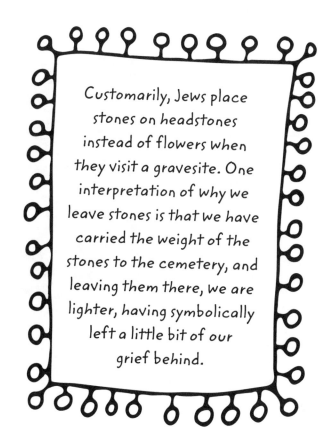

Customarily, Jews place stones on headstones instead of flowers when they visit a gravesite. One interpretation of why we leave stones is that we have carried the weight of the stones to the cemetery, and leaving them there, we are lighter, having symbolically left a little bit of our grief behind.

WHAT DO YOU WANT ON YOUR EPITAPH?

Gravestones (or tombstones, headstones, or tablets) in Jewish cemeteries have often chronicled the history of a Jewish community and provided information for future genealogists. They sometimes include Jewish symbols, such as a Star of David, a Torah scroll, a menorah, or in the case of someone who traces her lineage to the ancient priestly caste, the "hands of blessing." It used to be common to have an acronym of the initial Hebrew letters for the phrase "May his/her soul be bound up in the bond of life."

The epitaph on your gravestone, should you have one, is an opportunity to express your most cherished values and/or personality traits. "Devoted father, husband, son, friend" emphasizes the importance of relationships. At the end of a life, it turns out that what many of us cherish most are our relationships. Not what we did, but who we were to the people whose lives we touched.

Backside of Maxine Menster's gravestone in Iowa. Every time someone asked for her cookie recipe, she said, "Over my dead body."

But maybe you want your gravestone to reflect something else—your sense of humor, a passion, your personality. Do you want your epitaph to capture what was most important to you: "She bore witness to the Holocaust" or "Teacher, Community Activist, Pioneer"? Do you want one that highlights something you were famous for?

Occasionally, epitaphs say something funny. Legendary ones include "See, I told you I was sick!" or "There goes the neighborhood." W. C. Fields's reads, "On the whole, I would rather be in Philadelphia," and George Bernard Shaw's reads, "I knew if I stayed around long enough, something like this would happen."

Sholem Aleichem, the great Yiddish writer, wrote out instructions for his burial and mourning. About his tombstone, he directed: "Wherever I die I should be laid to rest not among the aristocrats, the elite, the rich, but rather among the plain people, the toilers, the common folk, so that the tombstone that will be placed on my grave will grace the simple graves about me, and the simple graves will adorn my tombstone, even as the plain, good people during my lifetime illumined their *Folksschreiber* [people's writer]."

Write It Down and Pass It On

Planning for this major event, like for births, *b'nei mitzvah*, and weddings, gives us a sense of empowerment and a modicum of control that, at a later time, might elude us. The important thing is to think about and discuss the issues with loved ones, come to some decisions, write down instructions, and make sure that family, friends, and clergy know about the plans. It need not be morbid; with a bit of imagination and a sense of humor, it might be a gratifying experience. By having those we love know what we want, we will ease their stress. Even more important, thoughtful planning will help those we love transform the pain of loss into the blessing of memory.

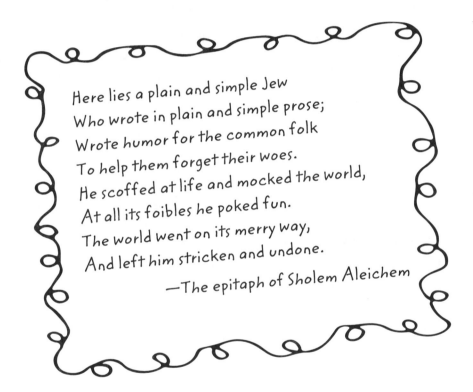

Here lies a plain and simple Jew
Who wrote in plain and simple prose;
Wrote humor for the common folk
To help them forget their woes.
He scoffed at life and mocked the world,
At all its foibles he poked fun.
The world went on its merry way,
And left him stricken and undone.

—The epitaph of Sholem Aleichem

From a Mother to Her Girls

By Rabbi Karyn Kedar

The morning you wake to bury me
you'll wonder what to wear.
The sun may be shining, or maybe it will rain;
it may be winter. Or not.
You'll say to yourself, black, aren't you supposed to
wear black? Then you will remember all the times we went
together to buy clothes: the prom, homecoming,
just another pair of jeans,
another sweater, another pair of shoes. I called you my Barbie dolls.
You will remember how I loved to dress you.
How beautiful you were in my eyes.

The morning you wake to bury me
you will look in the mirror in disbelief.
You'll reach for some makeup. Or not. And you won't believe that
this is the morning you will bury your mother.
But it is. And as you gaze into that mirror, you will
shed a tear. Or not. But look. Look carefully,
for hiding in your expression, you will find mine.
You will see me in your eyes, in the way you laugh
You will feel me when you think of God,
and of love and struggle.

Look into the mirror and you will see me in a look, or in
the way you hold your mouth or stand, a little bent, or maybe straight.
But you will see me.

So let me tell you, one last time, before you dress,
what to wear. Put on any old thing. Black or red, skirt or pants.

Despite what I told you all these years, it doesn't really matter
Because as I told you all these years, you are beautiful the way you are.
Dress yourself in honor and dignity.

Dress yourself in confidence and self-love.
Wear a sense of obligation to do for this world,
for you are one of the lucky ones and there is so much to do, to fix.
Take care of each other,
Take care of your heart, of your soul.
Talk to God.
Wear humility and compassion.

When you wake to bury me,
Put on a strong sense of self, courage, and understanding.
I am sorry. Forgive me. I am sorry.
Stand at my grave clothed in a gown of forgiveness,
dressed like an angel would be, showing compassion
and unconditional love.
For at that very moment, all that will be left of me to give is love.
Love.

Thoughts from a Jewish Communal Leader

Many of the funerals I attend are replete with stories of strength and courage. Acts of generosity. Creative genius. I leave feeling even more grateful for the precious gift of life, intent on finding new ways to express this gratitude.

But it seems that growing numbers of people have come to believe that the number of eulogizers directly correlates with the honor accorded the deceased. Children, grandchildren, colleagues, friends, dignitaries, and more are expected to speak. Stories overlap; funerals have become longer and longer.

A funeral is designed as the public occasion to pay tribute to the deceased by recounting his life story and the acts of kindness and generosity that shed light on the life he lived. It is not about speaking at length about our relationship to the deceased.

The pressure to line up multiple speakers is also unfair to the family. The Jewish funeral is held soon after death, when emotions are still raw. For a child or a sibling to speak requires distancing to gather one's thoughts. To find eloquence in the midst of devastating grief is nearly impossible.

That is not to say that family members need be silent. But perhaps the best way for their voices to be heard is by the rabbi sharing words written by family members that capture the qualities that made this beloved person so special.

I have always found the Jewish laws on death to be acutely attuned to human needs and emotions. They are designed to help us grieve, to honor the dead, and to allow us to continue living. The Mourner's Kaddish does not actually mention death or dying—it is a declaration of faith. And so let us honor these traditions, and in doing so, affirm the beauty and sanctity of life.

— John Ruskay, former president of the
UJA-Federation of New York, in a message to his leadership

CHAPTER 21

Talking about Life and Death
by Rev. Rosemary S. Lloyd
and Harriet Warshaw

Rosemary's Story

At the end of a visit to see my parents and grandparents, who lived several hundred miles away, I realized that the tears that came with saying good-bye were tinged with some fear. My paternal grandfather was in his late 80s, and I had begun to worry as I left that this could very possibly be my last good-bye. I mean, we never know, right?

I felt nervous about saying it, but I couldn't keep the thought to myself any longer. Before getting in the car and heading north, I looked at him and said, "Grandpa, I am sad to think that this could be the last time I see you . . ."

Without hesitating, he replied, "I'm an old man now. I've had a good life. I'm not afraid to die. So don't worry about me, OK? And if I don't see you, I'll see you."

That was it. Short and simple, but it said so much. From then on, with a smile and eyes brimming at the end of every trip—*for years*—one of us would say, "I'll see you," with special meaning.

I was with my grandfather on the last day of his life. He loved hard work in the gardens he tilled with my mother; he had spent hours outside planting a young fig tree with two of his grandsons. He enjoyed dinner with the family and went to bed. In the middle of the night, he called out from his room next to mine. I went to him and turned on a lamp. "What is it, Grandpa?"

"I'm cold," he said, with a faraway look in his eyes.

I roused my mother, also a nurse. As we bundled him in a blanket, our eyes met in a knowing look. I woke up my father and told him to go to Grandpa, that he might be dying.

In our research for this book, we became aware of the Conversation Project, an innovative organization cofounded by Pulitzer Prize-winning journalist Ellen Goodman to help individuals talk with their families about their end-of-life decisions. Harriet Warshaw is the executive director of the Conversation Project, and Rosemary S. Lloyd is their advisor to faith communities.

Words of Wisdom

Can we talk?
—Joan Rivers

Imagine being awakened from a deep sleep like that! Startled and afraid, my father said, "Call 9-1-1!" Recalling my grandfather's clear message over the years, I paused and sat down on the edge of the bed. Placing my hand on my father's shoulder, I said, "Dad, Grandpa is 94. He has had a good, long life. He told me he is not afraid to die." As gently as I could, I explained what would happen if he was taken to the hospital and his heart stopped. "I would hate to think of his 94-year-old body treated that way. This is a good way to die: at home, with all of us around him." Instead of dialing 9-1-1, I phoned my grandfather's other two sons and asked them to come quickly, and the three adult children circled their father's bed as he took his final breaths.

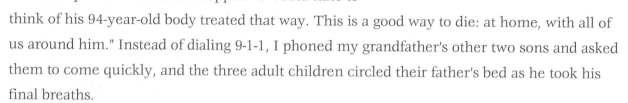

My grandfather died the way so many Americans say they wish to die: at home, peacefully, with loved ones surrounding them. But too often we see people struggling in intensive care units, undergoing unwelcome treatments. I am so grateful we had that conversation years before and over time. We quietly and comfortably acknowledged that our time together was precious because we knew it was limited. Knowing he was not afraid helped us all to face his death unafraid. Our conversation all those years ago is a legacy of consciousness and courage I carry with me to this day, and his dying moments granted me the hope that I too may have such peace when it is my turn.

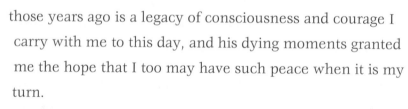

Part of aging well is planting wisdom trees for future generations. My grandfather's frank and faithful example of how to speak—elder to child or grandchild—is one I hope I am wise enough to emulate. Some of us will want "everything" at the end. Some will want limited treatment. The gift of alleviating confusion—and possibly conflict—amid crisis arises from telling those we will ultimately leave behind what grounds us as we age.

Talking about What We Want with Those We Love

One of the paths to mastering getting good at getting older is learning how to talk to our children, partners, friends, and doctors about the kind of care we want—or don't want—at the end of our one precious, unique life.

Although we hear all the time about the awkwardness or difficulty of this conversation, our years of experience sharing the mission and free tools of the Conversation Project tell us something else: When people are given time, a safe space, and an invitation to talk about matters of mortality, they tend to open up and have intimate, powerful, and meaningful conversations about what matters most to them about *living*.

The reluctance to have this conversation is understandable. It's not that we don't know on some deep level that we are going to die someday; it's just that there is so much life to live. Why talk now about the kinds of medical interventions we might want *someday*? Why not wait until we really need to talk?

Well, we are in control right now, for one thing.

Nearly half of people over 65 who are admitted to an emergency room will not be able to make decisions for themselves. A fall, medication errors, a stroke, a heart attack, or even severe pain can interfere with our ability to speak for ourselves. Designating a health-care proxy—someone who can speak for you—is essential. And central to that proxy's ability to advocate reliably for you is having conversations with that person about your wishes.

When we share our wishes for care with our loved ones, we are taking steps to preserve our voice, our autonomy, through them. We are also giving them a gift of knowledge and understanding so that they are not making crucial decisions in a crisis without our input. This decreases the chances that they will feel guilty, depressed, and uncertain about whether they did the right thing.

Starting the Conversation (Project): Ellen's Story

Ellen Goodman describes the relationship she had with her mother as "very close." It was the kind of relationship where they could talk about everything—children, politics, friends, heartache—except one thing. Ellen and her mother never talked about the kind of care her mom would want in the event that she could no longer choose for herself. And that turned out to be a problem.

When Ellen's mom developed late-onset dementia, Ellen reports that "she could no longer decide what she wanted for lunch, much less what she wanted for health care." So as her mother's disease progressed and her mental capacity declined,

Ellen was faced with making her mother's health-care decisions, such as whether her mom should be treated for another round of pneumonia, or whether to give permission to repair her mother's broken hip with surgery—a pain-causing, activity-limiting procedure her mother couldn't understand. Recalls Ellen, "I felt blindsided. I really didn't understand what my mother would have wanted in the situation she was in."

In these critical moments Ellen made the best decisions she could out of love and compassion. To this day, though, she says, "I just really wish I had had my mother's voice in my head telling me what to do."

Ellen's personal experience drove her to gather trusted friends and counselors to figure out how to ensure that others were not left in the dark about their loved ones' wishes. Inspired by her struggle, she cofounded the Conversation Project, a national public engagement campaign to support people in having their wishes for end-of-life care expressed and respected.

Early studies by the Conversation Project taught us that while 90 percent of Americans think it's important to have conversations with our loved ones about our wishes for care, *fewer than 30 percent actually have these conversations.*

What Gets in Our Way?

If we are honest, some of us harbor a superstition that if we talk about it, it might happen sooner. Moving beyond that fear, there are other obstacles. Parents may not want to worry their children—even if those children are adults—and may say things such as "Don't worry, honey. Your dad and I will handle this." On the other hand, adult children may be reluctant to bring up a subject so intimate and fraught; some worry that their parents will think they are expecting

When we cultivate the courage and compassion to face our finitude, we strengthen our capacity to live each day more fully, with gratitude and awareness.

or waiting for them to die. We may comfort ourselves with the notion that doctors are "in charge" or that the people who love us will make the right decisions when the time comes, so there's really no need to talk about it, is there? We generally think it's too soon. Until, of course, it's too late and we've missed a precious opportunity.

For most of us, though, we simply don't know how to begin the conversation. The steps

STEP 1: FIGURE OUT WHAT YOU WANT TO SAY

Make time in your busy life to pause and reflect on what matters most to you. "Someday" is not a plan. Reserve an hour or two on your calendar to do this. Remind yourself: "This is a gift I am giving my loved ones."

STEP 2: WRITE IT DOWN

Set out something to write on and with. Send a calming signal to your body and mind by taking a breath, feeling your feet on the floor, perhaps even closing your eyes. Then complete this sentence in your mind: "When I think about the end of my life, what matters most to me is . . ."

STEP 3: EXPLORE THE CHALLENGING IDEA OF BEING AT THE CLOSE OF YOUR LIFE

Where are you? Who is with you? What is going on around you? Is there music or prayers? Is someone holding your hand or is a favorite pet snuggled up with you? What is there left to be said? When you have pictured this in your mind, take a few minutes to write down what matters most to you.

STEP 4: CONSIDER YOURS AND YOUR LOVED ONES' ROLES IN YOUR MEDICAL DECISION MAKING

Assuming that you have already prepared an advance directive for health care (ADHC), how important is it that people do exactly as you wish, even if it makes them uncomfortable? Alternatively, do you want to grant them permission to do what brings them peace, even if it goes against your express wishes?

STEP 5: DECIDE WHO YOU NEED TO HAVE THE CONVERSATION WITH

This is really important. Make a full list of who you need to talk with. Your goal in speaking to your entire circle of care is to avoid conflict at the bedside. The last thing anyone wants to see is two siblings fighting in the ICU waiting room about their mother's care because one daughter is saying, "But Mom never told *me* that!"

STEP 6: SET ASIDE TIME TO TALK WITH YOUR LOVED ONES

Give yourself a deadline, because "soon" is not a time.

You may wish to practice expressing your thoughts with a trusted friend who is a good listener before asking your partner if he would be open to having the conversation. Or write a letter to the people you love, outlining what you have been thinking about.

described below are adapted from the Conversation Project's Conversation Starter Kit, which is used by millions of older people to help them start talking about what matters most to them about living, until the end. Knowing more about what matters to you—not just what's the matter with you—can help family members make decisions about medical interventions in the event that you cannot speak for yourself. That knowledge can be the gift that gives them peace of heart and mind in the wake of deep loss.

Harriet's Story

My mother survived six different types of cancer before emphysema overwhelmed her body. She lived with the possibility of dying for more than thirty years. This gave us plenty of time to talk about what type of living she wanted at the end of her life. I knew in no uncertain terms that she wanted to die with dignity, not in a hospital, hooked up to tubes and monitors. I knew she wanted us to be with her when the end was near. In the last few weeks of her life, I was absolutely clear about what to do. I told people at work they would just have to handle everything until I got back. I was a daughter first, and I was going to be there for my mother.

In the last few weeks of her life, I was at my mother's bedside sharing stories, reading to her, and being present. It was a time of serenity and pure joy, sharing such private and intimate moments. It was a gift to me—a legacy, really—to have a sense of purpose as we honestly faced the inevitable, together. I share this story with my adult children—and with total strangers—in the hope that more people will feel encouraged to give this gift of presence and clarity to their families, too.

Being willing to engage our loved ones in these intimate conversations about what matters, sharing the values that undergird our decision making, and acknowledging the truth of our human mortality (the death rate is still holding steady at 100 percent, after all) is part of getting good at getting older. When we cultivate the courage and compassion to face our finitude, we strengthen our capacity to live each day more fully, with gratitude and awareness.

Six Steps to Starting the Conversation

In approaching a discussion with your loved ones about how you envision the end of your life, think through how you'd like this conversation to proceed.

> What if you live alone? Twenty-eight percent of all American households comprise people who live alone. You may be widowed or divorced. Perhaps there are no adult children or close relatives in your life. To whom do you turn to ensure that your wishes for care will be respected? A health-care proxy (agent or durable power of attorney for health care) does not have to be "next of kin." You can choose a friend or someone you have come to trust. The important thing is to face your vulnerability and meet it with spiritual courage.

Consider the story of Miriam, whose mother left detailed typed instructions expressly limiting the kinds of medical interventions she wanted. At the bottom of the document, her mother had handwritten, "If you are reading this, you must be in a very difficult situation. I am so sorry. Please do your very best to respect my wishes. Love, Mom." When the time came to make a difficult decision, Miriam took out the letter. Seeing her mother's handwriting—the same neat, slanting script that her mother used to send birthday greetings and travel notes on postcards—gave Miriam the strength she needed to advise the medical team to act according to her mother's wishes.

Anticipating and Overcoming Objections

Still, we'll face obstacles in our minds and families. One man who was part of a small-group discussion on the topic explained, "I'm afraid that if I bring this up to my [adult] kids when we're together for the holidays, some of them may panic. They'll worry that there is something wrong with me, that I'm not leveling with them."

Anticipating how your loved ones might respond, try initiating the discussion with something such as "You know, I've been thinking. I'm feeling really fine now. Still, I know I may not always be this healthy. It would give me some peace of mind if I could tell you what would matter to me in the event that I got sick someday. Would you be open to hearing about it?"

It should not surprise you if the "kids" push back with something like, "Oh, Dad! You are the healthiest person I know! You are still running 5Ks and leaving us in the dust. We don't have to worry about you!"

Gently push back by modeling mature parenting (yes, even though the "kids" may be parents themselves now): "I like to think I'll still be shooting my age on the golf course for years to come, too. But, as sad as it is to think about, I won't be playing eighteen holes forever. It would be a help to me if you would listen to what I have to say."

If you encounter some resistance along the way, don't get discouraged or give up. Be patient and circle back when you feel ready to try again. Every attempt at having the conversation is valuable and signals to people around you that you are not afraid of the topic.

> What if a loved one has Alzheimer's disease or another form of dementia?
>
> It is especially difficult to start a conversation about end-of-life care when your loved one begins to lose her cognitive ability, along with her ability to function in the world. However, there is no greater time to have this conversation. See Part 4 Tools and Resources for information on the Conversation Project's guide for people who love someone who has Alzheimer's or another form of dementia. Individuals and families can use the guide to reflect on how their loved one would want to be cared for in the event they can no longer make those decisions for themselves.

Remember: It's not a marathon or a monolithic conversation. It may work best in your situation to keep it casual and drop a pearl of information here and there. For others, talking on a long walk or over a cup of coffee (or something stronger) may be the way to go. The conversation starts with you being willing to share first, and then invite your loved ones to talk about their wishes, too.

Keep in mind that as life circumstances change, so might your wishes. What you think you will want for care when you are 55 and healthy is likely to be different from what you are willing to fight for at 90 if you have multiple health issues. To ensure that your loved ones are keeping up with your evolving wishes for care, practice sharing at different points along the journey. Should your health status change, wonder together, "Now that we know what we know, what do you hope? And what do you fear?"

Modeling a growing comfort with talking about end-of-life issues and what matters most is a profound legacy for the generations that follow us. Normalizing these conversations—having them around the kitchen table, not waiting until there is a crisis in the ICU—is a way to help shift the culture from one that doesn't talk about dying to one that does. It offers us a spiritual practice for contemplating the reality of our mortality. And it is a gift to those we love: helping them get a good start on the path to getting good at getting older.

We don't want to wait too long to say "I love you" or "I'm sorry" or "Please forgive me."

So don't wait: It's always too early until it's too late.

New Yorker cartoonist Roz Chast's graphic memoir of trying to talk with her parents about what they want as they age is both a witty and poignant reminder about the power of denial when the subject is our own or our parents' aging. *Can't we talk about something more PLEASANT?* plumbs the absurdities and frustrations of trying to have the conversation with loved ones who resist your efforts.

Richard and Laura Bribe Their Kids into Having "The Conversation"

A couple of years back, we decided that it was time to have "The Conversation" with our adult children and their partners. Ours is a blended family. Our children didn't grow up together, and because we married when they were nearly grown, the kids don't really know each other. They live far away from each other and from us. It was important for us to gather them together, to have them hear what we wanted at the end of our lives.

So for the very first time, we took them away together—a weeklong vacation in Puerto Vallarta with just one condition: They had to sit through an end-of-life conversation with us. They all joked: There is no such thing as a free lunch or a free vacation!

When the time for the conversation arrived, we shared some wine and tequila. Then the two of us read a document we had prepared called "The Five Wishes." It asks five questions:

1. Who is the person or who are the people I want to make care decisions for me when I can't?

2. What kind of medical treatment do I want or don't I want?

3. How comfortable do I want to be?

4. How do I want people to treat me?

5. What do I want my loved ones to know?

Some of what the two of us wanted was the same; some of it was different. Laura wanted to have people in her synagogue told that she was sick, and she wanted them to pray for her, even if what they prayed for was an easy transition to death. Rich didn't want people to pray for him. If Laura were in a situation close to death and life support treatment would only delay the moment of her death, she didn't want that treatment. Rich would want it if his doctor thought it could help.

The kids and their partners asked lots of questions: What if you changed your minds? Would the situation be different if this happened before you got really old? The kids and their partners talked about their grandparents' deaths and their feelings about how they had died. Then they asked for blank copies of the Five Wishes because they realized it would be good for them to think about these questions for themselves.

We talked about organ donation and burial versus cremation, and whether the children thought "visiting" would be important to them. We talked about how we would want to be remembered. Finally, we talked about Alzheimer's and dementia.

Later in the week, just before we lit the Shabbat candles, we turned "The Conversation" into a short ritual. We read aloud our Covenant of Loving Partners, the promises we made to each other when we married. Then we added a new provision to our covenant:

> Now, ten years after we first entered into our brit ahuvim, we reaffirm the commitments we made then, and, in the presence of our children, we add another:

> We declare that if one of us should become ill with such serious dementia or Alzheimer's disease that it becomes

impossible to recognize our partner, and that this condition is attested to by two doctors and one rabbi, the other one of us should feel free to live as full a life as possible, including having other intimate relationships. That freedom in no way compromises the promise we have made to honor and to care for each other physically and financially as we grow older. We make this declaration because each of us believes that loving each other includes granting this freedom to pursue new intimate relationships, even as we honor our commitment to be present to each other as we age.

Then we lit Shabbat candles as we do each week: one for each of our children and their partners, along with the traditional two. We blessed our children and their partners, our hands on their heads, whispering the blessing that each of them is to us both.

"The Conversation" is not just a discussion; it is a sacred encounter. It is a blessing.

Tools and Resources

Chapter 18: Getting Your Stuff Together

Leah Bishop, who wrote this chapter, developed a personal affairs organizer that is available for download at www.behrmanhouse.com/ggago. Others are available online as well:

Cullen, Melanie, and Shae Irving. *Get It Together: Organize Your Records So Your Family Won't Have To.* Berkeley, Calif.: Nolo Press, 2016.

Dewey, Erik A. *The Big Book of Everything MK IIIa.* A free information organizer available in pdf or Excel formats. Go to www.erikdewey.com/bigbook.htm.

Higgens, Michele Perry. *The Everything Binder: Financial, Estate, and Personal Affairs Organizer.* Self-published, 2013. "Everything you need to document your important affairs."

Chapter 19: Planning for What You Don't Want to Plan For

There are numerous sources for advance health-care directives, from religious organizations and also from health-care institutions. The following are a few suggestions:

JEWISH RESOURCES

Conservative Movement. The medical directive was approved by the Committee on Jewish Law and Standards of the Rabbinical Assembly, which guides the Conservative movement in Jewish legal matters. Find it at www.rabbinicalassembly.org or www.behrmanhouse.com/ggago.

An Orthodox Perspective. The Rabbinical Council of America, the main US rabbinical association within Modern Orthodoxy, has a directive "to help ensure that all medical and post-death decisions made by others on your behalf will be made in accordance with Jewish law and custom." Find it at www.rabbis.org or www.behrmanhouse.com/ggago.

Reform Movement. Rabbi Richard Address, on his Jewish Sacred Aging website, offers *A Time to Prepare*, free forms designed "to help guide you and your family through a series of conversations about end-of-life plans and care plans," including a medical directive with six illness scenarios: www.jewishsacredaging.com.

Reconstructionist Judaism. Although there is no official advanced health-care directive for Reconstructionist Jews, Rabbi David Teutsch, a professor of Jewish ethics and former president of the Reconstructionist Rabbinical College, recommends the Five Wishes Advance Directive (see The Five Wishes on next page).

GENERAL RESOURCES

Compassion & Choices is a nonprofit support, education, and advocacy organization whose mission is to improve care and expand options for the end of life. Go to: www.compassionandchoices.org.

Considerations for Members of the LGBT Community. The Human Rights Campaign provides information to help members of the LGBT community receive fair and equal treatment. Search for advance health-care directives at www.hrc.org.

The Five Wishes. Developed by Aging with Dignity, a nonprofit organization advocating for quality care for those near the end of life, the Five Wishes is "America's most popular living will." Go to www.agingwithdignity.org/.

National Institute on Aging. The website of the National Institute on Aging is replete with helpful information, including its Advance Care Planning: Healthcare Directives. Go to: www.nia.nih.gov/health/.

What Health-Care Directives Are Called in Your State. In addition to offering legal resources for purchase, NOLO also has a lot of free information including a helpful listing by state. Look through "Legal Topics" on their website: www.nolo.com.

Chapter 20: Having the Last Word in Funeral Planning

BUILD-IT-YOURSELF CASKETS/UNCOMMON URNS

Instructions or kits for build-it-yourself caskets are readily available online, and there are even YouTube videos to help guide you through the process:

Casketplans.com: www.casketplans.com

Mother Earth News: www.motherearthnews.com/diy/how-to-build-a-handmade-casket

Natural Burial Company: www.funerals.naturalburialcompany.com

Northwoods Casket: www.northwoodscasket.com

If you are thinking about cremation, www.treehugger.com offers the Poetree, a designer urn "that infuses a poetic spirit into the mourning process" and lets you plant a tree from ashes.

GENERAL RESOURCES

The Funeral Rule, enforced by the Federal Trade Commission (FTC), makes it possible for you to choose *only* those goods and services you want or need and to pay only for those you select, whether you are making arrangements when a death occurs or in advance. Go to www.consumer.ftc.gov/ or www.behrmanhouse.com/ggago.

A good general source for information on the Jewish rituals of funeral, burial, and mourning is the nonprofit organization Kavod v'Nichum (Honor and Comfort). Go to www.jewish-funerals.org/.

Organizations in many communities provide free burials for the indigent. Check with your local **Jewish** Federation, Jewish Family Services, or Hebrew Burial Society.

JEWISH PERSPECTIVES ON THE AFTERLIFE

Soncino, Rifat, and Daniel Syme. *What Happens After I Die? Jewish Views of Life After Death*. New York: URJ Press, 1990.

Spitz, Elie Kaplan. *Does the Soul Survive? A Jewish Journey to Belief in Afterlife, Past Lives & Living with Purpose*. Woodstock, VT: Jewish Lights, 2015.

Chapter 21: Talking about Life and Death

Two good places to start talking about the realities and concerns of getting older with your family, friends, colleagues, and health-care professionals are:

The Conversation Project. Offers several easy-to-use starter kits, including one for "Families and Loved Ones of People with Alzheimer's Disease or Other Forms of Dementia" and "How to Talk to Your Doctor." Go to www.theconversationproject.org.

Death over Dinner. A simple format, with a step-by-step online guide and a wealth of articles, podcasts, and videos to facilitate discussion. There is also a Jewish edition. Go to www.deathoverdinner.org or www.deathoverdinner-jewishedition.org.

Chast, Roz. *Can't we talk about something more PLEASANT?* New York: Bloomsbury, 2014. A humorous—and poignant—take on the "Conversation."

Getting Good at Giving Back

David, a senior partner in a major law firm where he worked for most of his career, decided to retire when he turned 60. He didn't have to, but he was tired of the work and had enough money saved to maintain his lifestyle without a regular paycheck. Some of his friends were getting sick, a few had died, and he realized that he didn't want to spend the rest of his life negotiating mergers and acquisitions. His kids had launched their own careers; his wife was still happily engaged in her work.

He didn't know exactly what he wanted to do, but he knew he wanted to do something different. So he decided to take a "gap year," as some teenagers do between high school and college, to figure out what he wanted to do next. He took time to clean out the closets in his house, to organize everything on his computer, even to sort through years of photographs. He volunteered for a few different community organizations.

He spent a lot of time thinking about activities he enjoyed but hadn't really had time to pursue when he was working and raising his kids. The top two contenders were singing and golf. He began to take singing lessons and then joined a community choir. He also began to volunteer for an organization that trains adults to be coaches and mentors for kids who want to learn how to play golf. He describes the volunteer experience as changing his life as well as enhancing the lives of the kids with whom he worked. He loves the camaraderie with the other coaches, who mostly come from different

In the act of giving lies the expression of my aliveness.

—Erich Fromm, *The Art of Loving*

backgrounds and experiences than his. And he enjoys working with the kids and modeling the values that he finds in golf: perseverance, patience, and honesty. On top of all that, he feels healthier than he has in years—and his own golf game has improved.

Like so many others, David entered the stage of life that social psychologist Erik Erikson describes as "generativity," when the dominant motivation of our lives begins to shift from accumulating for ourselves—money, things, personal experiences—to giving back, to reinvigorating our natural inclination to do good for others. Some, like David, do something very different from what they had done before retirement; others apply their skills and experience in community service or other volunteer opportunities.

In part 5 we'll explore possible answers to the questions we increasingly ask as we take stock of our lives and tap into our generativity: How can I still make my life count? How can I continue to make a difference? What else can I do to make a meaningful contribution to the lives of others and to make the world a better place? We'll explore in this section how a generation raised in activism can redirect its time and resources to get involved in making change, one-on-one, locally, nationally, or globally.

According to the sages (BT *Shabbat* 127a), "The things whose fruits we eat in this world and whose full reward awaits us in the world to come include performing acts of loving-kindness . . . [and] making peace between people."

Enjoying fruits in this world and further reward in the world to come—it's just the rabbis' way of saying: You can have your cake and eat it, too—and change the world. Remember: Our hearts are in the same place as they were in the late '60s and '70s; it's only our hairlines (and waistlines) that have changed.

CHAPTER 22

Giving a Damn and Getting Involved
by Paul Irving

Paul Irving is a friend and mentor of ours who is a leader in the arena of purposeful aging. He is chairman of the Milken Institute Center for the Future of Aging, distinguished scholar in residence at the University of Southern California Leonard Davis School of Gerontology, and chairman of Encore.org.

DOESN'T GIVE A DAMN.

Words of Wisdom

There's no greater gift than thinking that you had some impact on the world, for the better.

—Gloria Steinem

Look up *retirement* in the dictionary and you'll see "withdrawal," "removal," "retreat," and "departure." These words signal societal expectations for our later years, images of aging that too many still accept. Do these images accurately reflect the goals and aspirations of today's older adults? For an increasing number of us, the answer is a resounding no.

Despite negative assumptions about frail bodies and diminished capacities, more older adults than ever are healthy, capable, and energetic; we are looking for new ways to become involved, make a difference, and leave a legacy. We know the value of our wisdom and experience, and we're not too old to raise our voices. Borrowing from Facebook executive Sheryl Sandberg's message to the women of her generation, we want to "lean in," not step back from a meaningful life.

More and more of us baby boomers—members of the generation that marched for civil rights, ended a war, and powered the modern women's movement—long to regain that sense of social mission, to reenergize our activism and involvement. We still give a damn, and we're eager to show it.

Increasing longevity has sparked a revolution that is altering every aspect of human existence, and we're just beginning to understand its implications. Longer lives offer more years of learning, work, intimacy, and involvement that can change families and communities in breathtaking ways. Of course, aging brings its health and financial challenges, but these extra years and new opportunities deserve celebration. They offer great possibilities that are not yet fully appreciated. Decades ago, Betty Friedan, the activist author of *The Feminine Mystique*, told us that "aging is not 'lost youth' but a new stage of opportunity and strength." How can we realize the potential of this new stage? What can we do to add more meaning and purpose to a longer life?

There Are No Rules, But There Are Choices to Make

For some, leisurely pursuits may seem like the ideal way to fill these extra years. Enjoying family and friends, new experiences, travel, walks in the park, and, yes, even golf can be good and good for us. There is an understandable sense that we deserve the downtime, that we've earned it.

Rob Reiner

But some of us feel called to do more. Inequities in health, wealth, justice, and opportunity are fraying our social fabric. Divides between race, gender, class, and religion mask our fundamental kinship. The natural world is fragile and at risk. Young people need our support. Partisanship, political dysfunction, and deficits in leadership undermine our confidence and trust. We recognize that older adults bring unique talents to the public arena and to the fight for a brighter future for us all through social action.

Many of us believe that if we're fortunate enough to be able to help, we must respond. The words of the rabbinic sage Hillel resonate: "If I am not for myself, who will be for me? If I am only for myself, what am I? And if not now, when?"

Gloria Steinem

With the urgency of our social challenges and the realization that fewer years lie ahead than behind, we know that this is not a time to sit on the sidelines. We have to act for the benefit of others and for our own benefit as well.

By working to improve the world around us, we'll add depth to our later years, set an example for our children and grandchildren, and leave a legacy of service and purpose. And there's a bonus: Our actions can help us as much as they help our beneficiaries. Research on volunteerism identifies it as an essential ingredient in the recipe for healthy aging.

Many in the baby boom generation are already involved, acting on these generative inclinations to contribute and serve. We're making a difference every day, embracing our older years with creativity, passion, and purpose. We're teaching and mentoring in our communities and doing caregiving for our neighbors. (See chapter 26, "Touching the Future through Mentoring.") We're volunteering in a wide range of public service organizations, and we're involved in socially focused encore careers. We're working to advance environmental initiatives and going back to school to learn new skills that can increase the impact of our work. We're involved in advocacy and political campaigns—knocking on doors, making calls, and even running for office.

As critical as our contributions are, we often encounter roadblocks as we try to share our talents to make the world a better place. Researchers tell us that millions want to help. But the frustrating reality is that many of us have trouble finding pathways to engagement.

Doing Well by Doing Good

Our aging correlates with increasing "generativity," the developmental characteristic defined by psychologist Erik Erikson to capture our need to nurture and guide younger people and contribute to the next generation. This generativity surge is not only good for our society, but it also can be good for us personally. Dan McAdams, a professor of psychology and human development at Northwestern University, notes that "a growing body of psychological research shows that being highly generative is a sign of psychological health and maturity. People who score high on measures of generativity tend to report higher levels of happiness and well-being in life, compared to people who score low. High generativity is also associated with low levels of depression and anxiety."

There's a supply and demand mismatch—a gulf between the growing number of older adults expressing a desire to get involved and the opportunities available to them.

The Scourge of Ageism

What is holding baby boomers back from getting involved in social activism? One answer is the rampant ageism that infects our culture—a culture that continues to denigrate age and extol the virtues of youth.

As older adults, we're often overlooked, excluded, marginalized, or caricatured. We're viewed as out of date and out of touch, as yesterday's resource. These stereotypes about older adults, reinforced by media and other institutions,

AARP is a leading voice against ageism in our society. The organization's legal advocacy initiatives, conducted by AARP Foundation Litigation (AFL), help to ensure that those 50 and older have a voice in the laws and policies that affect their daily lives.

ignore the strengths and potential of our aging population. They impede opportunity for those who seek work, exacerbate financial insecurity, and intensify costly health risks. This ageism is not just based on poor information; it is morally wrong. Ageism's practical consequences are real, and they are suffered all too often by the most vulnerable among us.

As Jo Ann Jenkins, the CEO of AARP, says, "Today it is socially unacceptable to ignore, ridicule, or stereotype someone based on their gender, race, or sexual orientation. So why is it still acceptable to do this to people based on their age?" But it's not just others who are the problem; it's also our own internalized ageism. As Jenkins further notes, "It's bad enough that ageism can influence public policy, employment practices, and how people are treated in society, but what's worse is that we accept the ageist behavior ourselves and start acting it out."

Of course, we must help others, but we must also stand up for ourselves. It's time for us to tackle ageism.

We can call out ageist language, out-of-date policies and practices, and denigrating humor. We can elevate awareness through social media campaigns, storytelling,

YOU DON'T HAVE TO BE A HERO...

OY! MY BACK HURTS.

TO MAKE A DIFFERENCE.

and letters to the editor. We can support age-friendly businesses and spurn those engaged in ageist practices. By exerting constructive pressure in meetings with and advocacy directed at leaders in the private sector, public policy, and other domains, we can challenge conventional wisdom and change hearts and minds. We can ensure that opportunity is available throughout our lives and create a better future for both old and young.

What's Next?

Through our faith institutions, political and academic establishments, and social networks, we can identify and join organizations committed to change in our neighborhoods and communities. We can bring up issues of ageism and social justice around the dinner table with family and friends. We can encourage our colleagues and coworkers to speak truth to power and stand up for what's right. We can learn throughout our lives to enhance our knowledge, communications skills, and effectiveness.

Taking a stand is rarely easy. Taking it to the streets is even harder. But our times demand it; change is necessary. Our talents are needed and we're uniquely equipped to help. Many of us feel compelled to respond. It's time to step up and step out, even if our involvement in social action is uncomfortable as we begin; even if we're unsure about our abilities. Maggie Kuhn, who in 1970 founded the Gray Panthers after she was forced to retire at age 65 from a job she loved, famously said, "Stand . . . and speak your mind—even if your voice shakes."

We're able to contribute and want to make a difference. We give a damn and we're ready to step up. We can become a force for social action once again, and now is the time to do it, for our generation and for generations to come.

CHAPTER 23
Making Purpose Your True North
by Marc Freedman and Marci Alboher

You may have heard that a "gray wave" of aging boomers heralds a new era of cross-generational conflict and economic despair.

Don't believe it. People post-midlife are poised to invent an entirely new stage of life, which we call the "encore years," when personal interests often turn to making the world better than we found it, shifting from "me" mode to "we" mode. This whole post-midlife period is simply new territory, and those of us flooding into this phase constitute a phenomenon unique to the 21st century.

Inventing life stages, however, is far from new. A hundred years ago, "adolescence" was first identified as a life stage by psychologist G. Stanley Hall. Before Hall, we recognized only two life stages: childhood and adulthood—no tweens, no adolescents, and certainly no adult-escent 20- and 30-somethings. Look further back and we barely recognized childhood. Retirement as we know it is a concoction of the post–World War II era. Today, with close to 10,000 Americans daily crossing the midlife divide, it's high time to recognize the "encore years."

Life after 50 is a distinct period, with its own character. We become more empathetic, we get better at synthesizing ideas, making connections between disparate elements, and solving complex problems. We actually grow smarter in some ways; there are good reasons wisdom is linked with age. Millions today are trading in the old dream of "freedom" from work (and the attendant social isolation in retirement) to put this wisdom to use in encore roles, productive engagements that contribute to the greater good.

Marc Freedman, CEO and president of Encore.org, is a pioneer, innovator, entrepreneur, and winner of the Eisner Prize for Intergenerational Excellence. He has become a friend of ours as we have worked on ChaiVillageLA and other initiatives. His most recent book is *How to Live Forever*.

Marci Alboher is a vice president at Encore.org and the author of *The Encore Career Handbook: How to Make a Living and a Difference in the Second Half of Life*, from which this chapter is adapted.

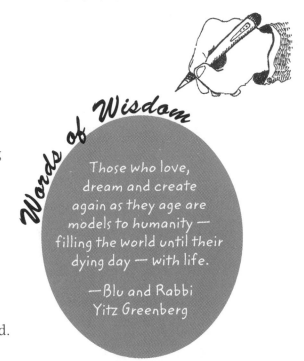

Words of Wisdom

Those who love, dream and create again as they age are models to humanity — filling the world until their dying day — with life.

—Blu and Rabbi Yitz Greenberg

Purpose is an animating force in this season; people seek work that speaks to issues beyond personal ambition and address pressing social challenges.

The truth is, society needs us, the most experienced segment of our population, particularly as our country faces serious challenges in areas such as education, health, social services, and the environment. The encore movement can help turn this all around, and it can do so on a grand scale, delivering the biggest potential human capital windfall since women entered the workforce en masse two generations ago. Today's encore pioneers are at the vanguard of a permanent change. We are the first wave, charting a new path beyond the "golden years" cliché.

Making Purpose Personal

Still, finding our way to an encore is neither quick nor easy. Oftentimes, the transition is a slow metamorphosis, with baby steps and detours that require persistence and creativity. As more of us move in this direction and more organizations step up to provide assistance and

A Retirement Snapshot
by Rabbi Everett Gendler

My wife Mary and I defined *retirement* to mean redirecting energy, not dropping bovine-like onto green pastures, grazing as time scurried rapidly onward. Instead, *retirement* to us meant being open to unscheduled, unanticipated opportunities for further involvement in the great life experiment. While we looked forward to possible new adventures, we were also worried about losing the connections with the future that our occupations—psychologist, rabbi, teacher, chaplain—had provided. How quickly this concern was answered. By virtue of blessed guidance—or chance, if you insist—in less than half a year we found ourselves engaged with the Tibetan exile community in India. For these past 15 years, we've been traveling regularly to India to help the followers of the Dalai Lama develop a community-wide educational program on strategic nonviolent struggle for the Tibetan cause. This Western, pragmatic, how-to-apply-it complement to his idealistic, inspirational advocacy of nonviolence has been welcomed and facilitated by His Holiness.

pathways, these shifts will get easier. But someone has to blaze the trail—maybe it's you.

How do you know if you're ready for an encore? Everyone is different, of course, but there are familiar patterns for reaching an "encore moment." Some people come to their encore after experiencing burnout—disenchantment (and plain exhaustion) after decades of the same old grind. Others' encore is sparked by a vague itch to make a change, even though they don't know what's ahead. An old passion or a new awareness of injustice could become all-consuming, and there's finally time to right the wrongs. Sometimes the encore moment is imposed—a layoff, a buyout, a hint of obsolescence in a changing marketplace; you sense it's time to get out. And sometimes a health setback, a loss, or the threat of loss illuminates your true priorities, away from the hamster wheel of endless work.

Keep the following factors in mind as you find your way:

- Oftentimes, you get to your encore years and don't know what's next.
- There's no right or wrong way to move into your encore. Some people plan for years. Others slide into encore careers. Some will work for extra decades; others for a few years.
- Transitions take longer than you think.
- You don't need to go it alone.

Are You a Leaper or a Planner?

Once you arrive at your encore moment—regardless of how you got there—there are essentially two ways you can go forward: You can leap or you can plan.

If you're a leaper, you plunge in when the opportunity strikes. After the initial leap, you may find that you dig in for a long period, having found your place. Equally likely, you may step back to reassess and adjust—or find that the initial leap was just the first step on a longer journey.

ARE YOU A LEAPER?

OR A PLANNER?

Ready for Your Encore?

Weigh these 10 questions. An abundance of yeses suggests that the time is likely ripe to consider shifting to work with a different purpose—your encore career—whether as a volunteer or a paid professional.

1. Are you in a place in your life where you can comfortably move forward in your encore without having to deal with other pressing aspects of your life (that is, where you live, caring for someone else, navigating a health issue yourself)?

2. Do you have some ideas about what you might want to do next?

3. Is there some issue you can't stop thinking about?

4. Do you have a sense that retirement from paid work is right around the corner?

5. Do you feel financially secure enough to make a shift?

6. Do you have someone you can comfortably talk to about your ideas and plans?

7. Are you open to the idea of taking classes or doing some other kind of on-the-job learning to update your skills or learn something new?

8. Do you know what kind of environment you want to work in and how much time you want to work?

9. Do you know if you want to work for yourself or for an organization?

10. Can you succinctly describe where you are in your encore process?

If you're a planner, you do your homework and come up with an idea, then research options about how to make it happen. You may be waiting to hit a milestone—last child off to college, eligibility for early retirement, sufficient savings to make you feel comfortable taking a risk. You may modify the way you work so that you have some free time for an immersion experience, such as an internship or volunteer work. You may need some new skills or even a certificate or a degree. Whatever the case, if you're a planner, you're thinking of the steps to an encore before you make the first move.

Reality Check

Those of us who have the financial freedom may find fulfillment in volunteer roles or as mentors to young people—sometimes for a modest stipend, sometimes gratis. Even if we need additional income, we may find a way to earn a living doing something that makes a difference in the world. But it's not always easy or obvious. If you love playing the ukulele, it might be harder to find a social-purpose encore than if you love fund-raising. But people find ways to knit together something that matters to them with another talent or skill. The skills you've mastered in your primary career—or in your life outside of work—may be transferable to a new setting. Or you may aim to master a new skill for a new stage of life by going back to school for a certificate or a degree.

That said, let's not sugarcoat things. If you're hoping to find an encore that includes full- or part-time work, age discrimination is real and can profoundly limit opportunities for people in and beyond midlife. (See the discussion on ageism in chapter 22, "Giving a Damn and Getting Involved.") It's illegal, but many employers just don't consider older people for some positions. Plus, stereotypes about age suggest that older employees aren't nimble or adept enough to learn new things, new technologies in particular. You can counter those expectations by making sure that your skills are up to snuff. Tailor your résumé to showcase your strengths as an advisor and mentor. Don't be shy about using LinkedIn; posting your profile telegraphs your understanding of how today's job market works. But don't just dismiss a bad interview as a fluke: If an employer doesn't value your experience, the organization might not be a good fit. Better to focus on places where older, experienced people are already part of the team.

Remember: You don't need to be a hero to make a difference. And you can't single-handedly solve all the problems of the world.

Purpose can be big and bold, or it can express itself in quiet ways. Perhaps you seek the spotlight; perhaps you prefer working behind the scenes. Perhaps you find meaning in venues beyond work: your community, your neighborhood theater group, the school board, the library board, a soup kitchen, a food co-op, your family. Whether you prefer to keep your private and personal lives distinct or blend the boundaries to a friendly blur, finding work that inspires you and helps others is within your reach. You'll need creativity to discover the right setting; resilience to stand up to outdated cultural norms; and belief that what you are doing next is right for you and contributes to the greater good. But you are not alone on this path. The people who have walked the encore road before you have discovered that work with purpose and meaning enriches life, health, and well-being in immeasurable ways.

AARP reports that "with low unemployment rates, companies are using creative recruitment strategies to attract older workers." Such companies include the CVS pharmacy chain, UnitedHealth Group, AT&T, and the Hartford insurance company. Check out over 460 employers who have signed the AARP Employer Pledge, publicly stating that they value experienced workers and believe in equal opportunities for workers of all ages.

CHAPTER 24

Volunteering with Its Joys (and Occasional Oys)

by Susan K. Stern

The most urgent and persistent question, according to Martin Luther King Jr., is "What are you doing for others?"

Particularly for those of us who are in the "next stage" of life, these words are a call to action, to serve, and to find purpose in life. We all have the capacity to change the world; it is within each of us to find our own path. This is particularly true for boomers.

Service is nothing new. It is part of the DNA of this country, from the signers of the Declaration of Independence, pledging their lives, their fortunes, and their sacred honor to their vision of a more perfect world, to the tens of thousands who today serve all over the country as VISTA and AmeriCorps volunteers. As President Barack Obama observed in a 2009 speech honoring volunteers and community service: "Service binds us to each other—and to our communities and our country—in a way that nothing else can. That's how we become more fully American. That's what it means to be American. It's always been the case in this country—that notion that we invest ourselves, our time, our energy, our vision, our purpose into the very fabric of this nation. That's the essence of our liberty—that we give back, freely."

Service is also at the core of being Jewish. We are commanded to do all we can in every generation to repair the world (performing acts of *tikkun olam*), and our Torah is filled with imperatives for social justice. As the contemporary theologian Rabbi Arthur Green writes in *Judaism's 10 Best Ideas*, "The notion that we are here to do God's work, treating those in need with decency and justice, remains essential to our faith. It is our task to fix the broken world, to get it ready

Richard met Susan Stern at the North American Jewish Forum in the mid-'80s when they were both "young leaders" in the American Jewish community. She has since served as a prominent Jewish lay leader on both the local and national level and has served on task forces and commissions about volunteerism on the state and federal level, including chairing President Barack Obama's Advisory Council on Faith-Based and Neighborhood Partnerships.

Words of Wisdom

Our sages taught that every person must say, "The whole world was created for my sake" (BT Sanhedrin 37a). Therefore, since the whole world was created for my sake, I must always be concerned with improving the world, fulfilling the needs of humanity, and praying for its benefit.

—Rabbi Nachman of Bratslav

for a messianic era that is still to come. The dream of an earthly era when all will live together in the harmony of a restored Eden is a dream that has never left us."

There is much to repair in this world, and it will take all of us together to make meaningful, lasting change. This is why more and more Americans are answering the call to serve. We are asked to volunteer, to lend our voices, skills, and ideas so that we may bring about real positive outcomes that address the toughest problems of our communities.

Once you have volunteered at a food bank, it's hard not to care about poverty and unemployment. Over time the needs of the people you serve become your stake in the challenges of our time.

—President Barack Obama

Volunteering is good for the organizations served, the community, and the recipients of our work. It is also good for the volunteer. Having examined the impact on those who give their time, energy, and talents, researchers determined a clear connection between volunteering and better health. Older volunteers in particular experience increased life satisfaction. People of all ages report a sense of purpose and positive feelings. Some even note a "helper's high," that special feeling we have when we see the smile of a child we have been tutoring who finally succeeds, or the tears of joy from an isolated, homebound person when we arrive to deliver a meal.

In recent years, more organizations are recognizing the transformative role service can have in engaging individuals and communities and providing real solutions. If well managed and targeted to real need, the experience can be life-changing. We experience joy when we realize that, through our efforts, another's life is made a little easier and more dignified. That action can have a ripple effect that lasts long beyond our service.

My own experiences are a case in point. I was part of a group of 20 volunteers who transformed an empty lot into a fruit and vegetable garden in a Brooklyn neighborhood that rarely had access to fresh and healthy food. We created individual plots for local residents to plant gardens for their families. When the first of the neighbors came by and I explained what we were doing, her whole face lit up: "You mean I can plant my own vegetables for my own family?"

She shared the news with her friends and within minutes the entire block was excited by the possibility of growing fresh food for their families. Watching their reactions, I knew we had changed their street. It was a powerful reminder that we change the world one person a time, one block at a time, and one community at a time. When we volunteer we *feel good* and *do good*.

The Changing Landscape of Volunteering

The barriers to meaningful volunteering are many, but not insurmountable. For example, even if we commit to volunteering, we are not guaranteed a positive experience. Our talents and expertise may not be well used, or our assigned work may not pique our interest. The project may be poorly organized, lack a clear articulation of its goals, and provide inadequate direction of volunteer efforts. In such circumstances, we may serve without knowing if we are making an impact or if our presence makes a difference.

Several years ago, Points of Light, the national volunteer organization founded by President George H. W. Bush, launched Reimagining Service, a multisector coalition of representatives from nonprofits, government, education, faith-based organizations, funding entities, and corporations, aimed at making volunteer experiences more meaningful and productive. The goal of the program is to use human resource techniques to screen and "hire" volunteers, based on their interests and abilities, and apply best management practices to ensure that volunteers are positioned to promote real and positive outcomes.

The work is based on the understanding that volunteers have good outcomes depending on the quality and effective management of those experiences. If the experience is poorly organized or seen as "busywork," volunteers may not feel they are making a difference. When they perceive the work as important and helpful to the community, however, volunteers are more likely to want to learn more about the issues and organizations they are serving. And with learning comes deeper involvement and the real possibility of making a long-term commitment to volunteer and engage even more with their community.

VOLUNTEERING

For boomers who are searching for meaningful ways to spend time and give back to their community, the challenge is to identify organizations equipped to provide well-planned and well-managed volunteer experiences, make good use of volunteers' time, and address causes that resonate with them.

The UJA-Federation of New York sponsors a service called Time for Good that matches prospective volunteers and organizations looking to engage them. One special initiative is the Engage Jewish Service Corps, specifically designed for baby boomers as they transition from working full-time to being retired. Engage seeks to transform outdated perceptions of older adults as people who only need services to a positive view of older adults as people who can also provide services. Engage is also creating community—among the volunteers themselves, many of whom are looking to develop new social networks in this stage of life, and between the volunteers and the people they serve in New York City.

How to Begin

If you are interested in volunteering, first identify your goals, passions, and skills. You also need to think realistically about how much time you plan to commit to this work. Are you making a weekly commitment (and for how long) or a one-time effort for a few hours? Could that one-time experience be a gateway to long-term involvement?

If you have a favorite nonprofit or cause, talk with professionals or veteran volunteers associated with your chosen organization about volunteer opportunities. Ask if they have someone in charge of volunteers and a commitment to making volunteering meaningful.

For the best results, determine the answers to the following questions:

- Does the organization have the flexibility to involve you in ways that suit your lifestyle, interests, and schedule?
- Are the organization and the volunteer opportunity good fits for your expertise and experience?
- Will the organization enable you to connect with others who share your interests and values?
- Is the organization committed to providing well-managed, meaningful volunteer experiences?

FINDING A GOOD VOLUNTEER OPPORTUNITY

There are several websites (see Part 5 Tools and Resources) that will match your interests with volunteer programs in your area. For most of them, all you need to do is enter your zip code and information about your interests. If you want to work with family members, colleagues, or friends, many of them will help facilitate that as well.

In the Jewish community, your local Jewish Federation, synagogue, JCC, or Jewish Family Service will be able to point you to meaningful volunteer opportunities in the area, whether within their institution or in the larger community.

I once ran into the county district attorney at an event where I was the speaker. I assumed that she was also slated to speak, but it turned out that she was there as a volunteer for the organization. Every Friday morning, despite her packed schedule, she reads to two young boys to help them improve their reading skills. She told me, "I wouldn't miss it for anything. It is the most important thing I do all week." Today she is a judge and continues to read to children at risk.

It is never too late to begin to volunteer, to make the world a kinder and gentler place, and to add purpose to your life.

Cities of Service is an intergenerational, civic-minded volunteer program that uses service and volunteering to help meet the city's needs. Activities range from driving people for flu shots, to painting blackened rooftops white to conserve energy, to delivering energy-saving light bulbs. In the decade since it was created in New York City, Cities of Service has expanded to a coalition of more than 215 cities whose mayors and chief executives represent nearly 55 million people in 45 states. (Find a link for your city at www.citiesofservice.org.)

Changing the World through Voluntourism

by Richard Siegel and Rabbi Laura Geller

Service travel programs (also called "service learning" or "voluntourism") are short-term commitments that take us beyond our own backyards. Many organizations offer these opportunities for volunteers of all ages, with some providing help to struggling communities in the United States, and others focusing their work in developing countries. In addition, there are specialty trips designed for volunteers over 50 through organizations like Global Vision International. Check out www.volunteerforever.com for an extensive list of projects where you can not only do good work with and for other people but also have fun through structured activities to explore the culture of the countries where you volunteer.

For many American boomers—Jewish or not—volunteering to give something back to Israel can be a profound and meaningful experience that provides you with a dramatically different perspective from what you could get as a tourist. Taking the time and making the effort to travel to and volunteer in Israel also sends a strong statement of support and commitment to the country and its people. A really excellent way to do this is through Skilled Volunteers for Israel.

That's what Don Goldman of Kansas City did. He describes his experience on the SVI website as an English tutor working with disadvantaged middle and high school students in Jerusalem: "What was really interesting to me about my volunteer experience was the way many Israelis treated me when I told them about the work I was doing. The programs I volunteered with touched on real issues within Israeli society, so Israelis cared about what I saw and would engage with me fully. That helped me get a glimpse of real Israeli society. . . . Going to Israel as a volunteer and being part of a real community gave me a more powerful experience than I've had before."

Along with all the factors that go into pursuing any volunteer opportunity, when volunteering abroad you also need to think about your projected length of stay, differences in cultural and workplace norms and environments, and your language proficiency. In Israel, for example, you do not typically need Hebrew or Arabic language skills, since colleagues and staff generally speak English. However, clients or students may not. But being able to read the alphabet of the country in which you volunteer is useful for decoding street signs or reading product names in shops.

You will also want to decide whether to set up your trip through established volunteering programs or make your own arrangements with a local organization directly. If you're interested in the latter, focus on organizations that are used to working with volunteers from abroad, such as those listed in Part 5 Tools and Resources. And whether you're participating in an established program or going it alone, be sure to ask direct questions relating to age criteria, vetting processes, and documentation. Or maybe you want to create your own opportunity, as Stuart Himmelfarb did.

In 2006, just a year after Hurricane Katrina devastated the Gulf Coast, Himmelfarb and two friends created the Klean-Up Krew, an intergenerational volunteer corps that has visited New Orleans more than 20 times since then to help the community rebound from the hurricane. He says, "This experience intensified my appreciation for significant volunteer engagement as a personally meaningful path to greater involvement in—and commitment to—Jewish life."

They focused on renovating homes, clearing debris (a tough assignment) and helping out at food banks and urban farms. They've also planted trees, tended compost heaps, and organized Mardi Gras beads for a fund-raiser.

Many of the initial participants were boomers. They were eager and committed, and they expressed Jewish values by working in areas of real need, like the lower-income areas Ninth Ward and St. Bernard Parish.

Fueled by their successful first trip in '06, Himmelfarb and his friends quickly organized a second—and stumbled upon an even better strategy: Five women asked if they could bring their daughters, all of whom were about to graduate from high school, for a mother-daughter experience. He recalls being amazed by the power of combining significant volunteer endeavor with intergenerational connections. Every invite since then has included a request to bring teenaged, college-aged, and other young adults. And, as an added bonus, some families used a Klean-Up Krew trip as their kids' b'nei mitzvah projects.

In the years since that first trip, Himmelfarb has brought more than 400 people to New Orleans, accounting for about 8,000 hours of work. Fields have been cleared, drywall and roofing have been installed, and food has been distributed. But, even more important, families have grown closer, and kids and parents have shared a deeply meaningful experience. And that includes Himmelfarb and his son, who's been on nine of these trips.

CHAPTER 25

Giving with No Possibility of Being Repaid
by Rabbi Stuart Kelman with Dan Fendel

Stuart Kelman has been a fellow-traveler of Richard's since the days of the 1960s-70s Jewish counterculture. A rabbi, educator, and author, Stuart is the founding rabbi of Congregation Netivot Shalom in Berkeley and dean of the Gamliel Institute, a center for study, training, and advocacy concerning Jewish end-of-life practices. Dan Fendel is dean of students of the Gamliel Institute.

Words of Wisdom

Remembering death in the proper way can bring a person to the ultimate joy.

—19th-century rabbi, Simcha Zissel Ziv

If we keep our eyes open for ways to give back, we might discover new possibilities that can enrich our own lives and deepen our engagement with the world around us. Participating in a *chevrah kaddisha* (literally, "holy society," or Jewish burial society) is a kind of volunteering that many of us may never have considered—or even heard of before—but that has the potential to be deeply powerful and personal.

Serving as part of a Jewish burial society requires a certain amount of special training, but, more importantly, it requires a special attitude of awe and reverence. Until recently, this mitzvah was primarily performed by Orthodox Jews. Now more and more non-Orthodox congregations and communities are creating Jewish burial societies to care for their own members.

According to Jewish tradition, there is no mitzvah more important than caring for the dead because it is the only one that can never be repaid. Being part of a *chevrah kaddisha* means being with and preparing a body for its final earthly journey. It is grounded in Judaism's understanding of the immutable nature of *kedushah* ("sanctity"), which holds that the body is a holy vessel into which the soul is placed. Like all holy vessels, it retains its essential holiness even when it is physically damaged or even after death. A *chevrah kaddisha* was so central to Jewish life that, since at least the Middle Ages, whenever a new community took root, this holy society was one of the first groups established.

Judaism's view of how to care for and respect the body from the time of death until burial consists of two parts: watching or guarding the body (*sh'mirah*) and purification (*taharah*), including the physical preparation of the body. Volunteers play central roles in both.

Being with the body means that it is never left alone—the fulfillment of the principle of honor or respect. Volunteers typically serve for two- or three-hour shifts and often read psalms while they are present with the body. Generally, this will happen at the mortuary or funeral home (or at the site of a tragedy, such as the Twin Towers rubble, where a volunteer corps of more than 200 people, including many college students, took shifts for seven months).

Purification involves reciting special prayers, washing and dressing the body, and placing it in the casket. Traditionally, family members cannot volunteer for the *taharah* ritual because of the emotional challenges as well as the effect of their presence on the rest of the team.

Serving in a *chevrah kaddisha* prompts us to take stock of our own mortality and frailty and of the enormity of the mitzvah that we have just performed. As Steven Foldes, a member of a Conservative synagogue explains:

> Walking into the room with the deceased and uncovering the body to begin the process of washing and sanctifying it, my breath is always taken away. It is truly an existential moment, and I realize again the razor-thin line between life and death. Here is someone from my community, someone with whom I may have prayed not long ago . . . and it is him and no longer him. He is there, but his life is gone, and my job as a member of my synagogue's *chevrah kaddisha* is to prepare his body for his casket with the same care and reverence with which I hope my body will be treated.

The end of life is part of a continuum that begins with visiting the sick, and therefore anyone can become a participant in a *chevrah kaddisha* anywhere along this continuum. You do not have to participate in preparing the body for burial to be a member. Anyone can visit the sick, be a guard, or do any of the myriad tasks of loving-kindness that need to be done before and after someone dies. In so doing, the words that are often said about the deceased become even more true: "May his [or her] memory be a blessing."

THE CHEVRAH KADDISHA Society

Memory has a powerful function in our tradition. As one of our teachers said, "People don't wind up in the ground, people wind up in people." Those we have accompanied on their final journey become a part of us.

CHAPTER 26
Touching the Future through Mentoring
by Richard Eisenberg

Richard Eisenberg is editor of the Work & Purpose and Money & Security channels on Nextavenue.org. He came to our attention from his always informative articles on this public media site for people age 50 and older. The following is an expanded version of one of his articles.

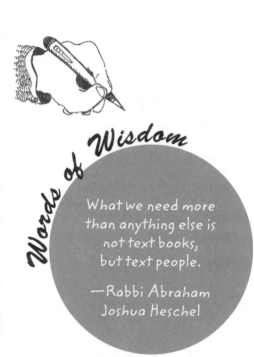

Words of Wisdom

What we need more than anything else is not text books, but text people.

—Rabbi Abraham Joshua Heschel

Four years after retiring from working as a St. Louis social work administrator, Elzora Douglas, at age 65, wanted to "try to give something back" to children. "Many times, children are not responsible for what's going on around them, but they're impacted more than anyone else," she said.

So Douglas signed up to tutor first- through third-graders weekly through Oasis, a national nonprofit educational organization for people age 50 and older. She's been doing it ever since and currently tutors students every Tuesday—one at a time, for 45 minutes each. "The students have a chance to be accepted where they are academically, without shame, without ridicule, and without judging," Douglas said. "What I get is the reward of seeing them grow and advance."

Mentoring is described by Michael Zeldin, a professor of Jewish education at Hebrew Union College–Jewish Institute of Religion, as "a long-term relationship, where the focus is on supporting the growth and development of the mentee. The mentor is a source of wisdom, teaching, support, and perspective. The essential dimensions of mentoring are the centrality of relationship and building trust."

Mentoring makes a difference to both the mentee and the mentor. According to a 2013 study, sponsored by MENTOR: The National Mentoring Partnership, 46 percent of at-risk youth with mentors are less likely than their peers to start using drugs, 52 percent are less likely to skip a day of school, and 55 percent are more likely to enroll in college. That same study showed that, sadly, one in three young people—more than 9 million kids in America—grow up without an adult mentor.

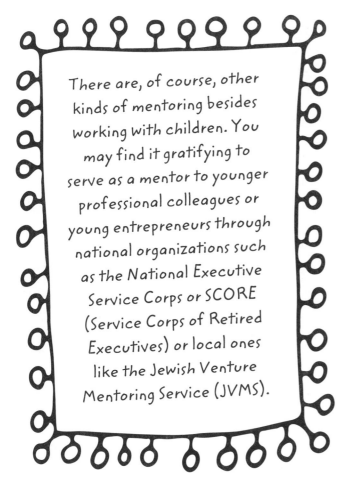

There are, of course, other kinds of mentoring besides working with children. You may find it gratifying to serve as a mentor to younger professional colleagues or young entrepreneurs through national organizations such as the National Executive Service Corps or SCORE (Service Corps of Retired Executives) or local ones like the Jewish Venture Mentoring Service (JVMS).

America has a "mentoring gap"—a lack of mentors to serve the nation's young people who need them.

David Shapiro, CEO of MENTOR, said he thinks adults over 50 make for ideal mentors. "They are relationship experts, based on their life experience, and have the wisdom of perspective. I think they also understand what it's like to walk alongside others as an empowering and supportive force, since they have often played this coaching, managing, mentoring role in life—personally and professionally."

Herb Moller exemplifies this description of the ideal mentor. He wanted to work with needy individuals after his long and rewarding career at Gillette. Today he's a mentor at UnidosNow, whose mission is to help students from low-income Latino families finish high school and go on to college. As he reflected to me, "That's what I feel called to do and to pay my many blessings forward."

Moller chose that nonprofit partly based on his poignant personal story. Born of German parents in Romania in 1941, he spent much of his early years in an orphanage and a Russian prison camp until his future stepfather got him and his mother out of Romania and into Germany when he was six. After his family moved to Philadelphia, he was abandoned by his mother and stepfather, and he lived on his own, with kindly interventions by others.

Moller's advice to people approaching retirement who would like to mentor: "Find something that you can do that would make a difference in a child's life. Look for the right match."

Meeting Your Match

Finding the right mentoring program for your goals, skills, and passions is easier than ever, thanks to recent initiatives from groups such as MENTOR and Encore.org. Those two groups have linked up as part of Encore.org's five-year Generation to Generation campaign, which pairs volunteers over age 50 with needy and at-risk children. The campaign's goal: mobilizing 1 million older volunteers to help children and youth thrive.

The qualities that make for a good mentor are:

- respect
- great listening skills
- empathy
- flexibility
- the ability to see solutions and opportunities

Challenges that can get in the way of good mentoring include lack of training, unclear expectations, too much or not enough structure and support, and tending to talk more than listen or to give advice rather than just being present. Mentors need to be patient; it might take as long as six months or a year to build the trust necessary for success. The biggest challenge is making the right match.

When searching for an appropriate mentoring program, some questions you'll want to ask include:

- What is the time commitment?
- How flexible is the program if I work full-time or travel?
- How will I be matched with the person I'll mentor, and what happens if it turns out not to be a good fit?
- What type of training and support does the program offer?
- Will I be working on my own, or can I get support from other mentors?
- Is the program a good match for my health?

Tutoring kids, mentoring millennials, being a foster grandparent—all are ways we can not only make a difference in the life of a young er person but change our own lives as well. It is a way we can touch the future.

MENTORING.
PASSING YOUR WISDOM FROM GENERATION TO GENERATION.

JANET'S STORY

I was stimulated and challenged during the 30 years I worked at a major academic medical center. However, during the last five years of my tenure there, the highlight of my workweek was leaving the office every Tuesday to work with Emily, who, when we first met, was a first-grader who had been identified by her school as needing help with reading.

After a half-day training, I embarked on a journey that would forever change my life.

Volunteering in an area for which I have great passion adds to my motivation and fulfillment. Reading soothes my soul, introduces me to other cultures, provides insights, and brings me joy. I began this work with more passion than skills, so I researched literacy tools online that would help Emily with reading, as well as related creative projects to reinforce her artistic talents. While we worked together, we began to share stories about our lives and eventually began going on "field trips"—often joined by my daughter, whom Emily adored. I began to evolve from a "tutor" to a "mentor." Emily's mother is a single parent of two children, and I became connected to their lives. I was often told how grateful they were that I came into their lives, but I'm not sure they understand their impact on my life as well. Not long ago Emily told me that we would always continue to read together and when I got older and had trouble reading, she would come to my house and read to me. I bet that she will.

—Janet Noah

Tools and Resources

Chapter 22: Giving a Damn and Getting Involved

A number of organizations—local, national, and international—offer opportunities for nonpartisan citizen activism. Websites such as Avaaz.org or Change.org make it easy to champion causes that are important to you.

Chapter 23: Making Purpose Your True North

An inspiring website to visit is Encore.org, www.encore.org. Just as inspiring is this book by its president Marc Freedman: *How to Live Forever: The Enduring Power of Connecting the Generations.* New York: Public Affairs, 2018.

Brooks, David. *The Second Mountain: The Quest for a Moral Life.* Penguin Random House, 2019. A powerful call to action for us to put commitment and relationship at the center of life, changing society in the process.

Chapter 24: Volunteering with its Joys (and Occasional Oys)

U.S.-BASED VOLUNTEERING

Visit these websites for assistance in finding local and U.S.-based volunteer opportunities:

All for Good (www.allforgood.org/)

HandsOn Network (www.pointsoflight.org/handsonnetwork)

Idealist (www.idealist.org/)

ReServe (www.reserveinc.org/)

Taproot (www.taprootfoundation.org/)

VolunteerMatch (www.volunteermatch.org/)

Nechama: Jewish Response to Disaster (www.nechama.org; *nechama* is Hebrew for "comfort"), based in the Midwest, provides cleanup and recovery assistance to homes and communities throughout the United States affected by natural disaster.

Senior Corps, (www.nationalservice.gov/programs/senior-corps), a program of the Corporation for National and Community Service, is composed of Americans age 55 and older who use their experience and wisdom to volunteer and make a difference in their communities. Current programs include Foster Grandparents; RSVP, the largest volunteer network in the country; and Senior Companions, which helps seniors remain independent in their homes.

Also check out your State Service Commission, which oversees federal programs operating in your state, such as AmeriCorps, VISTA, and Senior Corps. The Corporation for National and Community Service oversees these programs. Visit its website (www.nationalservice.gov).

PROGRAMS FOCUSED ON ISRAEL

Some of our favorites:

CAARI, Canadian American Active Retirees in Israel (www.caarivolunteers.com), combines volunteering in Tel Aviv schools and hands-on cleanup in Jewish National Fund sites with visits to Israel's landmarks. Takes place in January–February.

Conservative Yeshiva Volunteer & Study in Jerusalem combines Jewish study with volunteering in a nonprofit educational organization. Takes place during summer for two 3-week sessions.

Dental Volunteers for Israel (www.dental-dvi.org.il) places licensed dentists as volunteers in a clinic serving Jerusalem's indigent children, regardless of race or religion. Operates year-round.

GoEco (www.goeco.org/area/volunteer-in-the-middle-east/israel) offers a variety of affordable volunteer and ecologically minded vacations. Some programs are age-limited. Provides hostel-style accommodations. Operates year-round.

Jewish Agency's Partnership2gether Peoplehood Platform (www.jewishagency.org/p2g-eng) is a joint initiative of various Jewish Community Federations and the Jewish Agency of Israel.

Sar-El (www.sarelcanada.org) provides volunteer work on an Israel Defense Forces (IDF) base, performing noncombat civilian support duties, such as packing medical supplies, repairing machinery and equipment, building fortifications, and cleaning, painting, and maintaining the base. Volunteers work alongside soldiers, base employees, and other volunteers and stay in barracks Sunday through Wednesday. Operates year-round.

Skilled Volunteers for Israel (www.skillvolunteerisrael.org) provides meaningful volunteer opportunities by linking the interests and expertise of North American adults, including retirees, with the critical needs of Israeli nonprofit and educational organizations. Its visionary director Marla Gamoran has begun to change the culture of volunteering in Israel by focusing on older adults and offering a large variety of placement options, based on the skills, interests, experience, and geographical preference of the adult volunteers. Operates year-round.

WWOOF Israel, or World-Wide Opportunities on Organic Farms (www.wwoof.org.il), offers volunteer opportunities on a kibbutz, a moshav, or a small private family farm. Provides free food and accommodation. Volunteers learn from their hosts about organic gardening, winemaking, permaculture, green building, cheese making, gray water system, renewable energy, animal care, and more.

OTHER OVERSEAS VOLUNTEERING

A Broader View Volunteers (www.abroaderview.org) has 245 programs across the world, including some geared for mature travelers. The organization "openly welcomes doctors, nurses, dentists, and teachers at overcrowded and understaffed clinics, schools, orphanages, and hospitals."

Abroadly (www.abroadly.com, part of Volunteer Forever) is a clearinghouse of more than 150 programs committed to ethical and sustainable social impact in youth development, construction and community development, education, health and medicine, human rights, and wildlife and environmental conservation.

Globally focused, the American Jewish World Service Volunteer Corps (www.ajws.org/) provides substantive volunteer assignments in developing countries, ranging from two months to a year. Prior to service, volunteers participate in an orientation that includes Jewish text study relating to international development. When they return home, they are expected to advocate for community building and social change.

Global Vision International works in 13 countries, and all its programs are aligned with the 17 United Nations Sustainable Development Goals, as well as the objectives of local partners. It has a division for volunteers 50 and over.

Global Volunteers (www.globalvolunteers.org/community-projects/) specializes in ethical volunteer projects abroad, in special consultative status with the United Nations.

International Volunteer HQ (www.volunteerhq.org/) is a travel company that operates in 40 locations. Their placements include projects caring for abused elephants in the Elephant Village of Surin, Thailand, educational support in the schools of Kathmandu, and Great Barrier Turtle Conservation in Cairns, Australia.

Jewish Helping Hands (www.jewishhelpinghands.org/), founded by Rabbi Joel Soffin, reaches out to needy and vulnerable populations in the United States and abroad.

Projects Abroad (www.projects-abroad.org/volunteer-projects/grown-up-specials) offers two-week-long programs of global service. This organization has a division for skilled professionals, including those who are retired and have experience in teaching, care, conservation and environment, medicine and health care, journalism, law, and business.

Chapter 26: Touching the Future through Mentoring

Experience Corps (www.aarp.org/experience-corps) and Oasis (www.oasis.org/national-programs/intergenerational-tutoring) are both programs that place volunteers over 50 into schools as tutors for children in grades K-3. As career coach Nancy Collamer wrote on Next Avenue: "A striking 93 percent of teachers surveyed said their students' reading and literary performance improved under the guidance of AARP Experience Corps tutors."

The Foster Grandparent Program of Senior Corps (www.nationalservice.gov/programs/senior-corps) matches mentors with special-needs families to help with schoolwork, parenting, and care.

Gen2Gen (www.generationtogeneration.org), part of Encore.org, is dedicated to bringing the generations together and helping youth-serving organizations tap experienced talent. Click on Get Involved and follow the prompts to find a mentoring or volunteer opportunity.

Jewish Big Brothers and Sisters (www.jbbbsla.org/). Helps young people achieve their full potential through mentoring relationships and programs, offers college scholarships. The Los Angeles chapter owns and operates a 112-acre residential camp and retreat center near Glendale, California.

Mentor (www.mentoring.org). On the website, plug in your preferred geographic area, the age and type of youth you'd like to mentor (low-income, academically at-risk, LGBTQ), and be matched with a variety of options that meet your interest.

PART

6

Getting Good
at Giving Away

What endures after we've left the playing field? For some of us, our achievements have lasting impact, whether in our careers, with our families, in our volunteer work, or through any of the other myriad things that we do during our most productive years, however long they may be. Some of this may very well live on after us, either in some physical sense or in the hearts and minds of people whose lives we have impacted. This is part of our legacy.

> The purpose of life is not to be happy, but to matter—to be productive, to be useful, to have it make some difference that you have lived at all.
>
> — Leo Rosten

What else lives on after us? What, how, and to whom we give—money or our possessions, as individuals or as part of a group, in our lifetimes or after we're gone—transmits our values and so is also part of our legacy. When we share our stories—the experiences that shaped our personalities, values, and perspectives—we give the people we love greater insight into who we are, which may, in turn, give our loved ones deeper insight into who they are, too. As we each take a deep look at what values we want to pass on—in conversation or more formally in a recorded interview or a written document—we have the opportunity to recalibrate and make adjustments to how we currently live to be more fully in harmony with those truths we have already learned.

Rather than leave these transmissions to chance, we can make a conscious effort to articulate our values now so that those who live on and in generations to come will have a better understanding of who we are, what motivates us, what inspires us, where we've come from, and what we hope for the future. This is our true legacy and what truly matters. In part 6, we look at these four different ways to express our legacy through what we give away: money, things, stories, and wisdom.

CHAPTER 27
Giving Strategically to Make Real Change
by Andrés Spokoiny

Richard first met Andrés Spokoiny in Los Angeles when he delivered the keynote address at a Jewish Jumpstart symposium on funding innovation ("We need to invent a new way of inventing"). Andrés is president and CEO of Jewish Funders Network and a Jewish communal leader with a history of leading successful organizational transformations. Originally from Argentina, he has a multidisciplinary background including business, education, and rabbinical studies.

Words of Wisdom

Every dollar makes a difference. And that's true whether it's Warren Buffett's remarkable $31 billion pledge to the Gates Foundation or my late father's $25 check to the NAACP.

—Michael Bloomberg

Editors' note: *For some people, the word* philanthropy *might conjure up images of enormously wealthy individuals who created foundations to benefit social or humanitarian causes, such as the Rockefeller Foundation, the Ford Foundation, or the Bill and Melinda Gates Foundation. But philanthropy is actually something that all of us can engage in, regardless of the size of our wallets. Coming from the Greek* philanthropia, *meaning "the love of humanity," philanthropy is simply the practice of giving money and time to help better people's lives. Many of us already contribute to local or national charitable causes. Some of us are considering leaving a portion of our assets to charities. Whether we have a few thousand or a few million dollars, the following guide will help us approach philanthropic giving in a strategic and thoughtful manner.*

My assumption is that you have come to a point in your life when you want to "give back," and you want to make it count. In particular, you want to get serious about what you want to give away now and through your estate after you die.

You want to make real change, effectively applying what resources you have toward achieving some measurable impact. And whether your budget for charitable contributions is large or small, you want to be as careful with your social investments as you (hopefully) have been with your retirement account.

Many of us don't fit this description. We think of charity as a simple act, a coin in a *pushke* (collection box). We're happy writing a check to a worthy organization working for a good cause. And you know what? At the risk of speaking outright heresy as the president of an organization dedicated to rigorous, effective, and strategic philanthropy, that's okay. Better to give simply than to give nothing.

> If you are a regular contributor to a particular charity, you might consider leaving a gift to the organization in your will so that your support will continue after your death.

But I encourage you to take the next step by developing a strategic approach to giving. You can get so much more out of your giving—more impact for the world and more meaning for yourself and your family—if you're willing to put in the hard and deliberate work of pursuing effective philanthropy.

Here's some good news: You're never too old or too young to get started. For example, some of the most innovative Jewish giving today is coming out of teen philanthropy programs. On the other end, big changes in the Jewish community have been created by philanthropists in their golden years, such as Harold Grinspoon, who created PJ Library at age 76, and Charles Bronfman and Michael Steinhardt, who founded Birthright Israel in their 70s. And then there are those whose giving has continued throughout their adulthood, such as Barbara Dobkin, whose vision and philanthropy across the landscape of the American Jewish feminist community have empowered generations of Jewish women.

Start with Why

Why are you giving? This is different from asking why philanthropy is good in the abstract. How you answer this question speaks to what you personally want to achieve.

You probably have a mix of motivations for giving away money: personal, familial, communal, global. Maybe you're passionate about solving a particular problem or addressing an urgent social need. Maybe you feel a sense of responsibility or gratitude for the blessings you have received in life. Maybe you want to shape the way you're remembered when (someday) you're gone. Maybe you want a new way to connect with your kids and grandkids and instill your values in the coming generations. Maybe you feel anxiety about the future and want to create hope. Maybe you feel disengaged and want to create meaning. Maybe tzedakah is your favorite part of being Jewish—or your least favorite, and you want to change that. Maybe you want to do something for God or feel more engaged in your community.

THE JEWISH LINT SOCIETY. BELLY BUTTON LINT FOR ALL.

Out of that tangled mix of interests, emotions, and aspirations, you can begin the process of strategic giving by creating:

1. A mission
2. A team
3. A plan of action

Define Your Mission

Your mission comes from your motivations for giving that are focused on results beyond yourself and your loved ones. It comes from your values and priorities, from the changes you want to make.

Of course, you have to go beyond just picturing the changes. There's a difference between vision and mission. Vision is a desired state of the world. It's aspirational and far-reaching. Your mission, by contrast, is how you contribute to making that vision a reality. Break down your mission into distinct "problems to solve" and focus strategically on them. Where do you want to devote your precious time, energy, and passion? Where do you feel there is an opportunity for you to make a meaningful difference?

Your mission, once you have discerned and defined it, is your North Star, the way you navigate in any terrain and keep moving in the direction you want.

Put Together Your Team

It's not only big-money donors who need a team. No matter the dollar amounts, the process of clarifying your vision, mission, and strategy will be greatly enhanced by having other people involved in your deliberations. With whom do you want to do this? Many of us will turn to those relationships that motivate us to give in the first place: family, friends, community.

For most of us, family is either all or a significant part of who we want to help guide our giving. Family philanthropy is an incredibly powerful way for families to connect. It's a rare opportunity to discuss the family's shared values, achieve common goals, and shape legacies for individuals and the family as a whole. Many of us think about our philanthropic legacies only when we're planning our estate. But if we don't also consider giving during our lifetime, we miss out on opportunities for ongoing personal reflection and family dialogue.

Family philanthropy can also generate family conflict and intergenerational tensions.

> Ellen, one of Richard's friends, had become increasingly concerned about the impact of climate change on future generations. Inspired by Al Gore's award-winning documentary *An Inconvenient Truth* and the increasingly hot summers in Los Angeles and horrible hurricanes in other parts of the country, she was particularly moved by her rabbi's Rosh Hashanah sermon about humans being the trustees of God's creation. She organized a team of synagogue members who chose as their mission helping local Jewish institutions lower their environmental impact. The team financially supports initiatives by Jewish institutions that educate members, implement recycling programs, and make structural changes, such as installing solar-energy panels and low-water-use bathroom fixtures. The *Ner Tamid* (Eternal Light) at their synagogue is now powered by solar energy.

Don't let that put you off. The issues raised can provide an opening to improve family communication and improve mutual understanding in the long term.

As you consider who's on your team, think beyond your family, too. Look to giving circles (see chapter 28, "Mixing Community and Philanthropy"), committees, and boards of organizations on which you serve for others who share your goals. And if you have a lot of resources to devote to your giving strategy, you may also want to invite professionals—whether as paid staff or advisors—to help you figure it out.

Decide on Your Plan of Action

Your plan of action is motivated by how you see yourself: your legacy, your feelings, your personality. It comes, too, from your commitment to giving strategically and effectively. Be deliberate and explicit about how you'll decide to give, and evaluate your progress as you go along.

We have divided up our estate into five parts. If there is anything left after we both die, each of our four children will get one part, and the fifth part will go to charitable organizations. Rather than designate which charities will receive gifts, we have given our children the responsibility to meet, discuss, and distribute the funds to three types of organizations: progressive Jewish nonprofits in the United States and Israel, groups working for social justice, and those pursuing environmental protection. It's up to our adult kids to decide which ones.

—Richard and Laura

Evaluate Your Progress

Evaluation is critical to effective philanthropy. How can we improve if we don't know how we're doing? Many of us carefully evaluate who we're giving to, measuring and tracking how well the organizations are meeting our goals, but we don't often evaluate ourselves. However, we should try to buck that trend because it's hard to get honest feedback. Nobody wants to criticize the person doling out funds—a donor is always beautiful and charming, and his jokes are always funny—or tell a funder that she is being shortsighted in her grant giving, which often results in underperformance. Getting good at giving away is about proactively setting up mechanisms to receive constructive and insightful criticism from all directions: grantees, fellow funders, the broader community, and (ideally) the target population being helped.

Self-evaluation also points to a higher principle: accountability. Responsibility to those around us exists whether or not we choose it, but accountability is how we do or don't live up to it.

Keep Listening and Learning

For every step in this process—discerning your mission, building your team, crafting your process, evaluating your progress, holding yourself accountable—the most important skill is deep listening. Good philanthropy is social not only in its effects but also in its practice. To give well, you have to spend much more time listening than giving. Good philanthropy is conscious philanthropy. And through it, everyone benefits: the givers, the ones who receive, and the world that is changed through their partnership.

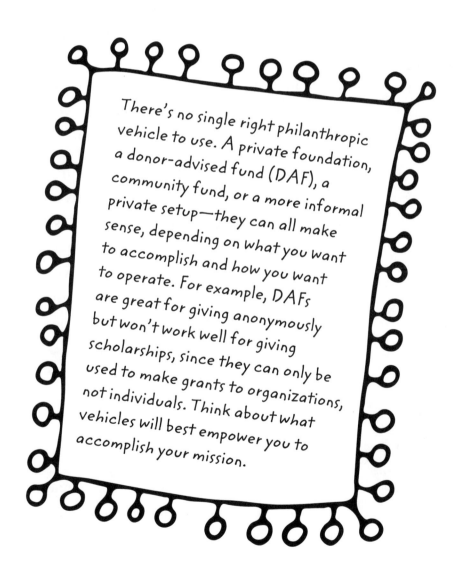

There's no single right philanthropic vehicle to use. A private foundation, a donor-advised fund (DAF), a community fund, or a more informal private setup—they can all make sense, depending on what you want to accomplish and how you want to operate. For example, DAFs are great for giving anonymously but won't work well for giving scholarships, since they can only be used to make grants to organizations, not individuals. Think about what vehicles will best empower you to accomplish your mission.

CHAPTER 28
Mixing Community and Philanthropy
by Felicia Herman

Felicia is the founder of Amplifier: The Jewish Giving Circle Project, "a network of giving circles motivated by Jewish values." Richard has been a fan of her work since 2005 when she took over as executive director of Natan, a group of young professionals who envision a new approach to strategic philanthropy.

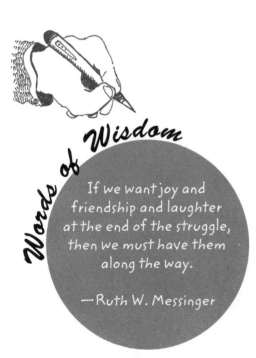

Words of Wisdom

If we want joy and friendship and laughter at the end of the struggle, then we must have them along the way.

—Ruth W. Messinger

In 2004 my husband and I joined a giving circle: a group of people who pool their charitable donations and decide together where to allocate their money. A simple but powerful way to bring people together to give, giving circles provide anyone—at any giving level, in any place, giving to any kind of cause—a way to come together to share and leverage the group's money, skills, and creativity. Circles might be made up of friends, colleagues, family, or neighbors—anyone who joins together to make a difference for their community or cause. A giving circle takes your mind, talents, and financial abilities seriously and makes giving a collaborative, social experience.

Natan, the New York City–based giving circle we joined, had just completed its first cycle of making grants to innovative Jewish and Israeli nonprofits, and it was recruiting new members as it embarked on its second cycle. My husband and I were drawn to Natan because it was a group of young givers who learned about and then invested thoughtfully in fascinating, emerging sectors of Jewish life: social entrepreneurs and start-up nonprofits that were engaging young North American Jews in new ways or who were developing creative approaches to economic development in Israel.

Giving circles are not new. In fact, collective giving enterprises date back to ancient times: in the Ancient Temple era there was the *kuppah* (community charitable fund), and the Talmud discusses the *tamchui* (communal food pantry), to which everyone contributed and the needy drew from as necessary. Jewish voluntary societies of the 18th, 19th, and 20th centuries—Jewish and secular—often included a mix of philanthropy and community service. Most recently, the tzedakah collective, enterprises popular in the 1960s and 1970s because of their countercultural ability to democratize giving, put the power in the hands of the givers and built a communal approach to social change.

Contemporary research on American giving circles confirms that their members give more, give more strategically, and are more involved in their communities than non–giving circle members. Giving circles are a growing phenomenon. There are now more than more than a thousand in the United States alone, involving thousands of participants and giving away hundreds of millions of dollars.

What Are the Benefits of Giving Circles?

Most people give on their own, responding to requests from charitable organizations or friends with favorite causes. To some, this kind of reactive giving is or becomes unsatisfying. Giving circles offer the opportunity to give proactively, strategically, and collaboratively, leveraging the money and wisdom of a community. Giving circles are:

Accessible. Anyone—at any giving level, at any age, in any place, with any funding interest—can start or participate in a giving circle. There's no minimum contribution level and no barriers to entry.

Hands-on. In addition to active engagement with philanthropic decision making, some giving circles offer members a chance to volunteer or provide pro bono professional assistance for the organizations they support.

Collaborative. Members make decisions together in a democratic process, leveraging each other's experiences and wisdom as equals and peers.

Communal. Members connect with each other and with their communities, building meaningful relationships with each other and with those they support.

Empowering. Members combine their dollars to do something bigger—and perhaps better—than they could on their own.

Educational. Members learn about the needs of their community or focus area and can be intentional and proactive about how they give to the causes they care about. They also learn from each other by exploring and welcoming diverse viewpoints.

Fun. Giving circles bring people together to accomplish some serious good in a joyful way. It's a social experience: In addition to giving together, members often share meals, stories, and their lives in meaningful ways.

The people, the content, the grantees, the impact: that's what drew my husband and I to Natan, and it's what has kept us there for 16 years. Natan has become a community of friends for us, a group of people connected by (many but not all of) our values, a shared desire to learn and grow, and a commitment to using our collective resources—financial, intellectual, and social—to strengthen the Jewish people and the State of Israel.

I don't have that much money. Is a giving circle right for me?

Yes! By joining together with others, you can leverage other people's contributions and together make a greater impact. The key to a successful giving circle of any size is having a realistic understanding of your impact and "rightsizing" your expectations for members and for the organizations that receive your support. (Many circles have a version of the mantra "Don't be a jerk!" referring both to how members get along with others and how they treat charitable organizations.)

Some groups focus more on the giving circle experience—Are we learning what we want to learn, happy with what we're giving to, and having fun?—than on the impact of their giving on the causes they support. Others focus on strengthening their philanthropic and grant-making skills, striving to be strategic, effective givers, sometimes by partnering or learning with local philanthropists, foundations, or community foundations.

From the grant recipient side, what matters is that circles respect the time and energy of applicants, right-sizing their requests from organizations (for applications, site visits) to the amount of money they're offering in grants.

How to Start a Giving Circle

Starting a giving circle couldn't be easier or more straightforward:

- Gather people together.

- Decide how much each person is willing to give (and where you will house the money).

- Discuss the values and interests that connect you and that will guide the circle; decide on a mission statement or set of criteria that will enable you to make choices from among many worthy causes.

- Decide on a process: How many meetings? Will you have a public call for proposals or will members nominate potential grantees? Will you use "one person/one vote" or establish voting proportional to giving level?

- Gather applications and material about potential grantees.

- Possibly meet with applicants and/or organize site visits.

- Decide how to allocate your collective funds.

> What's the minimum viable number for launching a group, and what's the ideal maximum size?
>
> Five to twenty people is optimal for a start-up giving circle, but it really comes down to what you hope to achieve, what your financial goals are, and how many different voices you can accommodate.

Within this basic framework, giving circles are infinitely customizable. The number of members, the amount of money you give, the issues and types of initiatives you focus on are all up to you. How many meetings will you have? Will you also host events to learn about issues and/or to be social together? Will you raise additional money from nonmembers? How many of the four "T"s will you offer to organizations: time, talent, treasure, ties (networks)? The rule of thumb is that form should follow function: create the giving circle that addresses the goals articulated by its members—and possibly by the needs of the fields in which you'll be investing.

Tips for Sustaining an Effective Giving Circle

A few words of advice for setting up a long-lasting and successful giving circle:

Recruit people who are fans of group decision making. Not every cause put forward by members will get funded, and not everything that gets funded will have unanimous or universal support. Members need to trust the group and its process and know that they may not get their way 100 percent of the time. They should be willing to engage in the give-and-take and compromise that come with being part of a team. And they should welcome and value different viewpoints, being curious about other people's perspectives and open to respectful debate. (This is a civic skill much in need.)

Giving circles take time. They take time for planning, meeting, reviewing applications, and voting. Some giving circles also organize site visits and networking and celebratory events. Make sure all members and prospects are aware of the time commitment and agree to do their best to show up consistently.

There's a cost of doing business. As your giving circle grows, so will its costs. Bigger events require more food and thus higher expenses. Maybe you want to develop a website or hire staff. Even if your circle starts small and members share or trade responsibility for expenses, you may one day need to raise money (from members or others), not only to make grants but also to operate your circle. This is good—it's a sign of success!—and it will give you an appreciation of the costs of doing business for the organizations you support, too.

Be realistic, stay humble, and respect everyone's time. Manage expectations about what your circle can accomplish, given members' contributions of money and time. Respect your members' time as well as that of your grant applicants and recipients. Shape what you ask of members to meet their expectations and goals, and don't ask more of grant applicants than what you are potentially giving them.

Strive for Ethical Giving

A giving circle is a combination of intentional grant making and providing excellent and meaningful experiences for members. It's often tricky to keep the needs and agendas of both in balance. Grant making is the process by which giving circles engage, educate, inspire, and empower their members, yet this process can impose substantial costs on the very organizations the circle hopes to support, for instance by placing time-consuming or onerous requirements on applying or evaluation. There is a power imbalance inherent in philanthropy—some people ask for money; others have the power to give or withhold it—that good giving circles can mitigate by being sensitive to this dynamic. Ideally, grant making is a partnership between the funder and the grantee. The funder provides the funds to do the work, and the grantee does the work every day. Neither's vision can be fulfilled without the other, and both have something to teach, learn, and give to the other. True partnership between the giver and the recipient is a deeply Jewish concept.

Giving circles democratize charitable giving, making it accessible and meaningful to anyone. They focus on collaboration between members, leveraging each others' resources and wisdom to achieve an impact greater than any one person could have done. They offer opportunities for an ethical, transparent, humble, and flat (that is, nonhierarchical) experience of giving that can bring tremendous benefit to the recipient, the giver, and, indeed, the world.

Leaving a Legacy, Not a Landfill
by Deborah Goldstein

Based in Brooklyn, Deborah assists seniors in the stressful process of downsizing and also offers coaching services for adult children who need help supporting their parents through a moving process.

Words of Wisdom

Who is rich?
Those who are satisfied with what they have.

—Pirkei Avot 5:1

As we get older, many of us find that we're more interested in getting rid of things than in acquiring more. At a certain point in our lives we look around and realize that we've accumulated a lot of stuff: shelves stuffed with books we'll never read; closets filled with clothes we'll never wear; and cabinets, attics, garages, and basements stacked with an array of leftover, left-behind, outgrown, slightly damaged things. There are a number of reasons to downsize or rightsize, the most common being a prelude to a move. But even if we're staying in our home, we may want to step back, evaluate what we have, and give away or get rid of what we no longer need or want. Although the experience can be physically, mentally, and emotionally exhausting, it can also be a satisfying and gratifying expression of our values and a gift to our heirs.

As a home organizer, I have supported people of all ages by helping them make thoughtful decisions about what to let go, what to hold on to, and what to give away. As they let go of the clutter and belongings blocking their space, internally and externally, they have gained a deeper appreciation for what truly holds meaning in their lives and a greater understanding of the symbolism and history of the belongings that are of true value.

The process of decluttering has a resonance with the pre-Passover preparations of removing *chameitz* (products that contain leavening) from our houses. Symbolically, *chameitz* is not just yeast or flour, but represents things that "puff us up." As we look around our houses, how can we get rid of the things that bloat us? Before Passover in my Brooklyn neighborhood, I witness families burning their bread in garbage cans in preparation for the holiday. It makes me think about my clients who at first are afraid that they will have to let go of things that matter to them, only to discover in the process what truly *does* matter to them.

Where to Start?

How do you sort through all your possessions and determine what do with them? I recommend starting in your home's storage units—the attic, basement, and garage; we often stuff items in these spaces because we don't want to deal with them—then move on to closets, cabinets, and drawers. Divide things into the following four groups.

GROUP 1: THINGS YOU WANT TO CONTINUE USING AND/OR ENJOYING

Items in this group are easy to identify because you know what you use and enjoy. When you're unsure about an item's usefulness or aesthetics, give it the time test: If you haven't used or worn something in a year, give it away. Or follow the advice of Marie Kondo in her best seller *The Life-Changing Magic of Tidying Up: The Japanese Art of Decluttering and Organizing* and consider whether the item "gives you joy."

GROUP 2: THINGS YOU WANT TO GIVE AWAY TO SPECIFIC PEOPLE

This category includes items you want to give away, either now or later, to specific people because they reflect values, experiences, or sentiments important to you. They tell the story of your life, so decisions surrounding them can be difficult. Before you begin, ask yourself: What do you want or consider to be your legacy?

JOHNNY CAN HAVE MY USED TUNA CAN COLLECTION. ♡

I asked both my mother and a long-term client this question. My mother is a Swedish minimalist, and my client is a "collector." In both cases, the question led to oral histories of family, love, and identity, and a list of their most important possessions—a museum catalog of their lives.

My mother put it simply but beautifully: "I want my legacy to be love: the love of my family and the love of my friends; the love I felt for them, and the love I received from them." She determined the value of things she loved by who gave them to her and whether they made her feel loved. For instance, she loved the furniture from my grandmother, my father's mother, who welcomed her into the family when she was not Jewish and who became a surrogate mother to her when she moved to the United States. My mother remembered and held on to this act of kindness and love even through the rough times. In the end, my mother identified about 5 or 10 items that she wanted my siblings and me and my children to have. Through asking my mother what her legacy was and what she truly valued, I gained a deeper appreciation for the purity of the love my mother gave us all, and I made a commitment to keep the few things that meant so much to her.

When I asked my client, the collector, what she wanted her legacy to be, her answer was "worthiness." Together we created a list of items to be given to friends and charities. For three years I had been helping this client sort and clear out items from her vast collection. A former actress, and a lover of words, she said, "I live in the word, whether spoken or written. It feeds me and it informs me and wraps itself around any material things I own." For her, any meaningful gift comes with a story. We decided that we would dedicate a portion of each session to writing dedications for heirlooms to be given to friends or relatives. My client then took it to the next level, not only writing descriptions of the objects, but also including letters to the individuals expressing the love she felt for them and how they influenced her life.

By letting your friends and family know what you would like to pass down to them, they will better understand the symbolism and meaning of the things that matter to you. Consider having these conversations one-on-one, and be mindful of the recipients' needs, interests, and capacities. When my collector client was considering leaving something to a dear friend who has himself become overwhelmed by his own stuff, she thoughtfully decided to leave him only one item.

Consider tagging important items with the names of possible recipients and brief descriptions of why they are meaningful. I cleared out a home with a woman whose mother was in a nursing home with severe dementia. As we were packing up the house, we discovered that her mother had left descriptions on the back of the most important items. At first this very moving revelation made the daughter sad, as she thought about how her mother was aware that she was losing her memory. But then she felt joy and love for her mother, whose notes helped her understand her mother's history and identify the real heirlooms.

Holiday gatherings or family get-togethers are great opportunities to have these conversations about leaving a legacy, although it is probably wise to let family members know in advance that this is part of your agenda. You may start by saying, "I have been thinking about my legacy and what I value, and this is why these things matter to me."

GROUP 3: THINGS THAT ARE USABLE BUT ARE NOT LEGACY ITEMS

We all have lots of beautiful, valuable, or usable stuff. But not everything will have such personal, sentimental, or symbolic value for you that you want to keep it in the family or give it (and its stories) to particular people. Trust your gut and keep a sense of humor. If your thought is "Why the heck did I keep this?" give it away or throw it away.

First, ask your friends and family if they would like anything that you are not keeping or giving to other people. If they don't respond, that is their answer. It does not mean your possessions are not valuable; they just might not fit into their physical spaces or lifestyles. Don't take it personally.

Second, donate. After decluttering, all my clients feel comforted by the idea that other people will benefit from their donations. Knowing that furniture, clothing, housewares, and other material possessions are going to worthy organizations makes letting go less painful. A dear friend of mine volunteers and contributes excess furniture to A Sense of Home, a Los Angeles–based nonprofit that sets up apartments for young adults who have aged out of the foster care system. My Swedish aunt and uncle donated their collection of traditional Christmas decorations to the ski club of which they were longtime members. A former client donated her civil rights academic library to a prison that was starting an education program. Another client donated her entire work wardrobe to an organization that helps women get back into the workforce after recovering from addiction and poverty.

> Recent cultural shifts are making this process more problematic or fraught than it used to be. Younger generations have different needs; that is, they have no use for the family china, less space to store large items; they may not find the objects meaningful or may have different aesthetic tastes. For more perspective on "unfurnishing" and advice on how to handle hurt feelings, see "Nobody Wants Your Parents' Stuff," in Part 6 Tools and Resources.

GROUP 4: THINGS THAT ARE BROKEN, UNREPAIRABLE, OR OF NO POSSIBLE VALUE TO ANYONE ELSE

What you cannot give away, dispose of in an environmentally positive way. Your local city or town has places where you can recycle fabrics, electronics, and toxic materials.

Additional Considerations

There is no one approach to decluttering. It helps to attune ourselves to special circumstances and be flexible in how we handle things.

Couples. Rarely do I find couples who have the same attachments to their possessions. One might be the collector, the other the minimalist (who might actually have spent decades resenting his or her spouse's collections!). I work with couples separately when downsizing a house. I encourage them to focus on their own "stuff" first and make joint decisions on shared items later.

Children's things. You may find that your home has become a storage unit for your adult children's memorabilia: yearbooks, trophies, sports equipment, school papers. Send your adult children photos of all the items that they have in the house and ask them if they want their stuff, or if it can be donated or trashed. If the kids want some of their things, set a firm deadline for them to pick up what they want or arrange with them to have the items sent.

Paperwork. Begin by buying a fireproof safe box. As you sort through your paperwork, secure in the box your important identity and financial papers, such as birth certificates, death certificates, military service records, long-term care instructions, wills, Social Security cards, passports, insurance policies, and the deed to the house. Decluttering can be exhausting and anxiety-producing. It is easy to become overwhelmed and forgetful. Knowing that all your documents are in one safe and secure container will bring you peace of mind. (See chapter 18, "Getting Your Stuff Together.")

Photos. Keep the photos, ditch the frames. Only keep photos and memorabilia that are truly significant to you. Make sure to write down the dates, the history, and the names of people on the back of photographs or frames of artwork. If you are looking at a photograph and have no idea who the person or people are in it, throw it out.

Organizing digital photographs is even more complicated and time-consuming than organizing physical photos. Because storage space on an external hard drive or in the cloud is so vast, you may tend to keep everything. This doesn't make for a coherent legacy, however. As with physical photos, it's worth going through them carefully. For this task, dedicate short periods of time over a number of days or weeks, so you don't get exhausted by the experience. Delete duplicates and only keep those photos that have value or meaning to you. Then label the files with information about who is in them, where they were taken, and when.

Journals. Clients often ask what I recommend they do with their personal journals. If your journals are simply travel logs and you don't mind your children or spouse reading them, go ahead and keep them. If your journals hold parts of your story that you would not want your loved ones to read, let them go. It is freeing.

Gifts and things passed down to you. We hold on to so many things that weigh us down. This is a time in your life when you deserve to focus on yourself and feel lightness and joy. Throw out the guilt and make thoughtful choices. If someone gave you a gift and it's not your style, donate it. If you have Aunt Esther's furniture in your basement and you hate it, donate it or put it out on the curb. You can find great peace in letting go of things that no longer have meaning or value to you.

I already know what I would like of my mother's: a blue blown-glass cat in her dining room. It's not because I am particularly fond of cats, but rather because I cherish the story attached to it. My mother, who is a giver and truly the most generous person I have ever known, was in Stockholm with my aunt and spotted this cat. She wanted it, but could not justify spending the money. My aunt grew tired of her indecision and told her, "If you don't buy it for yourself, I will." My mother bought it for herself. My mother told me it was her favorite thing now. To me it symbolized my mother giving love to herself, and that is something I want to hold on to.

Computer files, while not actually contributing to physical clutter, require some careful attention nonetheless. The process is the same as for paperwork: deleting duplicate or unimportant files and organizing the other files into coherent, easily identifiable categories so that others can find the information when and if needed. Then back up the files on an external hard drive or a cloud-based storage service or, ideally, both. And remember to make sure that key people in your life know your username(s) and password(s).

What is your legacy, and how do your things tell your story?

Telling Your Story

by Ellie Kahn

Ellie Kahn is a Los Angeles-based oral historian who writes periodically for the *Jewish Journal*, where we first encountered her work. She has extensive experience in recording life stories and producing videos and books based on the interviews.

Words of Wisdom

Everyone has a story. These stories, told to oneself and others, can transform the world.

Barbara Myerhoff, Number Our Day

Whether you were born in Poland or Chicago, survived the Great Depression, remember the Summer of Love and Woodstock, made millions or you're barely making ends meet, everyone has a story. But not many people get a chance to tell their stories, unless asked to do so. Some of us are not comfortable telling our stories, either. And, sadly, not everyone recognizes the value of recording such stories—until it's too late.

We needn't have had a traumatic or celebrity life for our stories to be important. The most ordinary life can seem extraordinary to our loved ones, because it is part of their family heritage, and they often want to know the details about this heritage and those who came before them.

Your story is just part of the intricate puzzle that makes you who are you are. Are you fortunate enough to still have parents or grandparents, aunts or uncles, lifelong friends or beloved mentors? Can they still recall events in their lives clearly and tell you about them? If so, they are also perfect candidates for being interviewed. And if you are the family's senior member, you have the chance to share your own personal stories.

What's Stopping You?

Too many people regret that they didn't get around to recording Mom's or Dad's stories or didn't make time to share their own. It's not uncommon to hear people say, "We thought Dad was healthy, so there was no rush. Then he had a stroke." While memories are fresh, and while older loved ones can enjoy talking about their life and experiences, take time to invite your family members to reminisce, or start sharing your own precious stories. What's stopping you?

We all are very busy. You have to be willing to invest the time for something that will last forever—maybe two to four hours for recording or writing down memories—plus prep time and editing the recordings, if you choose to.

You or your family elders are not comfortable talking about themselves. Let them know that they don't have to prepare because you will make it easy by asking them questions and agreeing to avoid subjects that you or they don't want to talk about.

Many people don't think their life story is worthy of being recorded. Your job is to convince them—and perhaps yourself— not only that family and friends are interested, but also that our life stories are *our most precious legacies*—gifts we give to our loved ones and beyond—and something that only *we* can offer future generations. These personal memories and stories are also part of the family history.

You think you already know everything about your family history. It is so rare for people to sit down for hours to listen to the details of a person's childhood, relationships, and the times in which they lived that it's likely you'll learn something new. Even if you're the one telling the story, you may learn something new. As you respond to the questions the interviewer is asking you, you may recall something you'd entirely forgotten or come to a new conclusion about how events unfolded.

You or your loved one typically listens rather than talks. In many families, there are talkers and listeners. The talkers might be great storytellers; some of them might be quite dominating. Listeners sit back and do just that—listen. However, many people who are good listeners will suddenly become very talkative when given the attention and opportunity to reminisce. Many families are surprised at what emerges from the quiet relative when she or he is free to talk without interruptions.

Create a List of Questions

Involve your children, siblings, and other family members and friends. What do they want to know about you or the subject of the interview? The best questions are open-ended, which means they push beyond a simple yes or no answer. For example, "Did you like high school?" is a closed-ended question. An open-ended version of the same question is "What are some of your memories about high school?" Words such as "Why," "What," and "How" are good ways to start open-ended questions. Other guiding prompts begin with "Tell me about" or "Describe." The internet is also a good source for questions; search QUESTIONS FOR ORAL HISTORY.

Some things to ask about:

Grandparents. Where did your grandparents come from? What did they do? What were they like as people?

Parents. What stories did you hear about your parents' childhoods? What were your parents' family lives like? How did they meet? How would you describe their personalities? Did they have any hobbies or special skills?

Personal details. What were some of the most significant world events during your lifetime? What did you want to be when you grew up? What were meals like in your family? What did you do for fun? What was your relationship like with your siblings?

Children. What are your favorite memories of each of your children? What was it like for you to be a parent?

Grandchildren. What do you want your grandchildren to know about you? What advice or words of wisdom do you have for them, in terms of your values or living a satisfying life?

Schedule the Interview and Extend an Invitation

Once you have a list of questions, set up the date for the interview. Allow two to four hours; the time will go faster than you can imagine.

Anytime is a good time to record yours or a loved one's stories, but family gatherings provide a special opportunity. Does your family have a seder or a Thanksgiving dinner every year? Holidays and special events can be an ideal time to record your stories or those of loved ones. It's convenient because everyone is there and it can add meaning to the occasion.

Prepare Your Interview Equipment and Setting

All you really need is a digital voice recorder or a digital video camera and tripod. Most of today's recorders have a built-in microphone that can pick up sound from two to five feet away. However, you might need an external microphone if the interviewer won't be sitting close enough to those who are speaking. Smartphones are not currently equipped to record audio or video of two to four hours, but this might change as the devices evolve in the future. If possible, try to have one person in charge of the equipment—for example, starting and stopping the video camera or audio recorder, making sure that the sound is being recorded properly—and another focused on asking the questions and keeping the conversation moving.

Consider bringing family photographs—looking at old photos of parents, grandparents, and one's childhood can stimulate memories and stories. It's also a great way to gets names of people in old photo albums who might otherwise not be identified.

There are two primary ways to conduct the interview: the one-on-one interview and the group interview.

The one-on-one interview, the most common technique, involves just the interviewer and the interview subject—and the person operating the equipment—and is focused on getting as many questions answered with as few distractions as possible. Pick a quiet, comfortable place, and turn off phones to let the subject know that the interview is the sole focus and priority during these hours.

The group interview involves the subject and friends or family asking the questions. With this dynamic setting, it's helpful to designate one person to be responsible for fielding the questions and making sure that the interview doesn't jump around too much.

Tips for a Successful Interview

Reassure everyone involved that conducting an oral history interview isn't a test. There are no right answers. The person sharing her oral history doesn't have to be entertaining or answer every question.

Allow time for answers. Once a question is asked, let the person talk. It's common for interview subjects to meander while reminiscing, and this often leads to some of the best memories and stories. The more details, the better.

Be sensitive to stamina. We all have a limit to our endurance for such interviews. If the person being interviewed is getting tired, take a break or stop for the day. Make a note where you left off.

Expect emotion. Reminiscing can conjure up strong emotions.

> Some talkers and listeners are married to each other. If you plan to interview such a couple, you might separate them at first so that each has a chance to speak. Then bring them together.

If the person you are interviewing cries, reassure him that expressing emotions is okay. Show him that you are comfortable with his emotions. Many people who have been through difficult times believe they need to shield others from hearing about their experiences. Allowing your interview subject to speak freely can create a tremendous connection and feeling of relief.

Be patient. Sometimes an interview like this can reveal memory problems. Be prepared for repetitions and confusion, and do not correct or criticize your subject when that occurs. Be patient and work around memory lapses by asking another question or asking the same question in a different way.

Show appreciation. When you are finished with the interview, let your subject know how much you appreciate her willingness to do this for you. She may say something like, "I really had nothing important to say"; reassure her that the stories she shared are meaningful and will be treasured.

After the Interview

Once the interview is completed, save the audio or video file to a computer and back it up. Share the file—either raw footage or an edited version—with loved ones or make CDs (audio) or DVDs to give to family and friends.

Videos can be enhanced with family photos to illustrate stories.

Video or audio recordings. If you are reluctant to edit the interview yourself, many people these days know how to use software for video and audio editing, and this could be a fun project for a grandchild or a friend. Or hire a professional or a film student at a local college to help edit your recording.

Books. The interview can be typed up by a loved one or professional transcriber and then organized and edited as a printed book, which can be illustrated with family photos and documents.

A recorded oral history—video, audio, or printed—is a priceless gift for future generations. Many years from now, when the people who were interviewed are gone—or when there are great-grandchildren who want to know about their ancestors—this will be a cherished family legacy. Just imagine if you had your great-grandmother's memoir. You are making sure that *your* descendants will have such a treasure.

CHAPTER 31

Remembering Me Like This

by Richard Siegel and Rabbi Laura Geller

In the Jewish cultural experience, one of the ways to answer for our life is by writing an ethical will. Since the days of the patriarchs and matriarchs, Jews have been leaving their families written documents outlining the values they want to pass on to future generations. An ethical will should not be confused with a legal will, that is, a last will and testament. The latter is a legal document detailing how you want to dispose of your physical property after death. An ethical will is a personal articulation of the nonmaterial values and wisdom you want to pass on.

The first Jewish ethical wills are recorded in the Bible. Jacob gathers his children around his bedside to tell them how they should live after he's gone. The entire book of Deuteronomy, particularly the final three chapters, is essentially Moses's ethical will to the Jewish people. David instructs Solomon to complete the tasks he had begun but was unable to finish. The Talmud, medieval sources, and modern Hebrew literature record many examples of ethical wills, some written by scholars, some by ordinary men and women. Some were written in freedom, and some in bunkers or trenches. Some were written in Hebrew, some in Yiddish, some in German, and some in English.

While writing an ethical will is a long-standing Jewish tradition, today the practice is promoted by other religious traditions and in secular life. In the 1950s, the acclaimed broadcast journalist Edward R. Murrow had a popular radio program, *This I Believe*, during which famous and everyday people shared five-minute essays about the values that motivated their lives. The program was reprised by National Public Radio from 2005 to 2014 and now lives on as a

Words of Wisdom

One should not search for an abstract meaning of life. Everyone has his own specific vocation or mission . . . everyone's task is as unique as is her specific opportunity to implement it. . .each person is questioned by life; and can only answer to life by answering for his or her own life.

—Adapted from Viktor Frankl, *Man's Search for Meaning*

nonprofit organization and website (www.thisibelieve.org). In 1993, Marion Wright Edelman, the visionary children's rights advocate, wrote *The Measure of Our Success: A Letter to My Children and Yours*, in which she imparts her wisdom for righteous living; the writer Ta-Nehisi Coates expressed his ideals in *Between the World and Me* as a letter to his son; and President Barack Obama shared his values in "A Letter to My Daughters," published the week before his inauguration in 2009. It begins:

> Dear Malia and Sasha,
>
> I know that you've both had a lot of fun these last two years on the campaign trail, going to picnics and parades and state fairs, eating all sorts of junk food your mother and I probably shouldn't have let you have. But I also know that it hasn't always been easy for you and Mom, and that as excited as you both are about that new puppy, it doesn't make up for all the time we've been apart. I know how much I've missed these past two years, and today I want to tell you a little more about why I decided to take our family on this journey.

Components of an Ethical Will

While many websites and organizations offer instructions, examples, courses, and other resources to help people write ethical wills or "legacy letters," writing an ethical will is actually a pretty straightforward process. Most ethical wills include some combination of the following five components:

1. Instructions for your end-of-life care, funeral, burial, and mourning. Today these are often handled in an advance directive for health care or in separate instructions about funeral arrangements.
2. A recording of your personal and family history: where you came from, how you got here, struggles or challenges you've overcome, significant people who made the journey possible.
3. Instructions or blessings to people you care about: expressions of personal hopes or wishes for your spouse/partner, children, grandchildren, business partners, and friends.
4. Efforts to tie up loose ends: repairing relationships, expressing gratitude, asking for forgiveness.
5. Wisdom learned; that is, your moral autobiography. This is the essence of the ethical will, summarizing the values by which you have tried to live your life, your personal achievements, your regrets and hopes for the future, significant events or moments that changed you, and thoughts on what still needs to be done.

Sam Levenson, a humorist and early television personality, wrote an "Ethical Will and Testament to His Grandchildren and to Children Everywhere" that begins:

I leave you my unpaid debts. They are my greatest assets. Everything I own—I owe:

1. To America I owe a debt for the opportunity it gave me to be free and to be me.

2. To my parents I owe America. They gave it to me and I leave it to you. Take good care of it.

3. To the biblical tradition I owe the belief that people do not live by bread alone, nor do we live alone at all. This is also the democratic tradition. Preserve it.

4. To the six million of my people and to the 30 million other humans who died because of people's inhumanity to each other, I owe a vow that it must never happen again.

5. I leave you not everything I never had, but everything I had in my lifetime: a good family, respect for learning, compassion for others, and some four-letter words for all occasions: words like "help," "give," "care," "feel," and "love."

Susan Turnbull, founder and principal of Personal Legacy Advisors, a firm that advocates nonbinding personal legacy documents, such as ethical wills, as a component of estate and philanthropic planning, offers some practical advice:

Tips for Creation of Your Ethical Will

Start today. If you were not here tomorrow, what is the most important thing you would not want left unsaid? Write it down—you've begun.

Relax. You are not trying to write for the Pulitzer Prize. What you create is a gift of yourself, made for those you love, not for an imaginary panel passing judgment on your life or your writing.

Ask yourself: What do I want to make sure my loved ones know and have in writing?

Consider the process a work in progress. Start by writing something short, and add more pieces or pages as you wish. It's natural that as you and your audience grow and change you might want to modify or add to what you wrote. Don't let the feeling that it has to be "perfect" from the beginning paralyze you. Just get started.

Be yourself. You cannot bequeath what you never owned to begin with, right?

Be careful. Be loving. The reach of your words is unknowable.

Make sure it is easy to find. Keep the file accessible, so you can add to it easily. Either keep it with your legal papers or affix a note there about where to find it. You want to make sure your words find their intended audience.

Share it! Consider sharing it during your lifetime, even as you know you may add to it or change it.

Write a Letter

It's not so hard, but not so easy, either: We're looking inward for the essential truths we have learned so far in our lives, facing up to failures as well as successes, and considering what really matters to us. The task of writing an ethical will is really a response to the challenge articulated by Viktor Frankl: to discover our own specific vocation or mission, and to answer for our own life. It is something we should all do—no matter how old we are.

Rabbi Edward Feinstein, spiritual leader of Valley Beth Shalom in Encino, California, captured both the urgency and poignancy of writing an ethical will in a message to his congregants called "Write a Letter":

> Write a letter. Address it to those you love—your spouse, your partner, your children and grandchildren, your friends, your community. Put into this letter what life has taught you: What have you learned from childhood, from growing up, from your education? What have you learned from your relationships, marriage, children, friendships? What have you learned from work, from your triumphs and successes in the world, and, more importantly, from your failures and disappointments? What have you learned from the death of loved ones, from the path of mourning and grief? What has life taught you? What is the meaning, the lesson, the wisdom of your life? What is your message?
>
> I ask you to do this for three principal reasons:
>
> *First, do it for yourself.* You deserve to know what your life has meant, what it has taught.

There are 5,485 verses in a Torah scroll; tens of thousands of words, more than a hundred thousand handwritten letters. According to tradition, if any one letter, in any word, in any verse, is defaced or erased, the entire Torah is *pasul*, invalid, and may not be read. A Torah missing even the tiniest *yud* is set aside. Why such an obsession? A Hasidic tradition teaches that each letter stands for one human soul. Each individual human being carries one letter of God's message into the world. Just as the loss of the tiniest letter invalidates an entire Torah scroll, losing one human being renders God's message indecipherable. You carry part of God's message. But do you know what it is? Have you discovered it? Have you decoded your part of the message? Have you delivered it?

Second, write the letter for your loved ones. As a rabbi, I frequently accompany families as they grieve. I ask them to share the stories and wisdom of their loved ones' lives. And I am frequently surprised how little they know. They can recount with precision the history of declining health, but they have no notion of the soul—the inner life, the moral struggles, the deepest values of the one whom they love. They know little of the poetry of the soul. "My dad was unremarkable," a son explains. "He worked all the time, cared for Mom, built us this home, but nothing heroic, Rabbi. I'm afraid there's little to say about him." Really? Nothing heroic in his devotion, commitment, care? Your loved ones deserve to know your inner truth. Leave it for them so they might cherish it.

Third, write the letter for your spiritual life. Our tradition begins with the commandment to Abraham, *lech lecha*, literally, "Go into yourself." Hearing the voice of God begins with hearing your own soul. There are many who believe that spiritual wisdom is far away— on some mountaintop to be wrestled from the mystery. But Torah, real spiritual truth, we are taught, "is not beyond your reach. It is not in the heavens . . . neither is it beyond the sea. . . . It is very close to you, in your mouth and in your heart" (Deuteronomy 30:11–14).

Write the letter. But know that it isn't easy. For so many, the heart is more inaccessible than the heavens, more forbidding than the sea. Denial, avoidance, endless distraction keep us from listening.

That's why we age. Without connection to the truth within, the spirit grows old, the soul grows tired. No one is old who knows the truth of his or her existence, the purposes of life. Write the letter.

Modernity has brought us many gifts. But one of the casualties of modern life is contemplation. Our ancestors lived in a much slower world. They walked to and from work. They had time to think, to meditate, to pray. At evening, their homes were not filled with television and internet. In the world before computers and cell phones, they had time to discover the meaning and lessons of existence.

With all our leisure and freedom, we must discipline ourselves to make time for contemplation. Otherwise we live from day to day, from appointment to project to vacation and back again to work, without ever stopping to wonder why. It takes a conscientious effort of the will to make the time, to find the quiet, to turn inward and to listen to what life has come to teach us. "If only you would listen," begs the Torah, then all of God's blessings would find you.

Write a letter.

I AM THE PURE LOVE IN YOUR TRUE HEART OF HEARTS.

I AM A FRESH START AND A NEW BEGINING.

I AM BABIES AND PUPPIES AND LITTLE CHILDREN.

I AM THE QUIET VOICE IN EVERY SOUL WHISPERING: YOU CAN DO IT, NEVER GIVE UP. I WILL NOT LET YOU FAIL.

I AM THAT FAVORITE OLD SHIRT YOU JUST CAN'T THROW AWAY.

©PALNIK 2013

KNOW THYSELF.

I AM THE STARS IN THE BLACK NIGHT SKY.

I AM YOUR HOME. I AM WHO I AM

I AM THE PATH OF LIFE THAT HAS LED YOU TO THIS MOMENT.

I'M A BIRD THAT SINGS MY OWN SONG

I AM THE GOOD PEOPLE THAT LOVE YOU FOREVER

I AM THE MIGHTY OCEANS, CLEAR LAKES, MOUNTAIN BROOKS, RIVERS, PUDDLES AND SWEET HOLY RAIN.

I AM THE STRANGER THAT NEEDS YOUR HELP.

I AM THE HEAVENLY HANDS THAT GUIDE AND PROTECT.

I AM AN ENEMY OF THE CRUEL AND A FIERCE FOE OF THE UNJUST.

I AM ALL THE MUSIC YOU HAVE EVER LOVED.

I AM THE MIRACLE OF LIFE.

I AM THE NOW OF NOWS. I AM THE PRESENT THAT IS ALL AROUND YOU.

MY ETHICAL WILL ☆ ☆ ☆

Tools and Resources

Chapter 27: Giving Strategically to Make Real Change

Jewish Funders Network (www.jfunders.org). A national organization of Jewish funders, both large and small, that provides free educational materials about different forms of philanthropy, such as private foundations, donor-advised funds, giving circles, giving in Israel, and impact investing.

Siegel, Danny. *Giving Your Money Away: How Much, How To, Why, Where, and To Whom* (www.dannysiegel.com). Danny Siegel (no relation to Richard) is a force of nature known for his unrelenting writing, teaching, and general talking about Jewish values and giving at synagogues, JCCs, Federations, day schools, and college campuses across the country. This is his one-volume guide to personalized tzedakah.

Smith, Wendy. *Give a Little: How Your Small Donations Can Transform Our World*. New York: Hyperion, 2009. Recounts inspiring stories of how modest donations helped to make a real difference in the lives of people around the world, with information on where and how to give.

21/64 (www.2164.net). An independent nonprofit providing advice, assistance, and training for multigenerational engagement in family philanthropy. It offers tools to help facilitate the conversation about values within families or among giving circle members.

Chapter 28: Mixing Community and Philanthropy

Amplifier (www.amplifiergiving.org). In 2014 Natan launched Amplifier: The Jewish Giving Circle Movement to help people create and sustain new giving circles. Amplifiergiving.org offers free resources with detailed practical information and also lists existing giving circles in case you want to join one, rather than start your own.

Chapter 29: Leaving a Legacy, Not a Landfill

Eisenberg, Richard. Sorry, Nobody Wants Your Parents' Stuff. www.nextavenue.org, 2017.

Jameson, Marni. *Downsizing the Family Home: What to Save, What to Let Go*. New York: Sterling/AARP, 2016. A step-by-step guide based on the author's personal experience.

Kondo, Marie. *The Life-Changing Magic of Tidying Up: The Japanese Art of Decluttering and Organizing.* Berkeley, CA: Ten Speed Press, 2014. A Japanese organizing consultant, Marie Kondo explains the KonMari Method, which includes a unique categorization system and a general principle of assessing what "sparks joy" for you.

Magnusson, Margareta. *The Gentle Art of Swedish Death Cleaning: How to Free Yourself and Your Family from a Lifetime of Clutter.* New York: Scribner, 2018. Introduces a process for steadily and methodically reducing the amount of stuff that you leave behind so that it does not become a burden for others.

Chapter 30: Telling Your Story

Interviewing Techniques. YouTube offers a variety of videos with helpful tips about interviewing techniques and the use of equipment for recording another person's life story. Search ORAL HISTORY.

The Last Act (www.lastactseries.com). This project of Reboot.org is a series of short documentaries that celebrates how we can "live better while living longer." Contribute your own short video interviews of someone "who is living their years to the fullest," using the DIY #TheLastAct toolkit.

StoryCorps (www.storycorps.org). For examples of moving life stories, beautifully told, there is no better repository than StoryCorps, a nonprofit whose mission is to provide people of all backgrounds and beliefs with the opportunity to record, share, and preserve the stories of their lives. You too can record a StoryCorps interview: Just invite anyone you choose to one of the StoryCorps recording sites to share a 40-minute conversation. Or if you can't get to a recording site, you can use the StoryCorps App to record anywhere.

Storytelling Tips. National Public Radio provides a variety of storytelling tips and best practices through its NPR Training site, www.training.npr.org/topics. Although primarily for people interested in producing radio format programs or podcasts, many of the resources are applicable to personal oral history projects.

Audio and Video Editing. While simply having the raw video footage or audio recording is a valuable document for future generations, you might want to edit your oral history interview to make a shorter or more coherent final project, perhaps interspersing it with photographs or contextual comments. There are a number of audio and video editing tools available for download over the internet.

Chapter 31: Remembering Me Like This

Whether they are called "ethical wills" or "legacy letters," there are many books, websites, and classes providing instruction on creating a document that expresses your personal values and perspectives on life.

From a particularly Jewish perspective:

Riemer, Jack, and Nathaniel Stampfer, eds. *Ethical Wills and How to Prepare Them: A Guide to Sharing Your Values from Generation to Generation.* Woodstock, VT: Jewish Lights, 2009.

Zaiman, Elana. *The Forever Letter: Writing What We Believe for Those We Love.* Woodbury, MN: Llewellyn Publications, 2017. A gorgeously written and thoughtful guide to creating a "forever letter," by rabbi and chaplain Zaiman, who speaks and teaches on this subject throughout the United States and Canada. Includes writing prompts, goals to strive for, pitfalls to avoid, and examples from private and public figures. See also www.elanazaiman.com.

From a broader, humanistic perspective:

Baines, Barry K. *Ethical Wills: Putting Your Values on Paper*. Cambridge, MA: Da Capo Press, 2006. Written by a doctor and hospice director, this book offers practical advice on both expressing and passing on your deepest held beliefs. See also www.celebrationsoflife.net.

Turnbull, Susan. *The Wealth of Your Life: A Step-by-Step Guide for Creating Your Ethical Will*. Wenham, MA: Benedict Press, 2005. A practical guide to creating a written document or recording, from finding a focus to telling your stories. See also www.personallegacyadvisors.com.

Epilogue

I used to study the bigger kids—
they'd show-and-tell me
how to wiggle my hips,
how to razz the boys.

Now I'm watching my cohort
master the skills at each grade
of incapacity
and get promoted to the next.

To the oldest I'm a novice.

"These seventy-five-year-olds,
they think they know everything,"
says Cousin Leo. He's ninety.

Who thinks, Leo? Who knows?

We're too busy reading "Gratitude"
and "Being Mortal,"
passing around the revised edition
of "Dying for Dummies,"

still trying to get it right.
And the young study us.

—Chana Bloch

Notes

Part 1: Getting Good at Gaining Wisdom

5   "Life is about not knowing": Gilda Radner, *It's Always Something* (New York: Simon & Schuster, 2009).

5   "Lots of old people don't get wise": Erik Erikson, in Daniel Coleman, "Erikson, in His Old Age, Expands His View of Life," *New York Times*, June 14, 1988.

5   "As you become more skillful in harvesting the fruits of a lifetime": Zalman Schachter-Shalomi and Ronald S. Miller, *From Age-ing to Sage-ing: A Profound New Vision of Growing Older* (New York: Warner Books, 1997).

Chapter 1: Changing Your Life for (the) Good

6   "Most of us have clearer strategies": David Brooks, *The Road to Character* (New York: Random House, 2016).

6   "a path of spiritual self-development": Alan Morinis, *Everyday Holiness: The Jewish Spiritual Path of Mussar* (Boston: Trumpeter Books, 2008), p. 15.

7   "[Those] who have aged most successfully": Dr. George Vaillant, *Aging Well* (Boston: Little, Brown, 2002).

7   "Each trait is practiced for one week": Edith Brotman, *Mussar Yoga: Blending an Ancient Jewish Spiritual Practice with Yoga to Transform Body and Soul* (Woodstock, VT: Jewish Lights, 2014), p. 15.

12   "Mindfulness is paying attention to what is true": Rabbi Rachel Cowan and Dr. Linda Thal, *Wise Aging: Living with Joy, Resilience, and Spirit* (Springfield, NJ: Behrman House, 2015)

15   "the deepest yearning": Parker Palmer, *A Hidden Wholeness: The Journey toward an Undivided Life* (San Francisco: Jossey-Bass, 2004).

Chapter 2: Cooking Up New Rituals

23   "There are moments you remember": From "This Is One of Those Moments," soundtrack of *Yentl*, lyrics by Alan Bergman, Marilyn Bergman, and Michel Jean Legrand.

36   "Becoming a Crone: Ceremony at 60": Marcia Cohn Spiegel and friends, Lilith 21 (Fall 1988): 18–19. This appeared in *Lilith* magazine; used here with permission. For more, and to subscribe, visit www.lilith.org.

Chapter 3: Putting the Life in Lifelong Learning

38   "When you stop learning, you start dying": Thomas Brooks Fletcher, Assemblymember (D-Ohio), congressional testimony (adapted), Congressional Record, p. 7969, U.S. House of Representatives, May 26, 1936.

39   "My 'project' continues": Henry Saltzman, used with permission.

43   "Wisdom is not a product of schooling": Albert Einstein, Letter to J. Dispentiere, March 24, 1954, Einstein Archives 59-495.

Chapter 4: Discovering Your Inner Pilgrim

44   "We depart seeking our most valuable treasure": Rabbi Adina Lewittes, "Travel as a Spiritual Practice," *Hadassah Magazine*, March 2018.

45   "I felt uprooted, cried, and longed to turn back": China Galland, *Longing for Darkness: Tara and the Black Madonna* (New York: Penguin, 2007).

47 "deceptively simple things": Phil Cousineau, *The Art of Pilgrimage: The Seeker's Guide to Making Travel Sacred* (San Francisco: Conari Press, 2012), p. 102.

48 "I don't want to end up": Mary Oliver, "When Death Comes," in *New and Selected Poems,* vol. 1 (Boston: Beacon Press, 1992), p. 33.

48 "Tourists": Yehuda Amichai, "Tourists," in *The Selected Poetry of Yehuda Amichai*, edited and translated by Chana Bloch and Stephen Mitchell (New York: Harper and Row, 1986), pp. 137–138. Reproduced with permission of University of California Press and with permission of the author's estate.

Chapter 5: Exercising for Sages in Training

Chapter 5 is adapted from Zalman Schachter-Shalomi and Ronald S. Miller, *From Age-ing to Sage-ing: A Profound New Vision of Growing Older* (New York: Warner Books, 1997), pp. 81–82, 267–285. Reprinted by permission of Grand Central Publishing.

Part 2: Getting Good at Getting Along

68 "Hell is other people": Jean-Paul Sartre, trans. Gilbert, *No Exit and Three Other Plays* (New York: Random House, 1946).

68 "social capital": Robert Putnam, *Bowling Alone: The Collapse and Revival of American Community* (New York: Touchstone Books, 2001), p. 314.

Chapter 6: Honoring Your Father and Mother

73 "In Facing the Finish": Sheri Samotin, adapted from *Facing the Finish: A Road Map for Aging Parents and Adult Children* (Minneapolis: Bascom Hill, 2014), pp. 19, 22, 23, 117–119. Reprinted by permission of the author.

75 "The National Institute on Aging offers": "Older Drivers," National Institute on Aging, updated December 31, 2016, www.nia.nih.gov/health/older-drivers.

77 "Believe me": Thomas Moore, "Believe Me, If All Those Endearing Young Charms." *A Selection of Irish Melodies* (London: J. Power, 1808).

Chapter 7: Caring for (and Feeding) Adult Children

78 "The legend engraved": Philip Roth, *Portnoy's Complaint* (New York: Random House, 1969), p. 109.

83 "Each year, parents spend": Age Wave, www.agewave.com/what-we-do/landmark-research-and-consulting/research-studies/the-financial-journey-of-modern-parenting-joy-complexity-and-sacrifice.

84 "According to a 2016 NPR report": Camila Domonoske, "For First Time in 130 Years, More Young Adults Live with Parents Than with Partners," *NPR News*, May 24, 2016.

85 "According to the *New York Times*": Quoctrung Bui, "A Secret of Many Urban 20-Somethings: Their Parents Help with Rent," *New York Times*, Feb. 9, 2017.

Chapter 8: Teaching Your (Children's) Children Well

88 "relationship between grandparents and grandchildren": Kurt Lüscher and Karl Pillemer, "Intergenerational Ambivalence: A New Approach to the Study of Parent-Child Relations in Later Life," *Journal of Marriage and the Family* 60, no. 2 (May 1998): 413–425

89 "an emotionally close relationship": David Coall and Ralph Hertwig, "Grandparental Investment: A Relic of the Past or a Resource for the Future?" *Current Directions in Psychological Science* 20, no. 2 (April 15, 2011).

89 "An American Grandparent Association survey": Sara M. Moorman, in American Sociological Association (press release), "Strong Grandparent-Adult Grandchild Relationships Reduce Depression for Both" (August 12, 2013).

90 "Data from the 'Littles' alumni": Big Brothers Big Sisters of America survey, 2009.

95   "all children need that one adult": Marc Freedman, quoted in Urie Bronfenbrenner, "What Do Families Do?" *Institute for American Values,* Winter/Spring 1991.

Chapter 10: Acquiring for Yourself a Friend

104   Shasta Nelson, *Friendships Don't Just Happen: A Guide to Creating a Meaningful Circle of Girlfriends* (Nashville: Turner, 2013).

104   "studies indicate that it is harder for men than for women to make friends": Geoffrey Greif, *Buddy System: Understanding Male Friendships* (New York: Oxford University Press, 2008).

108   "81 percent of older adults": Aaron Smith, "Older Adults and Technology Use," Pew Research Center Internet & Technology, April 3, 2014.

Chapter 11: Finding or Creating a Community

110   "the profound effects of loneliness": Carla M. Perissinotto, Irena Stijacic Cenzer, and Kenneth E. Kovinsky, "Loneliness in Older Persons: A Predictor of Functional Decline and Death," *Archives of Internal Medicine* 172, no. 14, (July 23, 2012): 1078–1083.

115   "ChaiVillageLA is the first synagogue-based": ChaiVillageLA, "Our Values," www.chaivillagela.org. Reprinted by permission.

116   "Developers are particularly bullish": Andrew Khouri, "A New Generation of Senior Housing Is Making 'Elderly Islands' Obsolete," *Los Angeles Times,* June 22, 2017.

116   "An article in the *Atlantic*": Alana Semuels, "Living, and Dying, at Home," *Atlantic,* May 1, 2015.

116   "*In Facing the Finish*": Sheri Samotin, adapted from *Facing the Finish: A Road Map for Aging Parents and Adult Children* (Minneapolis: Bascom Hill, 2014), pp. 19, 22, 23. Reprinted by permission of the author.

119   "Home sharing is a simple idea": National Shared Housing Resource Center, www.nationalsharedhousing.org. Reprinted by permission of NSHRC, a nonprofit clearinghouse of information regarding shared housing.

119   "The best community for you": Melissa Stanton, "Creative Housing Options," AARP Livable Communities, www.aarp.org/livable-communities/info-2014/creative-age-friendly-housing-options.html.

Part 3: Getting Good at Getting Better

Chapter 12: Staying Fit Is a Mitzvah

126   "I was reading a powerful and inspiring book": Chris Crowley and Henry S. Lodge, *Younger Next Year: Live Strong, Fit, and Sexy—Until You're 80 and Beyond* (New York: Workman, 2007).

129, 130   "I'm no athlete"; "The Ruth Bader Ginsburg Workout" Ben Schreckinger, as quoted by Gabe Friedman, "This Is Ruth Bader Ginsburg's Workout. Spoiler Alert: It's Ridiculously Hard," JTA.org, February 28, 2017. Reprinted by permission of JTA.

Chapter 13: Taking Care of Your (Emotional) Self

135   "My own good heart": Sylvia Boorstein, www.sylviaboorstein.com.

135   "we might benefit from adopting": Nancy K. Dess, "Tend and Befriend," *Psychology Today,* September 1, 2000.

136–139   "Self-compassion involves treating"; "Hiding our true selves": Kristin Neff, Self-Compassion: *The Proven Power of Being Kind to Yourself* (New York: Harper Collins, 2011), pp. 41, 49, 65, 85.

Chapter 14: Visiting Someone Who's Sick

142   "Here are seven lines sick people": Letty Cottin Pogrebin, *How to Be a Friend to a Friend Who Is Sick* (New York: Public Affairs, 2013), p. 45.

145 "Visiting patients with Alzheimer's": American Medical Association, "How Improv Is Helping Patients with Alzheimer's Disease," AMA, December 8, 2015, www.ama-assn.org/delivering-care/public-health/how-improv-helping-patients-alzheimers-disease.

Chapter 15: Living in the Land of the Sick

148 "Paul Cowan—a celebrated investigative journalist": Paul Cowan, "In the Land of the Sick: Letter to a Potential Patient," *Village Voice,* May 17, 1988. Reprinted with permission.

Chapter 16: Mourning and Moving On

159 "Over my career as a rabbi I have read": Sylvan Kamens and Jack Riemer, "We Remember Them," in *New Prayers for the High Holy Days,* edited by Jack Riemer and Harold S. Kushner (New York: Media Judaica, 1970), p. 36.

162 "Once a week": Nora Ephron, *I Remember Nothing: And Other Reflections* (New York: Random House, 2010).

165 "There is a certain need": Amy Lederman, "A Widow Examines Her Grief to Understand and Conquer It," *Arizona Daily Star,* February 9, 2016.

Chapter 17: Regarding My Body

166 "There's a crack in everything": From "Anthem," lyrics by Leonard Cohen, 1992.

Part 4: Getting Good at Getting Ready

175 "If you believe you can accomplish": Max Brooks, *The Zombie Survival Guide: Complete Protection from the Living Dead* (New York: Three River Press, 2003) pp. 158-9.

175 "By harvesting,": Zalman Schachter-Shalomi and Ronald S. Miller, *From Age-ing to Sage-ing: A Profound New Vision of Growing Older* (New York: Warner Books, 1997).

Chapter 20: Having the Last Word in Funeral Planning

188 "If Shaw and Einstein": Mel Brooks, *2000 Years with Carl Reiner and Mel Brooks,* comedy album (Capitol Records, 1960).

192 "Poetree is a funeral urn": Margaux Ruyant, "POETREE Funeral Urn," Designboom, www.designboom.com/project/poetree/. Reprinted by permission of Philippe Vahe.

200 "From a Mother to Her Girls": Rabbi Karyn Kedar, "From a Mother to Her Girls," *The Bridge to Forgiveness: Stories and Prayers for Finding God and Restoring Wholeness* (Woodstock, VT: Jewish Lights Publishing, 2011), pp. 94–95.

Chapter 21: Talking about Life and Death

212–214 "Richard and Laura Bribe": Laura Geller, adapted from "Talking End of Life with Next of Kin." *Jewish Journal,* January 7, 2014.

Part 5: Getting Good at Giving Back

Chapter 22: Giving a Damn and Getting Involved

221 "aging is not 'lost youth' ": Betty Friedan, "How to Live Longer, Better, Wiser," *Parade,* March 20, 1994.

222 "a growing body of psychological research ": Dan P. McAdams, "Generativity: The New Definition of Success," *Spirituality and Health,* Fall 2001, 26–33.

223 "Today it is socially unacceptable": Jo Ann Jenkins, *Disrupt Aging: A Bold New Path to Living Your Best Life at Every Age* (New York: PublicAffairs, 2016), p. 40.

224   "Stand . . . and speak your mind": Maggie Kuhn, *No Stone Unturned: The Life and Times of Maggie Kuhn*, (New York: Ballantine Books, 1991,) p. 159.

Chapter 23: Making Purpose Your True North

225   "Those who love, dream and create": Blu and Yitz Greenberg, "Elul 3," Jewels of Elul, August 17, 2015., www.jewelsofelul.com.

230   "with low unemployment rates ": AARP, "October AARP Bulletin Reveals How to Get the Best Medicare Coverage at the Least Cost in 2018 and Beyond," AARP Press Room, October 2, 2017.

Chapter 24: Volunteering with Its Joys (and Occasional Oys)

231   "Our sages taught that every person must say": Rabbi Nachman of Bratslav, *Likutey Moharan*.

231   "What are you doing for others": Martin Luther King, Jr. *Strength to Love*, (New York: Harper & Row, 1963).

231   "The notion that we are here to do God's work": Arthur Green, *Judaism's 10 Best Ideas: A Brief Guide for Seekers* (Woodstock, VT: Jewish Lights, 2014), p. 35.

232   "Once you have volunteered at a food bank": Barack Obama, "Remarks by the President at Points of Light 20th Anniversary" (speech, Texas A&M University, Collegeville, TX, October 16, 2009).

Chapter 25: Giving with No Possibility of Being Repaid

239   "Walking into the room ": Steven Foldes. Reprinted with permission.

Chapter 26: Touching the Future through Mentoring

240   "What we need more than anything": Rabbi Abraham Joshua Heschel, "The Spirit of Jewish Education," *Jewish Education*. Vol 24, no. 2, Fall 1953.

240   "Many times, children are not responsible": Elzora Douglas, quoted in Richard Eisenberg, "How to Stand Up and Show Up for America's Kids," Next Avenue , November 17, 2016, www.nextavenue.org/help-americas-kids-generation-to-generation.

240   "a long-term relationship": Michael Zeldin and Sara Lee, eds., "Touching the Future: The Promise of Mentoring," in *Touching the Future: Mentoring and the Jewish Professional* (Los Angeles: Rhea Hirsch School of Education of Hebrew Union College, 1995).

240   "According to a 2013 study": MENTOR: The National Mentoring Partnership, "The Mentoring Effect," www.mentoring.org (January 2014).

241   "They are relationship experts": David Shapiro, quoted in Richard Eisenberg, "For MLK Day, Here's How to Start Mentoring a Young Person," *Forbes*, January 15, 2017.

241   "That's what I feel called to do ": Herb Moller, quoted in Chris Farrell, "Make Your Retirement a Time to Give Back," Next Avenue , June 11, 2015, www.nextavenue.org/make-your-retirement-a-time-to-give-back.

Part 6: Getting Good at Giving Away

Chapter 28: Mixing Community and Philanthropy

257   "Contemporary research on American giving circles": Collective Giving Research Group, "Giving Circle Membership: How Collective Giving Impacts Donors," November 2018, https://scholarworks.iupui.edu/bitstream/handle/1805/17743/giving-circle-membership18.pdf

Chapter 31: Remembering Me Like This

274   "One should not search": Viktor Frankl, *Man's Search for Meaning* (New York: Simon and Schuster, 1985), p. 131.

275   "Dear Malia and Sasha": Barack Obama, "A Letter to My Daughters." *Parade Magazine*, January 18, 2009. Reprinted by permission.

276 "I leave you my unpaid debts": Sam Levenson, "Ethical Will and Testament to His Grandchildren and to Children Everywhere," in *So That Your Values Live On* (Woodstock, VT: Jewish Lights Publishing, 1991), edited by Jack Riemer and Nathaniel Stampfer, p.168. Reprinted by permission of Turner/Jewish Lights Publishing.

276 "Tips for Creation of Your Ethical Will": Susan Turnbull, "Tips for Creation of Your Ethical Will," Personal Legacy Advisors, LLC. Used by permission of the author.

277 "Write a letter": Rabbi Edward Feinstein, in a message to his congregants at Valley Beth Shalom, Encino, CA. Reprinted with permission.

Epilogue

285 Chana Bloch, "I used to study the bigger kids": "Dying for Dummies." New Yorker, July 3, 2017. Reprinted by permission of Georges Borchardt, Inc., on behalf of the Estate of Chana Bloch.

Acknowledgments

There are so many people whose support made this book possible. Among them are our literary agent Katherine Flynn of the Kneerim & Williams Agency, who helped us imagine the project and the many contributors who offered us the gift of their insight and experience. Many thanks to the team at Behrman House—David Behrman, who helped us structure and frame the book, Vicki Weber, who challenged us to think broadly about our audience, Dena Neusner, who put the right resources in place, and especially our editor Aviva Gutnick, who stuck with us through it all, coordinating the work of multiple authors, managing the design, reading the manuscript through multiple drafts, and making each version stronger. Most important was the work of of my friend Rabbi Beth Lieberman, who stepped in after Rich died as a thought partner, editor, and gentle nudge to keep me focused.

Our good friends Bill and Isa Aron were always willing to listen and advise. And when the project seemed overwhelming, they continued to remind me that finishing the book was my last gift to Rich. Rich and I shared many of the ideas we present here through teachings and study with our community of Temple Emanuel of Beverly Hills and with ChaiVillageLA, the project we cofounded to help boomers and beyond reimagine this next stage of our lives. After Rich's death, the Temple and the Village fed me, held me, comforted me, and enabled me to continue, as did so many of our friends. You all know who you are.

Many of our friends offered their own stories about getting good at getting older. Some we were able to incorporate into the book. Others helped us think about questions we otherwise might have ignored, including Len Lawrence, the former general manager of Mount Sinai Memorial Parks and Mortuaries. Among those who read parts of the manuscript were Diane Katz, Melissa Levy, and my Cohen Girl Cousins Group. Sharing the changes in our lives as we all get older has been an extraordinary blessing and has helped inform the issues of this book. Thought partners from the beginning were Rabbi Rachel Cowan (z"l), Rabbi Marion Lev Cohen, and Steven Cohen. And through the entire journey our cheerleaders have been Marian and Bill Siegel, each modeling getting good at getting older and maintaining a sense of humor through all the twists and turns along the way.

We learned about getting older from our own parents, Frieda and Ralph Siegel and Rosalie and Leonard Geller, and also from our children, Ruth and Andy Siegel, Joshua and Elana Goldstein, and their partners Janelle Goldstein and Zach Rausnitz, with whom we shared hours of conversation about what really matters. And Avery and Levi Goldstein, our first grandchildren, taught us how to touch the future.

About the Authors

Richard Siegel began innovating contemporary expressions of Jewish life during his involvement in 1969 with Havurat Shalom, an alternative spiritual community in Somerville, Massachusetts. He earned his master's at Brandeis University in contemporary Jewish studies with his thesis, "A Theoretical Construct for a Jewish Whole Earth Catalog." That led to the best-selling *The Jewish Catalog* (Jewish Publication Society, 1973), which he coedited. His extensive career as a Jewish communal professional began as Hillel director at SUNY at Stony Brook and continued from 1978 to 2006 at the National Foundation for Jewish Culture, where he was executive director for 15 years. His work at the NFJC helped re-conceptualize Jewish culture as an important medium for contemporary Jewish identity. In 2007 he was appointed director of the HUC-JIR Zelikow School of Jewish Nonprofit Management. Among his honors are the Bernard Reisman Award for Excellence in Jewish Communal Service from Brandeis University, the Jewish Cultural Achievement Award in Cultural Leadership from the NFJC, and the Career Achievement Award from the Jewish Communal Professionals of Southern California.

Rabbi Laura Geller, named as one of *Newsweek*'s 50 Most Influential Rabbis in America, was the third woman ordained by Hebrew Union College–Jewish Institute of Religion (1976). She began her career as the Hillel director of the University of Southern California and continued as Pacific regional director of the American Jewish Congress. In 1992, she was named senior rabbi of Temple Emanuel of Beverly Hills, the first woman to be called as senior rabbi of a major synagogue through a national search. She served on the editorial board of *The Torah: A Women's Commentary* and was featured in the PBS documentary *Jewish Americans*. She is the author of *The Torah of My Life: Forty Years in the Rabbinate and Still Counting*. A fellow of the Corporation of Brown University, from which she graduated in 1971, she serves on the board of the Jewish Women's Achive and Encore.org and as a mentor through Clergy Leadership Incubator. She was named in 2017 by Next Avenue as one of the top 50 Influencers in Aging.

Together, they are among the cofounders of ChaiVillageLA, the first synagogue-based "virtual village" that is changing the way we feel about growing older. Together they are the parents of Ruth and Andy Siegel, Joshua and Elana Goldstein, and the grandparents of Avery and Levi Goldstein.

About the Artist

Paul Palnik received a bachelor of fine arts and a master of arts degree in drawing, painting, and graphics from the Ohio State University. He has worked as an artist and writer for American Greetings, the *Jerusalem Post*, the *Columbus Dispatch*, *Muse* magazine (Smithsonian science magazine), Hebrew Union College Press, the Jewish Theological Seminary, Chabad Publishing, Dell Publishing, the Melton Center for Jewish Studies at the Ohio State University, and many more.

Paul taught graphic arts at the University of Arkansas in Fayetteville, Arkansas, and also taught drawing, design, and graphic arts at Anderson University in Indiana. He was artist-in-residence at Camp Ramah in Wisconsin for fifteen years. There he created more than twenty large murals that are currently hanging on numerous buildings throughout the campus.

Palnik Studios opened in 1968 and to this day is currently marketing and publishing Paul's cartoon art. Hundreds of original Palnik cartoons are in the permanent collection of the Ohio State University's Billy Ireland Cartoon Art Library. He exhibits in art shows throughout the United States and his work is represented in thousands of homes and numerous collections in the United States and abroad. The artist is always adding new works to his ever-increasing collection.

Paul lives quietly with his family in Columbus, Ohio.

To see more of the artist's work, please visit **www.paulpalnik.com**

About the Contributors

Marci Alboher is a leading authority on workplace trends. A former blogger and columnist for the *New York Times*, her latest book is *The Encore Career Handbook: How to Make a Living and a Difference in the Second Half of Life*. She lectures widely and has been interviewed by countless news organizations. Marci serves on the board of directors of Girls Write Now and as a mentor-editor for the OpEd Project.

Judith Ansara and **Robert Gass** are internationally known teachers, synthesizing rich backgrounds in spirituality, psychology, social action, and the arts. They have taught passionate aliveness and service for almost 40 years at centers such as Omega and Esalen and organizations ranging from the Sierra Club to General Motors to the White House. They are the creators of 15 recordings of sacred music, including the best-selling *Om Namaha Shivaya*, and their retreats for couples bring a depth of compassion and insight forged in the living laboratory of their 50-year marriage.

Leah Bishop is a partner at Loeb & Loeb LLP. She focuses her practice on estate and gift tax planning for high-net-worth individuals, the administration of estates and trusts, and charitable giving and tax-exempt organizations. Leah cochairs the firm's national practices in these areas. Leah has been married to Gary Yale for 43 years, and they have two grown daughters.

Rabbi William (Bill) Cutter was ordained at Hebrew Union College–Jewish Institute of Religion in 1965. He earned his PhD at UCLA in modern Hebrew literature and Jewish studies. During his more than 50 years teaching at HUC-JIR, he has helped develop several academic and public programs for the college and the Reform movement, but has especially enjoyed writing about modern Hebrew culture and humanistic-spiritual aspects of health and healing. He serves on several hospital committees supporting bioethics and pastoral care. Bill is married to Georgianne Fisher Cutter and—because of a remarkable son, Benjamin, and rabbinic daughter-in-law, Sari—enjoys especially the growth of his two grandchildren. He and Georgianne seek antidotes to the increasing commercialization of medical practice.

Helen Dennis, a nationally recognized leader on aging and the new retirement, has worked with more than 20,000 employees at corporations, at universities, and in Jewish communities, planning for the noneconomic aspects of retirement. Cofounder of Project Renewment, a movement of career women defining their next chapters in life, and coauthor of the *Los Angeles Times* best seller *Project Renewment: The First Retirement Model for Career Women*, she writes a syndicated column on successful aging for the Los Angeles Newspaper Group, reaching 1.6 million readers weekly. In 2016 she was recognized by PBS Next Avenue as one of the 50 Influencers in Aging.

Rabbi Elliot N. Dorff, PhD, is a distinguished service professor of philosophy at American Jewish University and, since 1974, visiting professor at the UCLA School of Law. He has served on three federal commissions—on the distribution of health care, diminishing the spread of sexually transmitted diseases, and research on human subjects—and now serves on the State of California's Ethics Committee governing stem cell research. His book *Matters of Life and Death: A Jewish Approach to Modern Medical Ethics* addresses many issues in end-of-life care.

Richard Eisenberg is managing editor of Next Avenue (www.nextavenue.org), a public media website for people aged 50 plus. He is also the editor of the site's Money & Security and Work & Purpose channels. He was formerly executive editor of *Money* magazine and front-page finance editor at Yahoo! He is the author of *The Money Book of Personal Finance* and *How to Avoid a Mid-Life Financial Crisis*.

Merle Feld is the author of a beloved memoir, *A Spiritual Life: Exploring the Heart and Jewish Tradition*; a book of poetry, *Finding Words*; and the award-winning plays *Across the Jordan* and *The Gates Are Closing*. She has pioneered teaching writing as a spiritual practice, serving lay seekers and mentoring rabbis across the denominations. Visit merlefeld.com and derekh.org for details about her forthcoming book, a how-to for journaling through our lives.

Dan Fendel is coauthor, with Rabbi Stuart Kelman, of *Chesed Shel Emet: The Truest Act of Kindness: Exploring the Meaning of Taharah* and *Nihum Aveilim: A Guide for the Comforter*. He cofounded the *chevrah kaddisha* at Temple Sinai in Oakland, California, was in the first graduating class of the Gamliel Institute, and has taught about the liturgy of *taharah* in various settings. He is also a spiritual care volunteer at Kaiser Hospital in Oakland.

Marc Freedman, president and CEO of Encore.org, is one of the nation's leading experts on the longevity revolution. The *Wall Street Journal* named his newest book—*How to Live Forever: The Enduring Power of Connecting the Generations*—one of the year's best books on aging well. An award-winning social entrepreneur, frequent media commentator, and author, Marc has been honored with numerous awards and fellowships, including the Eisner Prize for Intergenerational Excellence.

Deborah Goldstein is a Brooklyn-based home organizer with over 15 years' experience in helping her clients downsize and make thoughtful decisions about items that are truly meaningful to them. Her specialties are seniors, bereavement/estate cleanouts, and hoarding. Deborah's guiding principle is that what we truly value in our lives are the memories and the experiences we have had with the people we love. Visit Deborah at www.theartoforganizingnyc.com

Felicia Herman has been executive director of Natan, a giving circle supporting Jewish and Israeli social innovation, since 2005. She is the founder and advisory board chair of Amplifier, a network of giving circles inspired by Jewish values, and she serves on the boards of Sefaria, the American Jewish Historical Society, and the DreamStreet Theatre Company. She holds a PhD in American Jewish history and an MA in Jewish women's studies, both from Brandeis University, and a BA from Wellesley College. She lives in Brooklyn with her husband and three children.

Paul Irving is chairman of the Milken Institute Center for the Future of Aging, distinguished scholar-in-residence at the USC Davis School of Gerontology, and chairman of Encore.org. He is a director of East West Bancorp, Inc. and Pharos Capital BDC, Inc., and serves on advisory boards at USC, Stanford University, the Global Coalition on Aging, and WorkingNation. Paul is a member of the steering committee for the National Academy of Medicine Healthy Longevity Initiative and was a participant in the 2015 White House Conference on Aging. Paul writes and speaks about investment and innovation in the longevity economy; health, productivity, and purpose for older adults; and the changing culture of aging in America and the world.

Ellie Kahn (Living Legacies Productions) has been an oral historian since 1988, recording memories and stories for hundreds of families and organizations. Ellie is also a licensed psychotherapist, journalist, and documentary filmmaker. Though based in LA, Ellie often travels to other cities for her work. Her in-depth interviews are usually transformed into written and video treasures that will last for many generations. Visit her at www.livinglegaciesproductions.com.

Rabbi Naamah Kelman is a descendent of rabbis, becoming the first woman to be ordained by the Hebrew Union College in Jerusalem, where she is the Dean. Since moving to Israel in 1976 from New York, she has worked to promote pluralistic Judaism for Israelis and to strengthen the ties between Israel and world Jewry.

Rabbi Stuart Kelman, PhD, is the founding rabbi emeritus of Congregation Netivot Shalom in Berkeley, California. Together with David Zinner, he founded the Gamliel Institute, an online series of courses teaching the work of the *chevrah kaddisha*. His interests lie in the areas of liturgy, music, healing, and the work of the *chevrah kaddisha*, and he has written in all these areas. Ordained by the Jewish Theological Seminary, he holds a doctorate in education from USC.

The Reverend Rosemary Lloyd is dedicated to supporting clergy and congregations in having vital conversations about our unique wishes for care through the end of life. A graduate of Georgetown University and Harvard Divinity School, Rosemary has a lifelong interest in end-of-life care and ethics that is fueled by her experience as a registered nurse and hospice volunteer. She is an ordained Unitarian Universalist minister, a graduate of the Metta Institute for Compassionate End-of-Life Care, and an advocate for deepening the spiritual practice of embracing the reality of our mortality for the sake of having more joy in life.

Dr. Ruth Nemzoff, author of *Don't Roll Your Eyes: Making In-Laws into Family* and *Don't Bite Your Tongue: How to Foster Rewarding Relationships with Your Adult Children* is a resident scholar at Brandeis's Women's Studies Research Center. She holds a doctorate from Harvard University, an MA in counseling from Columbia University, and a BA from Barnard College. She is a board member of the Jewish Grandparents Network. To learn more, visit www.ruthnemzoff.com.

William Novak is probably best known as the ghostwriter for celebrity memoirs by Lee Iacocca, Tip O'Neill, Oliver North, Nancy Reagan, Magic Johnson, and Natan Sharansky. Prior to writing other people's books, he was the editor of *Response*, the Jewish student journal, and *New Traditions*, published by the Havurah movement. Together with Moshe Waldoks, he is responsible for *The Big Book of Jewish Humor*.

Rabbi Vanessa L. Ochs is a professor of religious studies at the University of Virginia. Her books include *Inventing Jewish Ritual*, *Sarah Laughed*, *The Jewish Dream Book* (with Elizabeth Ochs), *Words on Fire*, and *Safe and Sound*. She was awarded a creative writing fellowship by the National Endowment for the Arts. Ochs earned her BA from Tufts University, an MFA from Sarah Lawrence College, and a PhD from Drew University.

Ben Pomerantz, MSW, is a licensed clinical social worker in private practice in Los Angeles. He works with children, adolescents, and adults, specializing in teaching self-regulation skills, including clinical hypnosis. He has taught at the USC Graduate School of Social Work for many years.

Nessa Rapoport is the author of a novel, *Preparing for Sabbath*; a volume of prose poems, *A Woman's Book of Grieving*; and a memoir, *House on the River*. Her meditations are included in *Objects of the Spirit: Ritual and the Art of Tobi Kahn; Tobi Kahn: Sacred Spaces for the 21st Century;* and *Anointed Time: Sculpture and Ceremonial Objects*. She speaks frequently on Jewish writing, culture, and imagination.

Tiffany Shlain is an Emmy nominated filmmaker, author, and founder of the Webby Awards, and was honored by Newsweek as one of the "Women Shaping the 21st Century. Selected by the Albert Einstein Foundation for *Genius: 100 Visions of the Future*, Tiffany has had four films premiere at Sundance, including her feature documentary *Connected* and *The Tribe*. She is the author of *The 24/6 Life*, about her decade of tech Shabbats. Visit her @tiffanyshlain.

Rabbi Ruth H. Sohn is a rabbi, spiritual director, and writer. Ordained in 1982, she directs the Spirituality Initiative and the Leona Aronoff Rabbinic Mentoring Program at Hebrew Union College–Jewish Institute of Religion in Los Angeles. Ruth is an experienced teacher of Jewish mindfulness meditation and traditional Jewish texts. She codirects the Yedidya Center's Morei Derekh Jewish Spiritual Direction Training Program. Ruth's articles, biblical commentary, midrash, and poetry have appeared in various anthologies and periodicals.

Susan K. Stern's work as a community activist includes her appointment by two governors as chair of the New York State Commission on National and Community Service and her nomination by President Barack Obama as chairman of the President's Advisory Council on Faith-Based and Neighborhood Partnerships. She also served as founding chair of the UJA Federation's Time for Good, as well as chair of the board of the UJA Federation of New York, vice chair of the Jewish Federations of North America, a member of the American Jewish Joint Distribution Committee, and advisory liaison to Repair the World.

Harriet Warshaw has more than 35 years of management experience in both the public and private sectors, including senior positions at the Boston Hospital for Women, the New England Baptist Hospital, Genzyme Corporation, and the New England Healthcare Institute. She is the former executive director of the Conversation Project and now serves as a faculty member with the organization. In addition, she has held elected office in the Town of Wellesley, Massachusetts, including ten years on its Board of Health and nine years on the Board of Selectmen. She has served on numerous commissions and boards, including chairing the Combined Jewish Philanthropies' Commission on Caring and Social Justice and as president of the Temple Beth Elohim Board of Trustees in Wellesley, Massachusetts.

Index